REVOLUTION IN THE THEATRE

Etching by Célestin Nanteuil for *Le Monde Dramatique*, 1835. (Author's collection.)

REVOLUTION IN THE THEATRE

French Romantic Theories
of Drama

Barry V. Daniels

Contributions in Drama and Theatre Studies, Number 7

GREENWOOD PRESS
WESTPORT, CONNECTICUT • LONDON, ENGLAND

Library of Congress Cataloging in Publication Data

Daniels, Barry V.
  Revolution in the theatre.

  (Contributions in drama and theatre studies, ISSN
0163-3821 ; no. 7)
  Bibliography: p.
  Includes index.
  1. Drama—Addresses, essays, lectures. 2. Romanticism
—France—Addresses, essays, lectures. 3. Theater—
France—History—19th century—Addresses, essays,
lectures. 4. Dramatic criticism—France. 5. French
prose literature—19th century. I. Title. II. Series.
PN1633.R65D36 1983   842′.7′09145   83-1705
ISBN 0-313-22476-5 (lib. bdg.)

Library of Congress Catalog Card Number: 83-1705
ISBN: 0-313-22476-5
ISSN: 0163-3821

First published in 1983

Greenwood Press
A division of Congressional Information Service, Inc.
88 Post Road West
Westport, Connecticut 06881

Printed in the United States of America

10 9 8 7 6 5 4 3 2 1

CONTENTS

ILLUSTRATIONS

PREFACE

Revolution in the Theatre: French Romantic Theories of Drama. The title should be clear in its meaning: Romanticism in France meant revolution in the theatre, and the date of this revolution, 25 February 1830, as Théophile Gautier notes in his *History of Romanticism*, "remains engraved upon our past in blazing letters: the première of *Hernani*."

The majority of the selections in this volume were written prior to 25 February 1830. Romanticism was delayed in France, both because of political factors—the Empire—and because of the strength of neo-classicism in general in French culture. The latter was especialy true of the French theatre, which was dominated by the shadows of its first geniuses, Cornielle, Racine, and Molière. Thus, even after the French romaniticsbegan to publish in the 1820s, the theatre, especially the Comédie Française, was not open to them; hence the protracted critical discussions of the 1820s which precede the practical applications of the theory to the stage.

After 1830, after *Hernani*, there was little need for critical debate. The history of the French romanitic drama is a history of productions in the 1830s. Very little significant theory was written during this period.

The selections in this volume, then, present the French romantics' ideas about the theatre before they actually became involved in production. They provide a general understanding of the variety of factors that the romantics felt needed to be changed and give a good picture of what neo-classicism had become under the Restoration. They offer an idea of the variety of approaches to the theatre that the romantics envisaged.

In the Introduction I have attempted to place French romanticism in the context of the development of romanticism in Europe. I have also provided a general overview of the events in the French theatre during the Restoration. Finally, I have examined the major elements of romantic dramaturgy as they are developed in the selections. The Introduction is followed by a Chronology which summarizes the important events in the development of romanticism in France.

All the translations in this book are new. The Benjamin Constant essay, "On the Thirty Years War: Schiller's Tragedy, *Wallenstein*, and the German Theatre," and the selections by Alexandre Dumas (the elder), Emile Deschamps, Charles-Augustin Sainte-Beuve, and Alfred de Vigny are here translated into English for the first time. The translation of Constant's "Reflections on Tragedy" was first published, in a slightly different form, in *Educational Theatre Journal*, 23 (October 1971), 317-34. Notes in the text marked with an asterisk (*) indicate notes which appeared in the original works. All other notes are my own.

I would like to thank the editors of *Educational Theatre Journal* for their permission to reprint my translation of Constant's "Reflections on Tragedy."

I would like also to thank André Jarry, one of the editors of the new Pléiade edition of Vigny's works, for specific assistance in locating the references for the Vigny selection and for his general assistance when I needed information that could only be located in France.

Finally, I would like to acknowledge my gratitude for the assistance of Mary Daniels, who typed the manuscript, and whose editorial comments were always perceptive and generally followed.

REVOLUTION
IN THE
THEATRE

INTRODUCTION

Romanticism and French Romantics

For Stendhal, all good literature was romantic. He defined romanticism as "the art of presenting people with literary works which, given the current state of their customs and beliefs, are susceptible of arousing the most possible pleasure."[1] For Victor Hugo, romanticism was "no more than liberalism in literature."[2]

Unfortunately, defining romanticism is not as simple as Hugo and Stendhal would have it.[3] Jacques Barzun, in *Classic, Romantic, and Modern*, argues for a distinction between what he calls "historic" romanticism and "intrinsic" romanticism. He defines the former as "comprising those Europeans whose birth falls between 1770 and 1815, and who achieved distinction in philosophy, statecraft, and the arts during the first half of the nineteenth century."[4] He defines intrinsic romanticism as being "first of all constructive and creative" in its response to the "dominant problem" of the period which was "to create a new world in the ruins of the old.[5]"

Historic romanticism, in Barzun's definition, would include the majority of figures generally associated with romanticism: William Wordsworth, Samuel Taylor Coleridge, John Keats, Percy Bysshe Shelley, George Gordon, Lord Byron, Walter Scott, William Hazlitt, and Thomas Carlyle in England; Friedrich Schlegel (though not his brother, August Wilhelm, born in 1767), Ludwig Tieck, Friedrich Novalis, Heinrich Heine, Friedrich Hölderlin, and Heinrich von Kleist in Germany; and in France, Hugo, Vigny, Dumas, Stendhal, Alphonse de Lamartine, Théophile Gautier, and Alfred de Musset. I would quibble with Barzun's inclusive dates as they would exclude both Goethe and Schiller, but that would lead to the problem of defining "pre-romanticism." More important to the concept of a historical definition of romanticism is the chronological variation that occurs in the development of romanticism in the various European countries. Some critics see the German *Sturm und Drang* of the 1770s, and the early work of Goethe and Schiller, as the first wave of European romanticism, which is followed by a second generation of romantics whose work was appearing in the first and second decades of the nineteenth century, principally in England and in Germany. The French romantics would, then, constitute a third generation whose work does not begin appearing until the 1820s. Despite many varying opinions about the specific chronological parameters, there is general agreement that a major change in sensibility, in attitudes toward literature, begins to be felt in the last quarter of the eighteenth century and the first forty years of the nineteenth century. It is in this sense that the historical definition is useful.

A more difficult problem develops when an attempt is made to define what romanticism is: Barzun's "intrinsic" romanticism.[6] These definitions tend to isolate qualities which are generally associated with romanticism. Thus, René Wellek concludes:

If we examine the characteristics of the actual literature which called itself or was called "romantic" all over the continent, we find throughout Europe the same conceptions of poetry and the working nature of poetic imagination, the same conception of nature and its relation to man, and basically the same poetic style, with a use of imagery, symbolism and myth which is clearly distinct from that of eighteenth century neoclassicism.[7]

Wellek establishes three primary criteria: the creative imagination for the view of poetry, organic nature for the view of the world, and symbol and myth for the poetic style. Other critics attempt more comprehensive lists of criteria than those of Barzun and Wellek. Henry H. H. Remak, in his article "Western European Romanticism: Definition and Scope," arrives at the following qualities: (1) attitudes toward the past: interest in non-classical mythology, interest in folklore, medievalism, anti-neo-classicism, anti-unities of time and place, anti-eighteenth century; (2) general attitudes: imaginativeness, cult of strong emotions, restlessness, boundlessness, individualism, subjectivism, cult of originality, interest in nature, greater positive emphasis on religion, "mysticism," *weltschmerz* or *mal du siècle*, liberalism, cosmopolitanism, nationalism; (3) characteristics of the works: supremacy of lyrical modes and forms, re-awakening of national epic, historical drama and novel, greater flexibility of form, "vagueness," symbolism, rhetoric, "romantic irony," exoticism, realism (regionalism, local color).[8] Remak then proceeds, through a chart, to analyze the degree of presence or nonpresence of each of these qualities in the romantic literature of the various European countries. I have listed the qualities he analyzes to give an idea of the complexity and diversity of European romanticism.

French romanticism is perhaps easier to discuss.[9] Its outlines and issues are clear for a variety of reasons. The most important of these is the strength in France of neo-classicism. Unlike England with Shakespeare, Spain with Lope de Vega and Pedro Calderón de la Barca, and Germany with Goethe and Schiller, France's first major body of literature is neo-classical. It was, in fact, via seventeenth-century France that neo-classicism spread throughout Europe in the eighteenth century. The image of monarchy as developed by Louis XIV was an ideal imitated throughout eighteenth-century Europe. French became the language of diplomacy. The plays of Corneille, Racine, and Molière were translated and imitated throughout Europe. Thus, neo-classicism was very important to France's self-image as a world power. Napoleon Bonaparte's imperial image merely reinforced this concept of French neo-classicism. Thus, at the point after the revolution when France might have been open to radical change in literature, there was, rather, a strong re-affirmation of neo-classical values by the Bonapartist regime. Neo-classicism was the party line during the Empire and much that deviated from it was discouraged or actively suppressed by the government.

The most important literary figures during the Empire have proven to be Chateaubriand and Madame de Staël, both of whom are associated with romanticism (pre-romanticism). Chateaubriand's *René* (1802) with its doomed, melancholy hero was the first important French example of what would become a standard romantic type. Madame de Staël established a cosmopolitan salon in exile in Switzerland, where writers like Constant and A. W. Schlegel were regularly to be found. Her book *Germany* (written in 1810, published in London in 1813 and in France in 1814) introduced the basic premises of French romanticism, stressing the distinction between the literatures of the North, which were fundamentally romantic, with the basically classical literature of the South.

The restoration of the Bourbon monarchy in 1815 brought "freedom of expression, peace, and contact with foreign countries."[10] During the first few years of the Restoration much foreign literature which, because of war and Napoleonic policy, had been suppressed, was introduced into France. Translations of Byron began to appear in 1816, and between 1818 and 1824 an English edition of his works was published in Paris. Walter Scott's *Guy Mannering* was translated in 1816, and thereafter his works appeared regularly in France and were extremely popular. Pierre Letourneur's eighteenth-century Shakespeare translations were re-published in two editions in 1821, one of which was revised and provided with a lengthy introduction by the noted historian François Guizot. In 1822 the editor Ladvocat began publication of a series, *Masterpieces of*

..Dieu des Juifs tu l'emportes!
....
David, David triomphe, Achab seul est détruit.
Impitoyable Dieu, toi seul as tout conduit!
Acte V Scene VI

A Paris chez Martinet, Libraire, rue du Coq N.º 3 et 15

Mlle George in the Title Role of Racine's *Athalia*, 1808-1809.
(Author's collection.)

Foreign Theatre, which would include representative works of Schiller, Goethe, Lope de Vega, Calderón, and so forth. The dissemination of this literature, non-French in origin and non-classical in form, proved Madame de Staël's theories and helped introduce the new generation of writers to traditions other than that of French classicism.

After 1820 two distinct groups of writers who would call themselves "romantics" began to form. They shared similar attitudes toward the need for literary reform and an interest in foreign literatures, but differed in their politics.[11] The liberals, favoring historical subjects and prose, included Stendhal, Charles de Rémusat, Hygin-Auguste Cavé and Adolphe Dittmer, Ludovic Vitet, and Prosper Mérimée. The royalist group was distinguished by the poets Lamartine, Vigny, Hugo, Alexandre Soumet, Alexandre Guiraud, and Emile Deschamps. This latter group—with the exception of Lamartine—was responsible for the publication of the literary journal the *French Muse* (1823–1824) and formed what came to be known as the first *cénacle*, which met regularly in the salon of Charles Nodier, librarian of the Arsenal. These two groups were more unified in the last years of the Restoration, when the royalist poets began to support the liberal cause in reaction to the repressive regime of Charles X.

During the first few years of the 1820s both groups of French romantics began publishing original works. The most notable from the liberal group were Stendhal's polemic *Racine and Shakespeare* (1823–1825), Merimée's *The Theatre of Clara Gazul* (1825), Vitet's historical dialogues, *The League Trilogy* (1826–1828), and Cavé and Dittmer's *Evenings at Neuilly: Dramatic and Historical Sketches* (1827). The royalist group published an important series of collections of poetry, beginning with Lamartine's *Meditations* in 1820. They were followed by his *New Meditations* (1823), *The Death of Socrates* (1823), and *The Final Song of Harold's Pilgrimage* (1825). Hugo and Vigny led the *cénacle* with their publication in 1822 of *Odes* and *Poems*, respectively. Hugo followed his first collection with *New Odes* (1824) and *Odes and Ballads* (1826). Vigny published *The Trappist* (1822), *Eloa* (1824), and *Poems, Ancient and Modern* (1826). In addition to poetry, both Hugo and Vigny published historical novels in the manner of Walter Scott: Hugo's *Han of Iceland* (1823) and *Bug Jargal* (1826), and Vigny's *Cinq-Mars* (1826).

The period 1827–1830 was marked by an increase in activity as the climactic first night of *Hernani* approached. Hugo's mammoth drama *Cromwell*, with its important Preface, appeared at the end of 1827, and his definitive edition of *Odes and Ballads* was published in 1828 and was followed by *Orientals* in 1829. His plays *Marion Delorme* and *Hernani* were written in the summer and fall of 1829. Vigny published a complete collection of his *Poems* in 1829 and undertook several Shakespeare translations: first, a *Romeo and Juliet* (1827–1828) in collaboration with Deschamps, *Othello* (1828–1829), and *The Merchant of Venice* (1829–1830). Deschamps's collection of poetry and translations with its Preface appeared in 1828. Gérard de Nerval translated Goethe's *Faust* in 1827. Mérimée's historical dialogues, *The Jacquerie* and *A Chronicle of Charles IX's Times*, were published in 1828 and 1829. Sainte-Beuve, the literary critic for the *Globe*, published his *Historical and Critical Portrait of French Poetry and Theatre in the Sixteenth Century* in 1828, and a collection of poetry, *The Life, Poetry, and Thoughts of Joseph Delorme*, in 1829. Thus, by the end of the 1820s the French romantics had produced a significant body of literature including poetry, novels, historical sketches, and theory. It remained for them to conquer the theatre. This would be the work of the year beginning in February 1829 and culminating with the production of *Hernani* in February 1830.

The French Theatre, 1815–1830

The question of the theatre dominates theoretical writing during the 1820s in France, and the final battles of French romanticism were waged in the theatre.[12] This was due in part to the nature of the hierarchy of theatres established in France which, by the government allotment of privileges, gave the Comédie-Française the most prestige. The Comédie-Française was dominated by the neo-classicists and became to the romantics a symbol of all that was bad in French theatre. The success of romanticism in France would not be complete until this last bastion of neo-classicism, the "House of Molière," had been conquered. By its very public nature the theatre was an ideal battleground. The romantics hoped to use the theatre to reach the largest possible audience with their literary and extra-literary ideas.

At the beginning of the Restoration theatre-going was socially structured: popular audiences flocked to the popular or "boulevard" theatres, while the aristocracy and the intelligentsia supported the Comédie-Française, the Odéon, the Opera, and the Comic Opera. As the Restoration progressed the reactionary policies at the Comédie-Française would gradually alienate all but the most confirmed classicists from its audience, thus precipitating financial and artistic crises. The secondary theatres, on the other hand, flourished in the new freedom offered them by the Restoration.

Napoleon's Decree of 1807 had limited the number of secondary theatres in Paris to four: the Ambigu-Comique and the Gaîté, whose repertory was limited to melodrama, and the Vaudeville and the Variétés, where low comedy, parody, and peasant plays could be staged. The Comédie-Française held the monopoly of the classical repertory and, with the Odéon, was the only theatre in which standard tragedy and comedy could be played. After 1815 additional secondary theatres began to open. The most important of these were the Porte-Saint-Martin Theatre, which opened in 1815, and the Gymnase Theatre, which opened in 1820. The latter theatre's house playwright was Eugène Scribe, who became one of the most successful playwrights in France during the first half of the nineteenth century. He worked principally in the *comédie-vaudeville* form, moving it closer to traditional comedy and introducing into it material from contemporary social life. Scribe's success at the Gymnase was such that this theatre began attracting the audience of the Comédie-Française and thus contributed to the undermining of the neo-classical repertory.[13]

More important to the history of the romantic drama was the melodrama which flourished on the boulevard at the Porte-Saint-Martin, the Ambigu-Comique, and the Gaîté. For it was in this most popular nineteenth-century theatrical genre that many of the techniques and reforms advocated by the romantics would be developed, and, at the same time, the popular audiences were being accustomed to the elements of romantic dramaturgy. In a sense, the melodrama constitutes the real theatrical avant-garde of the 1820s.

Unity of time and place had long been disregarded in the boulevard theatres. Elaborate set designs and realistic effects were the stock-in-trade of the melodrama. Designers like Pierre Luc Charles Cicéri at the Porte-Saint-Martin Theatre, Louis Jacques Mandé Daguerre at the Ambigu-Comique, and Gué at the Gaîté abandoned the neo-classical conventions of design for the exotic locales, atmospheric effects, and local color advocated by the romantics. In fact, in scenic terms, the complete romantic iconography—natural vistas, melancholy ruins, historical accuracy—was to be found in the boulevard theatres of the 1820s. It was also on the boulevard that a new generation of actors was trained in a style both more "passionate" and more "realistic" than that of the actors at the Comédie-Française.

It is not at all surprising that, after the emblematic success of *Hernani* in 1830, the romantic playwrights abandoned the Comédie-Française for the boulevard theatres where they could work with such performers as Marie Dorval, Frédérick Lemaître, and Bocage. The production of Hugo's *Lucretia Borgia* at the Porte-Saint-Martin in 1833 is representative of this trend. It attracted the traditional audience of the Comédie-Française. The production was staged by the author and the leading actor, Lemaître. Cicéri designed the sets (including a moonlight view of Venice) which were accompanied by Louis Boulanger's historically accurate costumes. The play was staged with all the conventions of melodrama in the grandest of the melodrama houses.[14] It confirms Charles Nodier's statement that "the tragedy and drama of the new school are hardly more than melodramas elevated by the artificial pomp of lyricism."[15]

In opposition to the vigorous growth and popular success of the melodrama and the vaudeville, the official theatres, the Comédie-Française and the Odéon, were moribund. To the neo-classical faction change

THÉÂTRES DE PARIS.

Théâtre de l'Ambigu comique

ELODIE.

Décoration du 2me Acte.

par Daguerre.

Daguerre's Set Design for Act 2 of the Melodrama, *Elodie*, 1822. (Author's collection.)

meant rejection of the "glories" of the French stage: Corneille, Molière, and Racine. Yet, especially in tragedy, no lasting success had been introduced into the repertory since the time of Voltaire. The actors who governed the Comédie-Française tended to be conservative and understandably rejected material that required a different style of performance than that to which they were accustomed. During the first ten years of the Restoration, what success the Comédie-Française did experience was due to the attraction of star performers such as Talma, Mademoiselle Mars and Mademoiselle Duchenois. The retirement of the last-named and Talma's death in 1826 left neo-classical tragedy with no star actors to sustain it.

The most successful new plays presented at the Comédie-Française during the Restoration tended to break, albeit timidly, with neo-classical dogma. Thus, François Ancelot's *Louis IX* (1819) developed a subject drawn from modern French history; Pierre Lebrun's *Mary Stuart* (1820) was adapted from Schiller; while Etienne de Jouy's *Sylla* (1821) was, as Marvin Carlson notes, "probably the best tragedy of the period and certainly the most popular. For the first time a classic tragedy made extensive use of crowd scenes; for the first time a tragic hero lay down in a bed on stage."[16] To these should be added Alexandre Soumet's *Clytemnestra* (1822) and Népomucène Lemercier's *Jane Shore* (1824), the latter inspired by Shakespeare's *Richard III*. The Odéon also had a series of successes with transitional plays, beginning with Casimir Delavigne's *Sicilian Vespers* (1819), his *Pariah* (1821), and the work of two members of the *cénacle*, Alexandre Guiraud's *The Maccabees* (1822), and Alexandre Soumet's *Saul* (1822) and *Cleopatra* (1824).

The nomination of Baron Isidore Taylor as royal commissioner to the Comédie-Française in 1825 indicated the seriousness of the situation at this theatre. Taylor was empowered to intervene in the actors' administration of their organization. He had experience in the writing and staging of melodrama and was a partisan of the romantics. Thus, control of the Comédie-Française, to a degree, was removed from the conservative committee of actors and placed in the hands of someone who would be more open to reform.

Taylor inaugurated his administration with a production of Michel Pichat's *Léonidas*. Talma played the leading role in historically accurate costume. The two sets were the work of Cicéri and took their inspiration from the paintings of Jacques Louis David. The script was "moderately" romantic. The spectacular production was a great success.[17] Between 1825 and 1829 Taylor continued his reforms in stagecraft and had notable success in revivals of the standard repertory, but had less success with new plays. Until 1829 none of the romantic writers had written a script suitable for production at the Comédie-Française.

An event of great importance to the development of the French ro-

« J'ai gouverné sans peur et j'abdique sans crainte! »

Talma, Rôle de Sylla.

Miroir Journal

Talma in the Title Role of Etienne de Jouy's *Sylla*, 1821. (Author's collection.)

mantic theatre was the successful series of performances by a troupe of
English actors in the 1827–1828 Paris season.[18] Especially significant
were their Shakespearean performances, as Shakespeare was a symbol
to the romantics for all that was not classical and not French.

French translations and adaptations of Shakespeare had begun to
appear in the eighteenth century. The most important of these was the
Letourneur edition published in twenty volumes between 1776 and 1783,
a serious attempt to provide a literal and scholarly edition of Shakespeare, albeit in rather uninspired prose. The Letourneur text remained
the standard in France throughout the romantic period.

Letourneur's translations, however, were not intended for the stage.
The most important stage adaptations of Shakespeare were made by
Jean-François Ducis, with his *Hamlet* in 1769, followed by *Romeo and
Juliet* (1778), *King Lear* (1783), *Macbeth* (1784), *King John* (1791), and
Othello (1792).

Ducis's *Othello* is a fairly good example of how the Shakespeare text
could be twisted to conform to neo-classical conventions. It was among
the most successful of his adaptations and continued to be performed
at the Comédie-Française throughout the romantic period. In his *Othello*,
Ducis reduced the cast to seven characters and changed the names of
all but Othello. Brabantio became Odalbert; Cassio, Lorédan (son of
Moncénigo, the Doge); Iago became Pézare; Emilia, Hermance; and
Desdemona, Hédelmone. The changing of the characters' names is only
the first and most trivial of Ducis's deformations of Shakespeare's play.
More important are the modifications of the characters, the most drastic
of which affects that of Iago, whose villainous nature is not revealed
until the last act. Ducis explained that he felt certain that "the English
might be able to watch tranquilly the stage machinations of such a monster, but the French would not suffer his presence for a single moment.
Even less would they allow the development of the breadth and depth
of his villainy."[19] Thus, one of the key elements of Shakespeare's play,
the contrast between Othello and Iago, is destroyed.

The plot also undergoes extreme mutation. Shakespeare's complex
tragedy of emotions becomes a tragedy of intrigue which, apart from
the ending, most resembles a *comédie larmoyante*. Othello and Hédelmone
(Desdemona) are not yet married. Lorédan (Cassio) is in love with Hédelmone and, being a worthy suitor, is a valid threat to Othello. Com-
plications involve Odalbert (Brabantio)'s learning that Hédelmone and
Othello are not yet married and forcing her to sign a letter in which she
agrees to marry Lorédan. Odalbert, however, has openly defied the
Senate. In order to save her father, Hédelmone begs Lorédan to in-
tercede with his father, the Doge, on her father's behalf. She gives him
her *bandeau* of diamonds and the letter. When Othello announces that
the wedding plans are completed, Hédelmone begs him to postpone the

Décoration du 5.ᵉ Acte de Sylla.

Litho. de C Motte.

Cicéri's Set Design for *Sylla*, Act 5, 1821. (Author's collection.)

marriage and thus arouses his jealousy. Pézare feeds this jealousy by telling Othello that he has killed Lorédan and found the *bandeau* and the letter. At this point, Ducis's plot rejoins that of Shakespeare for the "Willow Song" and the final scene between Othello and Hédelmone. Othello only stabs her, however, as smothering would have offended the sensibilities of the French audience. This ending, even in Ducis's timid rendering, created a furor, and in the published text Ducis provided an alternative "happy ending."

Ducis, in reality, had written a neo-classical French tragedy with a love versus honor theme, in proper alexandrine verse, adhering to the unities and carefully observing decorum in characterization. Its lasting success reflects the continued force of the Academic attitudes.

It was on a different, and less ponderous, level than that of Ducis that Shakespeare began to infiltrate the French stage. Following the Revolution and during the Empire and Restoration, pantomime versions of Shakespearean plays began to be presented. Most notable among these were Louis Henry's *Hamlet* ("Tragic Pantomime in Three Acts, Intermixed with Dances," 1816) and *The Visions of Macbeth or The Witches of Scotland* ("Spectacular Melodrama," 1817), and Cuvelier de Trie's *Macbeth or The Witches of the Forest* (1817) and his *Moor of Venice, or Othello* ("Pantomime Intermixed with Dialogues, in Three Acts, Imitated from the English Tragedy," 1818). Needless to say, these pantomimes were hardly faithful to the letter, although because of the freedom from the classical conventions permitted in the minor Parisian theatres, they were often closer to the spirit of Shakespeare than were Ducis's imitations.

It should also be remembered that critical opinion in France toward Shakespeare had been changing since the Empire. Thus, at the same time that a popular audience was being exposed to Shakespearean form and subject matter in the theatre, the critical atmosphere was preparing a change in the literary climate. By 1821 two new editions of the Letourneur translations were published. The first of these, edited and introduced by François Guizot, involved revision and correction of Letourneur's texts.

The most important events in the history of Shakespeare in France during the Restoration were the performances in Paris of the English actors, first in 1822, then in 1827. The 1822 company, led by Penley, was brought to the Porte-Saint-Martin Theatre by its director, Jean-Toussaint Merle. The opening performance, *Othello*, took place on 31 July 1822. It was a fiasco, ending in a brawl. The actors, in an effort simply to get through the play, omitted most of the text, but the curtain was forced down during the scene of Othello's smothering of Desdemona. The afterpiece was driven from the stage. Two days later, despite the doubling of ticket prices, similar riots occurred. Penley was forced to move his company to a private theatre on the *rue* Chantereine where the troupe was able to continue performing from 20 August to 25 October. The failure of this first attempt of an English company to perform in Paris has rightly been attributed to political, rather than literary, considerations. French chauvinism and strong anti-British sentiments, heightened by the recent death of Napoleon, were the primary causes of the disturbances. The first of Stendhal's *Racine and Shakespeare* pamphlets was prompted by the French response to these performances.

Between 1822 and 1827 the attitude toward Shakespeare in France had changed. Political hostility to the English had waned. A wider acceptance and knowledge of foreign literatures—a major theme of romantic polemics—was reflected in critical essays in the press and in the numerous translations that began to be published during the 1820s.

On 6 September 1827 a troupe of English actors opened a series of performances in Paris that was so successful that the engagement was extended to July 1828. Prominent actors, including Charles Kemble, William Charles Macready, and Edmund Kean, joined the company for short runs of specific plays. The first Shakespeare performance was Charles Kemble's *Hamlet* on 11 September. Dumas's account of this performance gives an idea of the effect it had upon the romantic writers.

I must admit that the effect was much greater than I had anticipated. Kemble was wonderful as Hamlet, Miss Smithson adorable as Ophelia. I was overwhelmed by the scene on the battlements, the fan scene, the mad scene, the cemetery scene. From then, and only then, did I understand the theatre. . . . It was the first time I had seen on stage real passions animating men and women of flesh and blood.[20]

Of the eighty performances given by the English actors in the 1827–1828 season, Shakespeare's plays numbered thirty-three. *Hamlet* was performed seven times, *Othello* and *The Merchant of Venice* six, *Romeo and Juliet* five, *King Lear*, *Richard III*, and *Macbeth*, three each. Hugo, Dumas, Vigny, Deschamps, Musset, Hector Berlioz, Eugène Delacroix, the literary and artistic elite of Paris attended these performances. The Preface to *Cromwell* was in part inspired by them as were the Shakespearean translations of Vigny and Deschamps.

1829 was the critical year for the French romantics. Alexandre Dumas's prose history play *Henry III and His Court* was the first theatrical success of French romanticism. It was staged at the Comédie-Française in February 1829 with a cast that included the best actors from the disciplines of comedy and tragedy. Historically accurate sets were designed by Cicéri, with costumes by Edmond Duponchel. As Marie-Antoinette Allévy notes, "the historical genre, in the boulevard manner, i.e., with appropriate sets, exact costumes, numerous props, and sensational stage business, received its consecration in the House of Molière with *Henry III.*"[21] The production was a great success. Its forty-three performances in 1829 constituted one of the longest runs of the decade at the Comédie-Française.

Classicism was dealt a mortal blow by the success of *Henry III*. The actors were forced to acknowledge the financial potential of romantic scripts. The next move would be to stage a verse drama: Hugo's *Marion Delorme*. The play was written to fill this need following the success of *Henry III*, which proved the viability of writing for the Comédie-Française. To fill the gap when *Marion Delorme* was banned by the censor in the summer of 1829, Vigny's *Othello* translation, *The Moor of Venice*, was put into rehearsal and opened in October. It was given a production as spectacular as that of *Henry III.*[22] Its significance is outlined in Vigny's preface published in the text. It was only a moderate success however, which indicates that the time for translations and theories was past. Audiences were ready for a *French* romantic drama in verse. And this is what Hugo provided in *Hernani*.

The production of *Hernani* on 25 February 1830 brings to a close the history of the French theatre during the Restoration. It was an exemplary production.[23] The battle on the opening night signaled the triumph of romanticism over classicism.

1830, then, was a turning point for the French romantics. The most public of forums, the theatre, was theirs. The need for theory and defense had ceased. More practical concerns—how to keep and increase the audience they had won—were to be the important concerns of the 1830s.

The history of French romantic theatre after *Hernani* is ultimately a tale of failure and the reasons are too complex to detail here.[24] Dumas, Hugo, and Vigny—the major romantic playwrights—abandoned the Comédie-Française for the boulevard, where they could work with more sympathetic actors and producers. The boulevard audiences proved to be unresponsive to the generally antisocial or antibourgeois themes of the romantic plays. And the boulevard actors were more comfortable with prose than verse. Dumas met with the most success because he was the readiest to assimilate the material of the popular prose melodrama. Hugo attempted to ennoble the melodrama with *Lucretia Borgia* in 1833, but by 1835 both he and Vigny had returned to the Comédie-Française with *Angelo* and *Chatterton*, respectively. But their successes did not equal those of Scribe and Delavigne, whose plays dominated the repertory of the Comédie-Française in the 1830s. Their work successfully incorporated the freedom in form and the production reforms advocated by the romantics, while providing the audience with the innocuous middlebrow content they seemed to desire.

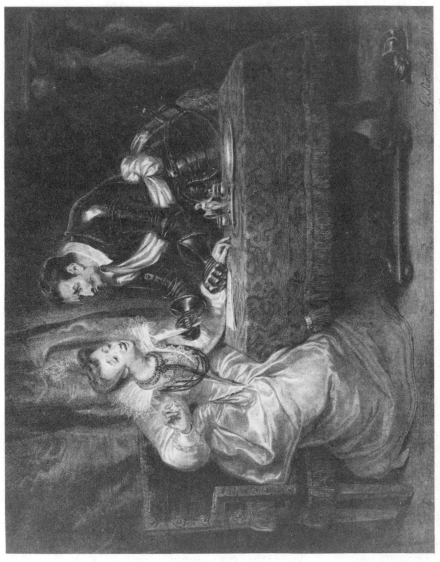

Alexandre Dumas's *Henry III and His Court*, Act 3, Scene 5, 1829. (Author's collection.)

Not form, but content, was the issue of the 1830s and the large middle-class audience of the July Monarchy had no desire to hear the radical social ideas of the romantics. The banning of Hugo's *The King Amuses Himself* after a single performance in 1832 at the Comédie-Française was a first sign. Dumas's *Antony* was considered too immoral for revival at the Comédie-Française in 1834. Dumas and Hugo collaborated in establishing a theatre of their own, the Renaissance, where Hugo's *Ruy Blas* was staged in 1838, but this venture failed. The revival of the classical repertory by Rachel in 1838 also contributed to the decline of romantic drama. The failure of Hugo's *Burgraves* in 1843 is generally cited by historians to mark the end of the history of romantic theatre in France.

Wellek's statement that "romantic drama seems today an episode of little importance which produced no works of enduring value"[25] certainly demands re-evaluation in light of the recent critical study of this subject.[26] It is especially in the area of theatre history and the development of dramatic literature in France that the importance of the romantic drama is clear. It is difficult to imagine the work of Emile Augier and Dumas *fils* in the 1850s, which was enormously influential in the development of late nineteenth-century realism, without the theatrical and dramaturgical reforms of the romantics. In this sense the romantic theatre was an important and necessary step in the development of nineteenth-century theatre.

The failure of the French romantics to produce "works of enduring value" for the theatre, albeit true in terms of a comprehensive examination of world drama, might best be attributed to the fact that, unlike the majority of the European romantics, they chose to work in the theatre, rather than in the study. If European romanticism is the first avant-garde, as many literary historians suggest, theatres and audiences receptive to the avant-garde did not exist until the independent theatre movement of the late nineteenth century. The failure of the French romantic theatre and drama, in fact, pinpoints one of the major issues in the history of nineteenth-century theatre: the conflict between the development of dramatic literature and the reality and economics of theatre production.

French Romantic Theories of Drama

A chronological organization of the theory and criticism in this volume could be outlined in the form of a *drame*.[27] Madame de Staël's *Influence of Literature on Society* (1801) would be our prologue. It introduced many of the themes of our play, but in many aspects looks back to the eighteenth century. Act I would consist of Constant's essay on *Wallenstein* (1809) and Madame de Staël's *Germany* (1810–1814). The former, even in the revised version of 1829, offers a good idea of the attitudes of the liberals during the Empire and their inability to dare extreme literary reforms. *Germany* brings this act to a dramatic conclusion, clearly establishing the term "romantic" in opposition to "classic" and outlining the need for change in French literature in line with other modern literatures. Although the ideas were not always original—A. W. Schlegel is a source for many of the concepts—the effect of *Germany* in Europe was far-reaching. Napoleon was correct in judging it anti-French: it effectively publicized France's loss of position at the forefront of European literature. Act II would consist of Stendhal's *Racine and Shakespeare* (1823–1825). This is the period of the first French romantic publications. Groups are beginning to form and theories to develop. Stendhal's witty and ironic pamphlet outlines the concepts of the liberal faction. Act III offers the point of view of the poets in Hugo's Preface to *Cromwell* (1827), the best known and most comprehensive attempt to develop a romantic theory of drama in France. It is the first major climax in our *drame*. Act IV reflects the increased activity which precedes the final climax. It includes Sainte-Beuve's article (July 1828) with its portrait of stagnant neo-classicism, Deschamps's Preface to his *Studies, French and Foreign* (1828), and Constant's "Reflections on Tragedy" (1829). Act V concludes with the productions of *The Moor of Venice, Othello* and *Hernani* and the prefaces to their published editions, January and February of 1830, respectively. They bring us a happy conclusion: victory for the romantics. The scene from Dumas's *Antony* forms the epilogue: the time for prefaces is over. The romantics' habit of theorizing in their prefaces is gently mocked by a character in the scene translated. The future is in the plays themselves and their nature is indicated by Antony's outburst. The epilogue is ironic.

It is important to examine the themes and ideas which are developed in the course of this *drame*. I will begin with the general concepts and then study the specific issues relating to the definition of drama.

In *The Influence of Literature on Society* Madame de Staël, with her eighteenth-century optimism, outlines a belief in the general progress of civilization. In such a view, change is a fact of life. "Nothing in life should be static, and art is petrified when it no longer changes."[28] Thus, the "law of progress," as Vigny calls it, is implicit in all the theories included in this volume. It is perhaps most systematically outlined in Hugo's Preface to *Cromwell*. Hugo's outline of the development of civilization incorporates many of Madame de Staël's concepts, notably the dichotomies of the North and South; the Christian and the pagan. In his schema, there are three ages of man—the primitive, the ancient, and the modern. The modern, Christian, age is the culmination of the gradual progress of civilization, and the modern form, the *drame*, as exemplified by Shakespeare, "is complete poetry."

The concept of progress is more obvious and easier to define than the attitude toward art. The eighteenth century is evident in Madame de Staël's statement that "the truly beautiful improves man," and that "it is not enough to stir the soul; you must enlighten it." She stresses the eighteenth-century French concept of "taste" throughout *The Influence of Literature on Society*. In *Germany* she continues to envisage a reconciliation between French classicism and romanticism. Thus, in discussing the actor Talma, who combines the best of the French and German acting traditions in his performances, she notes that "the domain of the arts is always composed of the union of the ideal and the natural."

Hugo's definition of art is more radical than Madame de Staël's and more characteristically romantic. For him, "everything that exists in nature exists in art." This is a radical break with the past and with the classical concept of ideal beauty. For Hugo, "True poetry...resides in the harmony of opposites. . . .The real results from the completely natural combination of two types, the sublime and the grotesque." This is the key to Hugo's theory: modern civilization introduced the grotesque in opposition to the sublime. The *drame* incorporates these opposites and all the opposing qualities found in life. Thus, it is "both full of depth and rich in surface, philosophical and picturesque."

In both Madame de Staël's books one of the principal ends of art is illusion. In *The Influence of Literature on Society* deviation from "good taste" destroys illusion. In *Germany* emotional truth is given more importance than material realism. Stendhal also assumes illusion to be a criterion of art, but, deriving his argument from Samuel Johnson, states that theatrical illusion is comprised of a series of "perfect" and "imperfect" illusions. During moments of perfect illusion we are caught up in the action on stage, emotionally involved in it, and actually forget that we are in the theatre.

Were Stendhal's ideas pursued to their logical conclusion, they would lead to a theory of realism. Hugo's theory, which stresses the real as a basic criterion for art, insists however that art is not realistic or illusionistic. Thus he states that "the theatre is an optical point. All that is found in the world, in history, life, in man, can and ought to be reflected in it, but under the magic wand of art." Art for Hugo is distinct from nature in that it combines the ideal and the real. In a key passage, Hugo defines the "ordinary" as a defect which destroys the *drame*. "For the optic of the theatre, all figures must be reduced to their most salient, their most individual traits. Even the vulgar and the trivial must have an intensity. Nothing must be neglected. Like God, the true poet is present everywhere at the same time in his work." Art, then, gives shape and meaning to nature. This is, in fact, an Aristotelian concept, and like Aristotle, Hugo uses it as a defense of poetry. Where Hugo differs from neo-classical theory is in his non-exclusive approach to subject matter and his rejection of *a priori* rules.

For Hugo, then, the poet, like God, is a creator. This concept of the godlike importance of the individual genius is found throughout European romantic criticism. Focus in criticism in this period shifts away from the concept of rules and toward the analysis of the individual creator.[29] Madame de Staël felt that a "work with a single touch of genius is preferable" to a work that is simply correct, that is, one that adheres to the neo-classical rules. For Hugo, genius transcends all rules. "Genius, which divines more than it apprehends, for each work finds the general laws in the general order of things and the special laws in the isolated whole of the subject treated." Content, then, is a determinant of form. Each work of genius establishes its own rules. Hugo adopts the organic metaphor: each work of art is a discrete organism free to develop unfettered as in nature.[30] This is the ultimate response to the neo-classical concept of rules.

One of the most important and original contributions of the European romantics to the history of criticism is their analysis of the relationship between art and society. Each age and each nation produces its own characteristic art. Early in the French romantic period this concept is used to explain the flaws as well as the beauties in Shakespeare. It is also Constant's defense for his adaptation of Schiller's *Wallenstein* to the conventions of neo-classical drama. For Stendhal all good art reflects its own epoch; hence all good art is romantic, Racine and Shakespeare. In Hugo's elaborate outline, the various aspects of the social, political, and religious orders in each of mankind's three epochs result in a specific art form. The primitive age is characterized by the ode, the ancient by the epic, and the modern by the *drame*. Vigny insists "that one ought to acknowledge each writer's work *in the context of its period*." All of the authors in this volume, then, do not deny the value of the great writers—that is, geniuses—of the past; they simply re-assert the need for each age and each nation to develop its own characteristic art.

The above explains why it is common to find the various specific reforms advocated by the romantics linked to the concept of revolution. The social upheavals of the late eighteenth century ought to be reflected in art. For a new society there ought to be new forms of art. Thus, writing in 1829, Constant admits that when he adapted Schiller's *Wallenstein* in 1809, he was wrong to make concessions to neo-classical taste. He "should have foreseen that a political revolution would carry over into a literary revolution." This also leads Stendhal to claim that he has "attempted in his own writing style to be suitable for the children of the Revolution, men who seek thought rather than beautiful phrases." Neo-classicism is associated with the tyranny of absolute monarchy, romanticism with democracy or constitutional monarchy.

One of the specific characteristics of French romanticism is the introduction of models from non-classical and foreign literatures. This cultural cosmopolitanism is a serious threat to French neo-classicism because it finds works of genius—valid models—in the "romantic" literature of the Elizabethan Age, the Spanish Golden Age, and in the contemporary literature of England and Germany. "Foreign models can generate new ideas," states Madame de Staël. Imitation in itself is inimical to the romantics. As Hugo proclaims, "there are neither rules nor models." In arguing against neo-classicism, however, examples are needed from works of proven merit. Shakespeare is a source of inspiration and an example of a possible form for romantic drama. This is, in fact, the purpose behind Vigny's *Othello* translation. He makes it clear that he is not offering an original work, but rather presenting a "foreign masterpiece" for the purposes of stylistic experiment.

Progress, the relationship between art and society, the artist as original genius, the organic growth of an art work, literary cosmopolitanism: these are some of the principal concepts which underlie the selections in this volume. The specific issue in the selections is the romantic theatre and, in France, this is always viewed in opposition to classicism or neo-classicism.[31] Neo-classical theory in France was formalized in the seventeenth century by such critics as François Hédelin, Abbé d'Aubignac, in *The Whole Art of the Stage* (1657) and Nicolas Boileau-Despréaux in *The Art of Poetry* (1674) and is exemplified in the plays of Corneille, Racine, and Molière.[32] Neo-classical dogma stressed verisimilitude in the appearance of truth which led, paradoxically, to concepts of reality and abstraction. The concept of reality results in a reduction of fantastic elements in the drama. The use of the chorus and the soliloquy is discouraged as not being realistic. The character of the confidant develops as a "realistic" means of allowing a character to speak his inner thoughts. Violence is not allowed on the stage, as the audience will be conscious that it is not really happening if it is merely simulated. Set changes would also draw attention to the "unreality" of the stage and are to be avoided. Abstraction is a function of the idea that truth is found not in details, but in the general characteristics shared by all things of a certain type. This leads to type characters and the concept of decorum in character. Characterization is thought of in terms of norms with respect to social status, age, profession, and sex. The unities of time, place, and action are all functions of verisimilitude. The dramatic genres are strictly defined and separated. The two major genres are tragedy and comedy. Tragedy deals with affairs of state or great actions; its characters are drawn from the ruling class; its style is noble. Comedy treats domestic or private situations; its characters are drawn from the middle or lower classes; its style is familiar. The tragic and the comic are kept strictly apart. Mixed genres exist but do not merit serious attention.

The eighteenth century saw a weakening in the attitude toward some of the specific tenets of the neo-classical dogma. Most important was the popular development of the intermediate genres, bourgeois tragedy and sentimental comedy. In France Denis Diderot is the most important theorist of these intermediate genres. The tendency in French romantic theory is to redefine the classical distinctions in romantic terms or to create a single dramatic genre: the *drame*.

Stendhal retains the strict separation of tragedy and comedy, but re-defines them in such a way that tragedy deals primarily with character and emotion while comedy is concerned with the details of existence. He would free tragedy of the limitation of verse and the unities of time and place and would open it to subjects from modern history. Vigny follows the Shakespearean model for tragedy, rejecting the unities, mix-ing the comic with the serious, using a style which ranges from the familiar to the epic, and making character more central than plot. Con-stant's essay, "Reflections on Tragedy," proposes a new form of tragedy which introduces "the action of society such as it is constituted in each epoch, and such as it affects character and passion, the latter being the traditional sources of the tragic."

It is Hugo, however, who most radically approaches the issue of the genres. For him there is only one genre, the *drame*, which "assimilates in the same inspiration the grotesque and the sublime, the fearful and the absurd, tragedy and comedy."

Also of note is the interest in history as a modern alternative to the limited classical or mythological subjects of traditional tragedy. Madame de Staël calls "historical tragedy...the natural trend of the age." She obviously had in mind not only Shakespeare's history plays, but more importantly, the plays of Goethe and Schiller—*Goetz von Berlichingen, Egmont, Don Carlos, Wallenstein, Maria Stuart, William Tell*, and so forth. It is evident from reading through the material in this volume that a majority of the subjects proposed or discussed are historical in nature. This is consistent with the general historical bias of nineteenth-century thought as well as with the growth of materialism.

Of the elements of drama, the romantics tend to emphasize character over the classical importance of plot. Madame de Staël's analysis of Shakespeare focuses on his characters, Richard III, Othello, and Mac-beth. Constant makes a distinction in his Preface to *Wallstein* which seems to have been generally accepted by the French romantics. For him French classical tragedy generalized character as passion while contemporary German plays portrayed individualized characters. Stendhal, Hugo, and Vigny consistently place the generalized characters of the neo-classical drama in a contrast to the "living" creations of Shakespeare.

The importance of character in romantic drama leads to one of the principal arguments for the rejection of the unities of time and place. As Constant notes, "the unities of time and place often compel the poet to neglect, in his events and characters, the truth of gradation and the delicacy of nuance." Vigny predicts that "in the future, the dramatic poet...will take in his broad hand a lengthy period of time and move whole lifetimes through it. He will create men, not *types*, but *individuals*." Constant is especially aware of this problem as he had tried to adapt Schiller's complex portrait of Wallenstein, developed over an extended period of time, to the neo-classical unities. Hugo, too, rejects the concept of the unities for similar reasons, although he also notes that more time is needed in the plays themselves to develop the richness and depth of characterization. Thus, although his *Cromwell* actually adheres to the unity of time, its scenic time is extended beyond the limits of the stage. Constant notes that Schiller's audience will accept a tragedy that is more than twice as long as a neo-classical play. Hugo advocates the replacement of the multiple playbill in the theatre with an evening given over to the performance of a single *drame*.

Setting is important as it reflects the environment in which the characters are developed. Constant defines setting as "the element which essentially characterizes the social state whose portrayal is the goal of dramatic writing." As Hugo states, "It is beginning to be understood in our time that exact localization is one of the first elements of reality....The place where this or that catastrophe occurred becomes a terrible and inseparable witness of it, and the absence of silent characters of this sort would make the greatest scenes of history incomplete in the drama." This attitude toward the set is one of the major contributions of romantic dramaturgy. Scenery for the romantics becomes a necessary element in the production, an environment for the action, which conveys important information as well as contributing to the atmosphere of the scene. The scene grows out of the action and changes as the action demands.

The final dramaturgical issue is the matter of language. Of the neo-classical concept of verse, Madame de Staël notes that "the pomp of alexandrine verse is an even greater obstacle than is the habit of conventional good taste to any change in the form and content of French tragedies....Any number of emotions and effects are banished from the stage, not by the rules of tragedy, but by the very exigencies of versification." Constant, Stendhal, Hugo, and Vigny outline at length the problems inherent in the traditional approach to French verse. Stendhal simply advocates prose, and, by 1829, Constant seems to favor this option. Hugo, Deschamps, and Vigny propose changes in the alexandrine which would make it more flexible and greatly increase the vocabulary that could be employed.

The battle that was waged for romanticism in France, then, was essentially a battle for freedom against the constraints of the neo-classical theory of art. Hugo sums this up nicely when he states in the Preface to *Hernani*: "Liberty in art; liberty in society: these are the double goals toward which all rational and logical minds must strive together." All the essays in this collection ultimately contributed to the achievement of this end.

Notes

1. Stendhal, *Racine and Shakespeare*. See Chapter 3, p. 126 in this volume.
2. Victor Hugo, Preface to *Hernani*. See Chapter 5, p. 191 in this volume.
3. René Wellek, *Concepts of Criticism* (New Haven, Conn.: Yale University Press, 1963), pp. 128–221, provides a general survey of the attempts to define romanticism.
4. Jacques Barzun, *Classic, Romantic, and Modern* (Garden City, N.Y.: Anchor, 1961), p. 8.
5. Barzun, *Classic*, p. 14.
6. See the Selected Bibliography for a list of titles dealing with romanticism.
7. Wellek, *Concepts*, pp. 160–61.
8. In *Comparative Literature: Method and Perspective*, ed. Newton P. Stallknecht and Horst Frenz (Carbondale, Ill.: Southern Illinois University Press, 1961), pp. 223–59.
9. René Bray, *Chronologie du Romanticisme: 1804–1830* (Paris: Nizet, 1963), is the best general introduction to the development of romanticism in France during the Restoration.
10. Guillaume de Bertier de Sauvigny, *La Restauration* (Paris: Flammarion, 1955), p. 7.
11. Bray, *Chronologie*, pp. 63–65.
12. The best studies of the French theatre during the romantic period are Marie-Antoinette Allévy, *La Mise en scène en France dans la première moitié du dix-neuvième siècle* (Paris: Droz, 1938); Maurice Descotes, *Le Drame romantique et ses grands créateurs* (Paris: P.U.F., 1955); and Marvin Carlson, *The French Stage in the Nineteenth Century* (Metuchen, N.J.: Scarecrow, 1977).
13. See Carlson, *French Stage*, pp. 52–53; and Neil Arvin, *Eugène Scribe and the French Theatre* (Cambridge, Mass.: Harvard University Press, 1924).
14. See Barry Daniels, "Victor Hugo on the Boulevard: *Lucrèce Borgia* at the Porte-Saint-Martin Theatre in 1833," *Theatre Journal*, 32 (1980), 17–42.
15. Charles Nodier, "Preface" to Guilbert de Pixérécourt, *Théâtre Choisi* (Paris: Tresse, 1841), p. viii.
16. Carlson, *French Stage*, p. 29.
17. See Léon Séché, "Les Débuts du Romantisme au Théâtre Français: Le Baron Taylor et le *Léonidas* de Michel Pichat," *Les Annales romantiques*, 5 (1909), 241–72.
18. For a history of English theatre in France, see Joseph-Léopold Borgerhoff, *Le Théâtre anglais à Paris* (Paris: Hachette, 1913); and Victor Leathers, *British Entertainers in France* (Toronto: University of Toronto Press, 1959).
19. Jean-François Ducis, *Oeuvres complètes* (Paris: A. Nepveu, 1826), II, p. 167.
20. Alexandre Dumas, *Mémoires* (Paris: Gallimard, 1954–1967), II, pp. 419–20.

21. Allévy, *La Mise en scène*, p. 88. See Marie-Antoinette Allévy, *Edition critique d'une mise en scène romantique* (Paris: Droz, 1938), for a study of this production.

22. See Barry Daniels, "Shakespeare à la romantique: *Othello, le More de Venise* d'Alfred de Vigny," *Revue d'Histoire du Théâtre*, 27 (1975), 125–55.

23. The staging has been analyzed by Marvin Carlson in his article *"Hernani's* Revolt from the Tradition of French Stage Composition," *Theatre Survey*, 13 (1972), 1–27.

24. James Smith Allen, *Popular French Romanticism* (Syracuse, N.Y.: Syracuse University Press, 1981), is an interesting study of the reading public in Paris during the romantic period, which clearly outlines the "industrialization" of literature and the shift from the elite public of the eighteenth century to a large popular audience in the nineteenth century.

25. René Wellek, *A History of Modern Criticism: 1750–1950*, vol. II, *The Romantic Age* (New Haven, Conn.: Yale University Press, 1955), p. 242.

26. French scholars are currently editing or have recently edited important critical editions of the work, including theatrical works, of Hugo, Vigny, and Dumas. The journal *Romantisme* was begun in 1971. The Comédie-Française staged extremely successful revivals of *Hernani* and *Ruy Blas* during the 1970s. Vigny's *Chatterton* and *La Maréchale d'Ancre* have been revived and filmed for French television. The work of Allévy and Descotes in France and more recently, my own work and that of Marvin Carlson, cited above, have contributed to our knowledge of the importance of romantic stagecraft to theatre history.

27. The English term *drama* does not adequately translate the French term *drame* for the intermediate genre between tragedy and comedy. It will be left in French throughout.

28. All quotations not otherwise noted are from the selections in this volume.

29. Sainte-Beuve's series of "Literary Portraits" and his book *Port-Royal* were influential in establishing the biographical method in criticism.

30. Hugo used this concept of original genius and organic growth to defend his aversion to revising and correcting his own works. Vigny seems to be answering Hugo on this point when he says that "any man who has ideas and doesn't organize them into a unified system is an incomplete man." Each system, however, is unique for Vigny; the product of an original genius dies with him.

31. In France, *classicism* can refer to the Greek and Roman theatre, as it does in other countries, but it can also mean the drama of the seventeenth and eighteenth centuries: Corneille through Voltaire.

32. See Jacques Scherer, *La Dramaturgie classique en France* (Paris: Nizet, 1968), for a detailed study of French classical dramaturgical practice. One of the best outlines of neo-classical theory is found in Oscar Brockett, *History of the Theatre* (Boston: Allyn and Bacon, 1982), pp. 158–60.

CHRONOLOGY

Titles given in all capital letters are included in this volume.

1800 Madame de Staël. THE INFLUENCE OF LITERATURE ON SOCIETY.

1801 Chateaubriand. *Atala.*

1802 Chateaubriand. *The Genius of Christianity.*
Madame de Staël. *Delphine.*

1803 Senancour. *Obermann.*

1804 18 May. Napoleon proclaimed Emperor.

1805 Chateaubriand. *René.*
14 May. F. Raynouard. *The Templars.* Comédie-Française.

1806 26 June. G. Legouvé. *The Death of Henry IV.* Comédie-Française.

1807 Napoleon's decree limiting the number of Parisian theatres.

Madame de Staël. *Corinne.*
A. W. Schlegel. *Comparison between the Phaedras of Racine and Euripides.*

1809 Constant. WALLSTEIN with first version of the essay "On the Thirty Year's War."
7 March. N. Lemercier. *Christopher Columbus,* a "Shakespearean Comedy." Odéon Theatre.

1810 Napoleon destroys all published copies of Madame de Staël's GERMANY.

1813 Publication of the French translation of A. W. Schlegel's *Lectures on Dramatic Literature* (1809–1811). Publication in London of GERMANY.

1814 11 April. Abdication of Napoleon.

Publication of GERMANY in France.

1815 June. Establishment of Louis XVIII as head of a constitutional monarchy. Reopening of the Porte-Saint-Martin Theatre.

1816 Constant. *Adolphe*. French translation of Scott's *Guy Mannering*.

1818 Publication in Paris of an edition of Byron's *Works*. Posthumous publication of Madame de Staël's *Considerations on the French Revolution*.

1819 23 October. Casimir Delavigne. *The Sicilian Vespers*. Odéon Theatre.
5 November. L. Ancelot. *Louis IX*. Comédie-Française.
December–March 1821. *Le Conservateur Littéraire*, edited by Victor Hugo.

1820 Gymnase Theatre opened.
6 January. C. Delavigne. *The Actors*. Odéon Theatre.
6 March. P. Lebrun. *Mary Stuart*. Comédie-Française.
Lamartine. *Meditations*.

1821 Publication begun of F. Guizot's revisions of the Letourneur Shakespeare translations.
1 December. C. Delavigne. *The Pariah*. Odéon Theatre.

27 December. E. de Jouy. *Sylla*. Comédie-Française.

1822 Ladvovat begins publishing its collection *Masterpieces of Foreign Literature*.
March. Alfred de Vigny. *Poems*.
5 June. A.-V. Arnault. *Régulus*. Comédie-Française.
14 June. A. Guiraud. *The Maccabees*. Odéon Theatre.
June. V. Hugo. *Odes*.
31 July–25 October. English actors perform in Paris.
October. Stendhal. Chapter 1 of RACINE AND SHAKESPEARE in *Paris Monthly Review*.
7 November. A. Soumet. *Clytemnestra*. Comédie-Française.
9 November. A. Soumet. *Saul*. Odéon Theatre.

1823 January. Stendhal. Chapter 2 of RACINE AND SHAKESPEARE in *Paris Monthly Review*.
February. V. Hugo. *Han of Iceland*.
March. Stendhal. RACINE AND SHAKESPEARE.
July-1824. *The French Muse*, edited by Deschamps.
October. Lamartine. *New Meditations*.
November. Stendhal. *Life of Rossini*.
6 December. C. Delavigne. *The School for Old Men*. Co-

médie-Française.
French translation of A.
Manzoni's *Count of Car-
magnola* and *Adelghis*, with
his "Letter to Mr. C. on
the Unities of Time and
Place in Tragedy."

1824   3 January. Charles Nodier
appointed Librarian at the
Arsenal. Formation of the
first *cénacle*.
February. V. Hugo. *New
Odes*.
April. A. de Vigny. *Eloa*.
20 April. N. Lemercier.
Jane Shore. Comédie-
Française.
24 April. Auger, President
of the French Academy,
gives a speech attacking
the romantics.
2 July. A. Soumet. *Cleopatra*. Odéon Theatre.
15 September–1831. *The
Globe*.
16 September. Death of
Louis XVIII.

1825   March. Stendhal. RACINE
AND SHAKESPEARE,
No. II.
29 May. Coronation of
Charles X.
June. P. Mérimée. *Clara
Gazul*.
9 July. Baron Taylor ap-
pointed Royal Commis-
sioner to the Comédie-
Française.
26 November. M. Pichat.
Léonidas. Comédie-
Française.

1826   January. V. Hugo. *Bug
Jargal*. A. de Vigny. *Poems,
Ancient and Modern*.
April. A. de Vigny. *Cinq-
Mars*.
19 October. Death of
Talma.
November. V. Hugo. *Odes
and Ballads*.
L. Vitet begins publication
of *The League*, a trilogy of
historical dialogues.

1827   May. M. Pichat's *William
Tell* accepted at the Comé-
die-Française.
19 June. V. Ducange.
*Thirty Years, or the Life of a
Gambler*. One of the most
successful melodramas of
the period. Established
Frédérick Lemaître and
Marie Dorval as star
performers.
August. Stendhal. *Armance*.
6 September–July 1828.
English actors perform in
Paris.
November. Gérard de
Nerval. Translation of
Goethe's *Faust I*.
December. V. Hugo pub-
lishes CROMWELL.
24 December. V. Hugo.
Amy Robsart. Odéon Thea-
tre. Failure of this play
adapted by Hugo from
Walter Scott, staged as
being by "P. Foucher."

1828   15 April. Vigny and Deschamps's *Romeo and Juliet*
translation accepted by the
Comédie-Française.

10 June. F. Soulié. *Romeo and Juliet*. Odéon Theatre.
June. P. Mérimée. *The Jacquerie*.
July. Sainte-Beuve. *Historical and Critical Portrait of French Poetry and Theatre in the Sixteenth Century*.
5 July. Sainte-Beuve. Article in the *Globe*: ALEXANDRE DUVAL OF THE FRENCH ACADEMY.
August. V. Hugo. *Odes and Ballads*.
November. E. Deschamps. STUDIES, FRENCH AND FOREIGN.

1829   January. V. Hugo. *The Orientals*.
11 February. A. Dumas. *Henry III and His Court*. Comédie-Française.
March. P. Mérimée. *A Chronicle of Charles IX's Times*.
April. Sainte-Beuve. *The Life, Poetry and Thoughts of Joseph Delorme*.
May. A. de Vigny. *Poems*.
30 May. C. Delavigne. *Marino Faliero*. Porte-Saint-Martin Theatre.

3 August. Rossini. *William Tell*. Opera.
August. V. Hugo's *Marion Delorme* banned.
September. V. Hugo writes *Hernani*.
24 October. A. de Vigny. *The Moor of Venice, Othello*. Comédie-Française.
B. Constant. *Literary and Political Miscellany* includes ON THE THIRTY YEARS' WAR.
November–December. B. Constant. REFLECTIONS ON TRAGEDY in the *Revue de Paris*.
December. A. de Musset. *Spanish and Italian Stories*.

1830   January. A. de Vigny. Publication of THE MOOR OF VENICE, OTHELLO.
25 February 1830. V. Hugo. HERNANI. Comédie-Française.
30 March. A. Dumas. *Christine*. Odéon Theatre.
May–June. A. Dumas writes ANTONY.
28–30 July. July Revolution. Louis-Philippe proclaimed king.

MADAME DE STAËL

Madame de Staël (1766–1817) was an outstanding figure in her age, not only in the realm of literature, but in politics as well. Her parents were Swiss Protestants. Her father, Jacques Necker, settled in Paris in 1756 at the age of eighteen and began a career in banking which was to make him a millionaire. He entered politics in 1767 as a minister of the Republic of Geneva to Versailles. From 1778 to 1781 and again in 1788–1789 he served as Minister of Finance to Louis XVI. Madame de Staël's mother, Suzanne Curchod, was poor, but well educated. As a young woman she was courted by Edward Gibbon and corresponded with Voltaire and Jean-Jacques Rousseau. Her salon in Paris was a meeting place for the literary elite of the 1770s and 1780s, frequented by Diderot, Jean Le Rond d'Alembert, Gibbon, Comte Georges-Louis Leclerc Buffon, Jean-François Marmontel, and Baron Friedrich Melchior von Grimm.

Madame de Staël, then, grew up in the highest literary and political milieus. At the age of twenty she was married to Eric Magnus Staël-Holstein, the Swedish ambassador to Paris. It was a marriage of convenience and after the first two years of the marriage the couple led virtually separate lives. Among her lovers in the next twenty years were Charles Maurice de Talleyrand-Périgord, Louis de Narbonne (to whom she bore two sons), and Benjamin Constant.

Madame de Staël's salons at the Swedish embassy in Paris and at her family residence, Coppet, in Switzerland, were centers for liberal political sentiments and revolutionary literary ideas. Her meddling in politics was important enough to bring about her exile from Paris in 1795 and again throughout the Empire. Napoleon, in fact, kept her under constant surveillance and had the original 1810 French edition of her Germany *destroyed.*

Madame de Staël wrote plays, short stories, and two successful novels, Delphine *(1803) and* Corinne *(1807), but, in retrospect, her most important literary works have been the two volumes of criticism from which our selections are taken. Of these two works the first,* The Influence of Literature on Society *(1800), is the less radical and more strongly reflects the influence of eighteenth-century French traditions. Her basic idea was to prove the perfectibility of mankind by considering the history of literature in the context of social and political developments and to prove the positive effects produced by literature on society. Although this idea did not originate with Madame de Staël, she became the principal source for its transmission to the French romantic writers of the Restoration. Of similar importance is her distinction between the literature of the South and that of the North. The former is associated with classicism, while the latter is associated with freedom, emotionality, melancholy, and mysticism. Although she tried to fashion a middle ground between these two extremes, the literature of the North tends to appear more progressive. A general point is made that the literature of the South needs to respond to the alternative forms and subjects to be found in Northern literature.*

This last concept is more thoroughly developed in Germany, *which she was finally able to publish at London in 1813. In this work the literature of the North is now clearly defined as being romantic. Her study of modern German literature and comments on English literature, especially Shakespeare, provided the coming generation of French romantic writers with one of their primary sources of inspiration.*

The Influence of Literature on Society (1800)

The first edition of The Influence of Literature on Society *was published in Paris by Maradan in April. A second edition, "revised, corrected and augmented," was published in December 1800.*

FROM THE PREFACE TO THE SECOND EDITION
. . . . . .

One can distinguish today, in French literary circles, two opposed opinions, each of which, through excesses, can result in the loss of literary taste or originality. One group believes that style can be strengthened by the use of confused images, neologisms, and extravagant phraseology. These writers diminish literature, adding nothing either to eloquence or thought. Such attempts overwhelm natural talents rather than refine them. The opposition would like to convince us that good taste consists in a regular, but general, style which clothes even more general ideas.

The second method is much less open to criticism. Its oft-repeated phrases are like old friends; one lets them drop without making any demands of them. But it is difficult to conceive of an eloquent or thoughtful writer whose style does not contain expressions which shocked his first readers, at least those who were not carried away by the loftiness of his ideas or by the liveliness of his sensibility.

. . . . . .

The most perfect of our poets, Racine, is he whose bold expressions aroused the most criticism. And that most eloquent of writers, the author of *Emile* and *Héloïse*, is supremely subject to criticism by those who are insensible to the charms of eloquence. Rousseau's style would no longer be recognizable if one were to cut his sentences in two; if one were to remove interest and movement from their development or if one were to isolate a few words which appear bizarre out of context but which are most effective in their proper place.

I repeat, a generalized style need not fear such attacks. Subdivide the sentences of such a style as much as you like—on their own the words that compose them will re-form into sentences, "accustomed as they are to find themselves together." But never has a writer expressed the sentiments he feels nor developed truly individual ideas without this originality being reflected in his style. It is this alone which arouses and captures the interest and imagination of his readers.

Paradoxes are without doubt general ideas. Usually one has only to reverse a banality to make it a paradox. Such it is with a certain type of exaggerated writing: frigid expressions are transformed into false expressions. But is it necessary to limit man's ideas to a closed circle? For there is no talent where there is no originality in thought or style.

Voltaire, whose patrimony was the century of Louis XIV, sought new beauties in English literature which he could adapt to French taste. Almost all out poets of his century imitated the English. . . . Why then would we disavow the merit of work so often imitated by our best writers?

Doubtless, as I have continually reiterated in this book, no literary beauty endures if it is not subordinated to the most perfect of taste. I was the first to employ a new word, "vulgarity," finding that there were not enough words to banish forever all the forms lacking elegance in their imagery and delicacy in their expression. But talent consists in knowing how to respect the true precepts of taste, while introducing into our literature all that is beautiful, sublime, and touching in that melancholy nature so well observed by Northern writers. And, if it betrays ignorance of art to have wanted to adopt in France all the incoherencies of the English and German tragic writers, we must be insensible to the genius of eloquence. We must be forever deprived of the talent to deeply touch the soul, if we do not admire the ability of the Northerners to feel and to communicate the passion of emotions and the depth of thought.

It is impossible to be a true man of letters without having studied ancient writers, without having an excellent knowledge of the classical writers of the century of Louis XIV. Henceforth, we must abandon the idea of continuing to produce great writers in France, if we criticize in advance all that can lead to the development of a new genre, or open new roads for humantiy, or, finally, offer a future for thought. A life devoted to literature will soon have little attraction if the century of Louis XIV is maintained as a model of perfection which no writer, however thoughtful or eloquent, can surpass.

I have carefully distinguished in this book what pertains to imaginative art from what concerns philosophy. I have noted that the former is not subject to infinite refinement, while the boundaries of thought cannot be foreseen. It has been said that I was insufficiently respectful of the ancients. Nevertheless, I have repeated, in diverse ways, the fact that the majority of poetic inventions came to us from the Greeks and that Greek poetry has not "been surpassed or even equalled by the moderns." It is true, however, that I did not say men have not acquired a single new idea for nearly three thousand years. And it is a great error to condemn mankind to Sisyphus' torture; always to fall back without having advanced.

. . . . . .

PART I: "ANCIENT AND MODERN LITERATURE"

Chapter XII. "Concerning the principal fault attributed
to Northern literature by the French"

In France Northern literature is criticized as lacking taste. Northern writers respond that this concept of taste is a purely arbitrary construct which often deprives feeling and thought of their most original felicities.

There exists, I believe, a just median between these two views. The rules of taste are not arbitrary. One must not confuse the basic principles on which universal truths are founded with concessions demanded by local circumstances.

The obligations of virtue, that code of principles unanimously approved by all mankind, admit some minor modifications in respect to the manners and customs of diverse nations. And, although the main premises remain unchanged, the prominence accorded to any specific virtue may vary as customs and governments vary. If taste can be compared to what is greatest in man, it would similarly be found to be fixed in general principles. National taste should be judged according to these principles: the more that it is in accord with them, the closer it is to truth.

It is often asked if genius must be sacrificed to taste. The reply is negative: taste never necessitates the sacrifice of genius. In Northern literature you will often find ridiculous scenes in juxtapostion with scenes of great beauty: what taste condemns should be eliminated. There is no necessary connection between the flaws and the felicities except that of human weakness which does not allow the constant maintenance of a lofty tone. The flaws are not a result of the beauties, although the latter can help erase the memory of the former. Rather than give any lustre to talent, these flaws often weaken the intended impression.

If you ask which has the more merit, a work with great flaws and great beauties, or a mediocre, but correct work, I would reply without hesitation, that the work with a single touch of genius is preferable. The nation is weak which is only interested in the ridiculous, so easily comprehended and avoided, rather than seeking above all in man's thought that which expands the mind and the soul. Negative merit can give no pleasure, but many men demand of life only the absence of pain; of writing the absence of flaws; of everything only absences. Hardy spirits want to live, but in order for them to exist they must encounter new ideas or passionate feelings in what they read.

There are works in French where one finds beauties of the first order without the intermixture of bad taste. These are the only models which at once manifest all the virtues of literature.

Among Northern men of letters there exists a peculiarity which is more dependent, so to speak, on factionalism than judgement. They value the characteristic flaws as much as the virtues of their writers. They ought to say to themselves, as a witty woman said of a hero's weakness: "He is great in spite of, and not because of, that."

Men seek agreeable effects in the masterpieces of the imagination. Taste is nothing but the art of understanding and anticipating the causes of such impressions. When you summon up disgusting situations you arouse an unpleasant reaction; something one would sedulously avoid in real life. When you transform moral terror into physical repulsion, by the depiction of intrinsically horrible circumstances, you lose all the charm of imitation. You provide only an emotional excitement, and you may not even achieve this questionable effect if you exaggerate too much; because in theatre, as in real life, when exaggeration is perceived, even the truth is no longer accepted. If you continue in this manner, if language is muddled or plot developments are unconvincing, you will lose temporarily or destroy completely your audience's attention. If you paint ignoble traits in heroic characters, you run the risk of hindering the maintenance of theatrical illusion, which has an extremely delicate nature: the slightest circumstance can wake the spectators from their enchantment. The simple gives the mind a chance to rest and revitalize itself; while the base might prevent the renewal of trust in noble and lofty thoughts.

In England, Shakespeare's beauties can triumph over his flaws. But these flaws diminish much of his renown in other nations. Surprise is certainly a good means of heightening an effect, but it would be ridiculous to conclude from this that one ought to precede a tragic scene with a comic one, to increase the effect of the former. A beautiful phrase, appearing in a careless composition, can make all the more impression on the mind, but the exception cannot, ultimately, overcome the effect of the whole. Surprise should be born of greatness in itself and not of its opposition to meanness, of whatever kind. Painting needs shadows, but not splotches, to set off the brightness of colors. Literature ought to follow the same principles. Nature offers the model: good taste need only be the rational observation of nature.

One could examine these developments much more fully, but it is enough to demonstrate that in literature, taste never necessitates the sacrifice of any pleasure: on the contrary, it indicates the means of increasing pleasure. And the principles of taste, far from being incompatible with genius, are discovered through the study of genius.

I shall not reproach Shakespeare with having disregarded the rules of art. These rules have infinitely less importance than those of taste, because the former prescribe what must be done, while the latter limit themselves to identifying what must be avoided. One cannot be mistaken in what is bad, but it is impossible to set limits on the ingenuity of a man of genius. A genius can take entirely new paths without, however, failing to achieve his goal. The rules of art are a compilation of the probable ways to achieve success. If success is achieved, it matters little whether the rules were follwed or not. But it is not the same with taste, for to place oneself above taste, is to stray from the very beauty of nature; yet nothing is above nature.

Let us not say, then, that Shakespeare knew how to dispense with taste and was superior to its laws. Let us admit, to the contrary, that he manifests taste when he is sublime, and that he lacks taste when his talent flags.

Chapter XIII. "Shakespearean Tragedy"

The English enthusiasm for Shakespeare is more profound than that any nation has ever felt for a writer. Free peoples have a proprietary attitude toward all types of renown which does honor to their country. This sentiment inspires an admiration which excludes all manner of criticism.

In Shakespeare there are beauties of the first order which appeal to all nations and all epochs. In Shakespeare there are also flaws which may be attributed to the Elizabethan period and peculiarities which are so popular with the English that they continue to have great success on the English stage. I want to examine these beauties and singularities as they relate to the national taste of England and to the genius of Northern literature.

Shakespeare did not imitate the ancients, he was not inspired, like Racine, by Greek tragedies. He wrote one play on a Greek subject, *Troilus and Cressida*, and in it he did not observe the manners and customs of Homer's day. He is much more successful in his tragedies on Roman subjects. Histories, or the *Lives* of Plutarch (which Shakespeare seems to have read with real care) are not merely literary studies; they offer an almost living portrait of man. When models of dramatic art from antiquity are the sole objects for study, there is less originality—an imitation of an imitation—than in that genius which paints from nature. This immediate genius, if I can so express myself, is what particularly characterizes Shakespeare. From the Greeks to Shakespeare all literatures start from the same source and are derived one from the other. Shakespeare begins a new tradition, doubtless marked by the spirit and general coloring of Northern poetry. He spurred the development of English literature and gave its character to English dramatic art.

A nation which has become free, whose passions have been powerfully stirred by the horrors of civil war, is much more susceptible to the emotion excited by Shakespeare than by that of Racine. When adversity weighs upon a people for a lengthy period, it gives them a character which even subsequent prosperity cannot erase. Although sometimes equalled by later English and German authors, Shakespeare was the first writer to portray moral suffering in the extreme. The bitterness of the suffering he renders could almost pass for an invention, if nature were not mirrored in it.

The ancients believed in a Fate which strikes and destroys like lightning. The moderns, and Shakespeare in particular, find the deepest sources of emotions in philosophic necessity, based on the memory of so many irreparable misfortunes, vain efforts, and deceived hopes. The ancients dwelt in a world that was too new, whose history was too brief, and they were so avid for the future that misfortunes portrayed were never as distressing as those in English plays.

Shakespeare portrayed the fear of death in all its aspects, a sentiment whose effects the ancients, because of their religion and their stoicism, rarely developed. Shakespeare makes us feel the fearful sense, the cold shudder that a man feels, when, full of life, he learns that he is going to die. In Shakespeare's tragedies old age and youth, virtue and crime, face death and express all the emotions natural to this situation. Do we not feel compassion on hearing the pleas of Arthur, a child sentenced to death by King John, or when the assassin Tyrrel comes to Richard III to announce the peaceful "sleep" of Edward's children?[1] When a hero is portrayed at the point of losing his life, our interest is captured by the memory of what he has done and by the grandeur of his character. But, when weak-willed men of ignoble fates such as Henry VI, Richard II and King Lear are represented at the point of death, the audience's attention is focused solely on the great debate between being and nothingness in nature. Shakespeare knew how to paint with genius that mixture of physical action and moral reflection inspired by the approach of death, when man is not swept away by overwhelming emotions.

Another feeling that Shakespeare alone knew how to dramatize is pity without any admixture of admiration for the sufferer,[2]* pity for an insignificant person,[3]* and, sometimes, even pity for a contemptible person.[4]* An unlimited talent is needed to transpose this feeling from life to the theatre while preserving all its strength. When successful, the effect that it produces is of a greater truthfulness than any other: one is interested not in the great man, but in the man; thus one is moved not by conventionally tragic feelings, but by an impression so close to the impressions of life that the illusion is even greater.

Even when Shakespeare portrays characters with illustrious fates, he interests his audience in them through purely natural feelings. The circumstances may be elevated, but the hero differs less from other men than in our tragedies. Shakespeare lets us penetrate intimately the greatness he depicts. Listening to him, we experience all the nuances and gradations which lead to heroism, and our soul itself achieves this loftiness.

The English national pride, a result of the jealous love of liberty, lends itself less to fanatical devotion to a few leaders than does the chivalric spirit of the children of the French monarchy. The English do recognize the services of a good citizen, but they do not have that penchant for limitless enthusiasm inherent in French institutions, customs, and character. That proud disdain for submissive enthusiasm, ever a part of the English character, must have inspired in their national poet the idea of deriving compassion from pity rather than from admiration. The tears which we shed for the sublime characters of our tragedies are aroused in Shakespeare for the lowly and forsaken sufferer, for that chain of misfortunes which cannot be met in Shakespeare without acquiring something of the experience of life itself.

Shakespeare excels in the depiction of pity, but what power there is in his depiction of terror! He derives terror from crime. One could say of Shakespeare when presenting crime, as the Bible, death, that he is "the king of terror." How artfully combined in *Macbeth* are an increasing superstition and remorse!

Witchcraft is in itself much more terrifying than the dogmas of even the most absurd religion. What is unknown, what is not guided by any intelligence, will arouse the most extreme fear. In whatever religious system, it is always understood at what point terror must cease; there is always some basis in rationality. The chaos of magic, however, throws the soul into complete disorder.

In *Macbeth*, Shakespeare admits fatalism, using only what is necessary to render the crime pardonable. But this fatalism does not make him dispense with the philosophic gradation of the workings of the soul. The play would be even more admirable if its great effects had been produced without the aid of the supernatural; but the supernatural consists only, so to speak, of phantoms of the imagination brought before the eyes of the spectators. These are not mythological beings imposing their supposed desires or selfish natures upon the affairs of man. These are the phantasms of a dreamworld, aroused when our passions are strongly agitated. There is always something of the philosophic in the supernatural as employed by Shakespeare. When the witches announce to Macbeth that he will be king, when they return to repeat this prediction at the moment he hesitates to follow his wife's bloody counsel, is it not clear that what the author wanted to represent in the terrifying figures of the witches was the internal struggle of ambition and virtue?

He did not have recourse to the supernatural in *Richard III*, though he painted Richard as even more a criminal than Macbeth. He wanted to show a Richard without remorse, without any inner struggle, ever-calculating, as cruel as a ferocious animal, and not as a guilty man whose first instincts had been honorable. The depths of crime are revealed in Shakespeare, and he knows the way of descent to this Taenarus to observe the tormented.

In absolute monarchies, great political crimes can only be committed through the will of kings; and it is forbidden to represent these crimes before their successors.[5] Civil strife, which in England preceded liberty and which is always provoked by the spirit of independence, gave birth, much more often than in France, to both great crime and great virtue. In their history the English have more tragic situations than do the

French, and nothing prevents them from exercizing their talents on these subjects of national interest.

Almost all European literatures began in imitation. Literature revived in Italy. The countries to which it was exported imitated the Italian style at first. The North was more quickly freed of this mannerism than France, though its traces may be found in the older English poets: Waller, Cowley, etc. Civil war and the philosophic spirit corrected this false taste: misfortune, whose impressions are all too true, excludes affected sentiments, and reason eliminates inappropriate expressions. Nevertheless, in Shakespeare one still finds some affected mannerisms in conjunction with the most forceful painting of passions. There are some imitations of the flaws of Italian literature in the Italian subject of *Romeo and Juliet*. But oh, how the English poet rises above that miserable model! How well he knows to set his Northern soul to the task of depicting love!

In *Othello*, love is characterized differently than in *Romeo and Juliet*. But how grand and strong it is in *Othello*! How well had Shakespeare grasped what forms the link between the sexes: courage and weakness! When Othello swears to the Venetian Senate that the only means he had used to seduce Desdemona was his account of the dangers to which he had been exposed, how all women would agree with him! They know that the most effective way of winning women's love is not in flattery. A man's most irresistible charm lies in the favorable protection he can grant the timid object of his choice; and in his renown, reflected by her powerless existence.

In Shakespeare's age, English attitudes toward women were not yet formed. Political unrest had precluded all social development. The position of women in the tragedies was, therefore, entrusted entirely to the will of the author: thus Shakespeare, when speaking of women, sometimes used the noblest language that love could inspire, and, at other times, language in the poorest, most popular taste. This genius, endowed by passion, was inspired by it, as priests by their gods. When excited, he was oracular; when calm returned to his soul, he was nothing but a man.

His plays based on English history, such as the two dealing with Henry IV, Henry V, and three on Henry VI, are very successful in England. I, however, believe them very much inferior, in general, to his original tragedies, *King Lear, Macbeth, Hamlet*, and *Romeo and Juliet*. In the former, irregularities of time and place are much more evident. In the former, Shakespeare caters to popular taste more than in all his other plays. The discovery of printing necessarily diminished the author's condescension to national taste: the opinion of Europe was to be considered. And, although it is most important that plays, which must be performed, have success in performance; then, so that their fame can extend to other nations, writers tend more to avoid allusions, pleasantries, and characters which can only amuse their own countrymen. The English, however, acquiesced at the last possible moment to the general idea of good taste. Their freedom was based on national pride even more than upon philosophic ideas. They reject all that comes from abroad, in literature as well as in politics.

In order to determine the effects in English tragedy suitable to our theatre, there remains one thing to be considered: this would be to distinguish in Shakespeare's plays his concessions to popular taste; the real errors that he committed; and the true beauties which the stringent rules of French taste exclude.

The majority of the English audience demands that tragic scenes be followed by comic scenes. Nevertheless, the contrast of what is noble with what is not, always produces, as I have already noted, a disagreeable impression in men of taste. The noble genre requires nuances, but too pronounced contrasts are merely ineffective extravagances. Puns, licentious ambiguities, popular tales, the accumulated proverbs of a long-standing culture which are, so to speak, the popular prejudices of a nation—reason criticizes all these means of attracting the applause of the masses. They have no relation to the sublime effects which Shakespeare derives from simple words and from skillfully employed commonplace situations which, wrongly, we would not dare allow on our stage.

In his tragedies, Shakespeare made allowance for base natures. He protected himself from the judgement of taste by making himself the object of fanatical popularity. Thus he acted as a party leader, but not as a good writer.

The people of the North had lived for centuries in a culture at once civilized and barbaric; thus traces of this coarse and ferocious past lingered in the popular consciousness. Shakespeare himself retains vestiges of these folk-memories. Several of his characters are drawn with traits only admired in those centuries when life consisted of combat and of the display of physical strength with military courage.

Shakespeare also evinces the contemporary ignorance of the principles of literature. His plays are superior to Greek tragedies in their analysis of passions and their knowledge of men, but inferior to them as artful compositions. Shakespeare has often been reproached for dull patches, useless repetitions, and incoherent images. In his time it was all too easy to interest the spectator for the author to have been as strict with himself as he ought. For a dramatic poet to achieve the fulfillment of his talents, he must not depend on the judgement of blasé old men nor on the merely subjective, personal response of the young.

The French have often condemned the scenes of horror depicted in Shakespeare. These seem to me to be susceptible to criticism, not for arousing too strong an emotion, but for their occasional disruption of theatrical illusion. First, it has been verified that the wholly terrifying situations that Shakespeare's poorest imitators chose to present only produce a disagreeable physical sensation and none of the emotions appropriate to tragedy. Furthermore, one finds many inherently moving situations which seem to demand representation, which result, however, in a diversion of attention, and thus, interest.

When the governor of the tower in which young Arthur is imprisoned orders a hot iron to blind his prisoner, apart from the horror of such a scene, an action is called for which it is actually impossible to present onstage. The spectator will pay so much attention to the action itself that the moral effect will be forgotten.

The character of Caliban in *The Tempest* possesses a singular originality, but the animal-like form given him by his costume diverts attention from the philosophic elements in the conception of his role.

One of the beauties in the reading of the tragedy of *Richard III* is what he himself says of his natural deformity. One feels that the revulsion it evokes must affect his soul, rendering it all the more perverse. What, however, is more demanding or closer to the ridiculous than the portrayal of a deformed man on the stage? Everything in nature is capable of interesting us; in the theatre it is necessary to handle visual oddities with the greatest of care for they can permanently destroy all serious effects.

Shakespeare also too frequently represents physical suffering in his plays. Philoctetes is the only theatrical precedent for it; and it is the heroic origin of his wound which allows the spectator to focus attention on his woes. Physical suffering can be described, but not presented. It is not the intellect, but the senses, which resist this type of imitation. It is not the author, but the actor, who cannot express it nobly.

Finally, one of Shakespeare's greatest flaws is lack of simplicity in the intervals between sublime sequences. He is often affected when he is not inspired by his genius. He lacks the art to sustain himself, that is, to be as natural in transitional scenes as in the portrayal of the magnificent workings of the soul.

Otway, Rowe, and other English poets, Addison excepted, have all produced tragedies in the Shakespearean manner. His genius almost met its match in *Venice Preserv'd*. But Shakespeare was the first to paint the two most profoundly tragic situations that men can conceive: madness caused by misfortune and isolation in misfortune.

Ajax is enraged, Orestes is pursued by the gods' wrath, Phaedra is devoured by love's fever; but Hamlet,[6]* Ophelia, King Lear, in different situations and with different characters, have the same quality of madness: suffering alone speaks in them.

Unhappiness alone speaks in these characters; this dominant emotion has replaced all other emotions; every faculty is affected except the capacity for suffering; and this obsession seems to tear the character from any self-consciousness and present himself without restraint, as an object of pity. Spectators might perhaps reject a voluntary plea for pity, but they completely succumb to emotion born of a disproportionate grief. Madness, as drawn by Shakespeare, is a beautiful portrait of the shipwreck of a moral nature when the tempest of life exceeds all bounds.

In the French theatre there exist strict rules of propriety, even for the expression of grief. It is grief itself on stage; friends serve as its attendants, enemies witness it. What Shakespeare painted with admirable fidelity and spiritual power is isolation. Next to the torments of grief he places man's forgetfulness and nature's calm, or better, an old retainer, the only being to remember that his master had once been king. This indicates a knowledge of what is most distressing to men, of what renders grief poignant. He who suffers, he who dies, while producing whatever effects of terror or pity, escapes what he has experienced through the observation of what he inspires. But what is strong in the poet's talent, what may even presume a character equal to the talent, is to have conceived grief weighing solely on the victim. While man needs to lean on those around him, even in his prosperity, the vigorous and somber imagination of the English draws for us the unfortunate person isolated by his misfortune—as by deadly infection—from all attention, all memories, all friends. Society takes what life there is from him before nature has given death.

Will the theatre of republican France admit, as in the English theatre, heroes drawn with their weaknesses, strengths, and inconsistencies; vulgar circumstances in conjunction with the most elevated situations? Finally, will tragic characters be taken from memory or from the imagination; from human life or from the beautiful ideal? That is the question I plan to address after having discussed the tragedies of Racine and Voltaire. I examine, in the second part of this book, the influence of the Revolution on French literature.

PART II: "THE PRESENT STATE OF KNOWLEDGE IN FRANCE AND ITS FUTURE"

From Chapter V. "Imaginative Works"

. . . . . .

Tragedy is always concerned with the same feelings and, since it portrays grief, the source of its effects is inexhaustible. Nevertheless, tragedy is modified, as are all the products of the human spirit, by the social institutions and customs which relate to it.

Classical subjects and their imitations have less of an effect in a republic than in a monarchy: distinctions of rank heighten the sense of pain attached to the reversals of Fate. Such distinctions placed an immense gap between misfortune and the throne which the mind could cross only with trepidation. The social order of ancient cultures, increasing the scale of existing inequities by the establishment of a class of slaves (with the accompanying elevation of the master class) thus provided their peoples with contrasting social conditions of truly theatrical proportions. Doubtless one can be interested in situations for which there is an analogy in ones' own nation. Nevertheless, that philosophic spirit, which is the natural result of free institutions and political equality, diminishes from day to day the power of social illusion.

Ancient governments had often *banished* or *destroyed* their kings, while in our age, they have been *analyzed*, which is most inimical to the imaginative effects to be derived from the notion of a monarchy. The splendor of power, the reverence it inspires, the pity one feels for those who lose it (if one admits their right to possess it), all these emotions affect the soul independent of the author's talent. The strength of these reactions would be greatly weakened in the political order which I have assumed. Man has already suffered too much as man to have the emotion caused by misfortune heightened by the dignity, power, or in the end, the circumstance particular only to the dignity of a few.

One must, however, avoid turning tragedy into *drame*.[7] A clear idea of the difference between the two genres is necessary to prevent this error. The difference does not rest solely, I believe, in the rank of the characters portrayed, but in the grandeur of these characters and the strength of the passions that are developed.

Several attempts have been made to adapt the beauties of the English genius and the effects of the German theatre to the French stage. And, excepting a very few, these attempts achieved only momentary success and earned no lasting reputation.[8]* For pity in tragedy, like laughter in comedy, is but a fleeting impression. If you have not been stirred to thought by this reaction, if the tragedy that brought tears brought to mind neither a moral lesson nor a novel situation aroused by the emotion itself, then the feeling aroused is no more complex than that aroused by a gladiatorial combat. Such emotion will not extend the range of thought and feeling.

In a German work I noted an observation which seems to me perfectly correct: that successful tragedies ought to strengthen the soul after tormenting it. In effect, no matter what the unfortunate situation may be, true grandeur of character inspires admiration in audiences. This leaves them more capable of braving adversity. The principle of utility is found in this genre as in all others. The truly beautiful also improves man. Without studying the rules of taste, you can be assured that a play possesses true genius, if you sense it positively affects your own character.

Such effects are produced in the theatre not by moral maxims, but by the development of characters and the manipulation of natural situations. Using this opinion as a guide, we will be able to determine which foreign plays can enrich our tradition.

It is not enough to stir the soul; you must enlighten it. You cannot allow yourself all the startling visual effects—tombs, tortures, ghosts, combats—unless they directly aid in the philosophic rendering of a great character or a profound statement. All the inclinations of men of thought lead toward a rational end. A writer does not merit true fame until he has employed emotion to illustrate some great moral truth.

The circumstances of private life suffice for the effects of *drame*. In general, for an event to be an appropriate subject for tragedy, it must involve events of national import. Nevertheless, one ought truly to seek tragic dignity in the loftiness of ideas and in the depths of feeling than in folk memory and historical allusions.

Vauvenargue noted that "great thoughts come from the heart." Tragedy puts this sublime truth into action. *Fénelon* is based on an event entirely characteristic of the *drame*; the role in the play and the memory of this great man suffice to make of this play a tragedy.[9] The name of M. de Malesherbes, his noble response to a horrible fate, would provide a subject for the most affecting tragedy imaginable. Lofty virtue, immense genius—these are new qualities that ought to characterize tragedy; and, above all else, the sentiment of grief as we have learned to experience it.

It does not seem doubtful to me that there are effects of a moral nature more powerful than have yet been expressed in our otherwise admirable French tragedies. The trappings of power and rank introduce a kind of restraint in tragic subjects which does not permit hand-to-hand combat between men. The use of veiled expressions and repressed emotions, together with the maintenence of decorum presumes a certain sort of skill, but passions cannot be successfully portrayed given these conditions; the reckless power and subtle insight inspired by complete artistic freedom will be lacking.

Under a republican government, what most impresses thought is virtue, and what most strikes the imagination is misfortune. I don't know if even the depiction of glory—the only pomp in life that the philosophic spirit honors—will stir the republican audience as strongly as the portrayal of emotions which touch the entire being through analogy with human nature.

A philosophic system which presumes universal concepts and a system of political equality will give a new character to our tragedies. This is not a reason to reject historical subjects. But it is necessary to portray great men with feelings that make them sympathetic to all and to use dignity of character to ennoble minor actions. It is necessary to ennoble the natural instead of perfecting conventional ideas. It is neither the irregularity nor inconsistency of English and German plays that ought to be imitated. But it would be a novel beauty for us and for foreigners to discover the art of providing commonplace circumstances with dignity and of painting great events with simplicity.

The theatre is life ennobled, but it must be life. And, if the most vulgar circumstance is useful as a contrast to great effects, then enough talent must be expended to make this acceptable—to extend the limits of art without outraging taste. Our earliest tragedians will never be equalled in the realm of ideal beauties. We must then endeavor more often to employ— with reason's guidance and the spirit's wisdom—dramatic means which arouse in men memories of their own past, for nothing moves so deeply.[10]*

The traditional conventions of the theatre are comparable to the hierarchy of ranks in government: you cannot maintain one without the other. Dramatic art, deprived of all these artful resources, can advance only through imaginative theory and sensibility. The possibilities, however, are limitless for grief, which is one of the most powerful means of developing the human spirit.

Life flows by, so to speak, unnoticed by the happy man. But when the soul is troubled, the mind contrives to search for hope, or to discover a cause for regret, to plumb the past, to predict the future. And this faculty of observation which, in calm and happy times, is directed almost entirely toward external objects, turns inward when misfortune strikes. The neverending effects of pain bring thoughts and emotions which appear and re-appear in our consciousness; tormenting us with new expressions of the same feeling. What an inexhaustible source of reflection for the imagination!

The laws of tragedy do not offer as many obstacles to the choice of subject as do the difficulties linked to the exigencies of poetry. What would be sensitive and true in everyday language would be ridiculous in verse. Metre, harmony, and rhyme exclude expressions which, in certain situations, could produce a great effect. The true decorum of the theatre lies in the dignity of moral nature; decorum in poetry is a function of the verse itself. Although decorum often enhances the effect of one kind of beauty, it limits the scope of genius—the observer of the human heart.

In reality, one would not believe the grief of a man who could express in verse his regret at the death of someone he had very much loved. A certain degree of passion inspires poetry; past a certain point, poetry is rejected. Thus there is necessarily a depth of suffering, a type of truth, that would be weakened by poetic expression. And there are commonplace situations, made unspeakable by unhappiness, which cannot be submitted to rhyme or dressed up in poetic images without incorporating ideas foreign to the natural sequence of feeling. We can think of no way to deny the fact that a tragedy written in prose, however eloquent it may be, would arouse much less admiration, at first, than our masterpieces written in verse. The merit of having overcome difficulties and the charm of an harmonious rhythm serve to doubly increase the worth of the dramatic author. But it is this conjunction of two talents that has been one of the principal causes of the great difference between French and English tragedy.

The minor characters in Shakespeare speak prose; his traditional scenes are in prose; and even when he employs the language of verse, his verse, being free, does not demand the almost continual poetic splendor of French verse. I do not suggest, however, attempting prose tragedy in France: the ear would be troubled attempting to become accustomed to it. But it is necessary to perfect the art of verse that is simple and so natural that is does not divert, even through poetic beauty, the profound emotion which ought to absorb all other ideas. Finally, in order to open a new source for theatrical emotions, it would be necessary to find an intermediate genre between the decorum of the French poets and defects in taste of the Northern writers.

Philosophical analysis applies to all works of the imagination, as well as to the works of the mind; today man is intrigued only by his emotions. Externally, everything is observed and evaluated: the individual, as a moral being, and his motivation, alone arouse either surprise or a powerful reaction. Tragedy—most powerful in touching the human heart—does not communicate the general ideas of common existence and does not draw characters and situations that are almost equally removed from nature as from the marvels of fairy tales. Tragedy would arouse in men the purest feelings they had ever known and would elicit from every audience memories of the noblest aspects of their lives.

. . . . . .

Germany (1810-1813)

Napoleon's police confiscated the first edition of Germany *published in 1810 by Nicolle in Paris. The London publisher, Murray, issued the work in 1813. It was published in France by Nicolle in 1814.*

PART II: "LITERATURE AND THE ARTS"

Chapter XI. "Classical and Romantic Poetry"

The term "romantic" has recently been introduced in Germany to distinguish that poetry whose origins are in the songs of the troubadours, which developed in the age of chivalry and Christianity. If you will not concede a division in the domain of literature between the pagan and the Christian; the North and the South; Antiquity and the Middle Ages; chivalric institutions and those of the Greeks and Romans, then you will never succeed in arriving at a systematic judgement of ancient and modern taste.

Sometimes the term "classical" is assumed to be a synonym for "perfection." I use it here in another sense; considering classical poetry to be that of the Ancients and romantic poetry to be that which is, in some way, related to the traditions of chivalry. This division corresponds as well to the world's two historical epochs: the one which preceded the establishment of Christianity and the one which followed it.

Along these lines, various German works have compared ancient poetry to sculpture and romantic poetry to painting.[11] And they have distinguished the progress of the human mind in its transition from materialist to spiritualist religions, from nature to the divine.

The French nation, the most cultivated of the Latin nations, tends to prefer classical poetry in imitation of the Greeks and Romans. The English nation, the most eminent of the Germanic nations, prefers romantic and chivalrous poetry and takes pride in her masterpieces in this genre. I will not examine here which of these two types of poetry is preferable: it is sufficient to show that the diversity of tastes, in this respect, derives not only from accidental causes, but also from the primitive sources of imagination and thought.

There is a simplicity in the epic poetry and tragedies of the Ancients which results from man's identification with nature in that era, and his belief in his dependency on destiny; as nature is dependent on necessity. Reflecting little, man always externalized the workings of his soul; conscience itself was represented by external objects. The torches of the Furies illuminated remorse in the eyes of the guilty. The event was all-important in antiquity; character is more important in modern times. The uneasy reflective quality, which often devours us like Prometheus' vulture, would have seemed foolish in the clearly defined relations which existed in the civil and social states of the Ancients.

In the earliest periods of art, statues were made only of isolated, individual figures; groups appeared later. With truth one could say that of all the arts: there were no groupings; the objects represented followed in succession as in bas-reliefs without connection and without any complication of composition. Man personified nature: nymphs dwelt in the waters; hamadryads in the forests. But nature, in turn, seized upon man. And one could have compared man to a torrent, lightning, or a volcano, so much did he act on involuntary impulse, without reflection in any way altering the motives or the results of his actions. The Ancients possessed, so to speak, a corporeal soul, all of whose actions were strong, direct, and coherent. It is not the same with the human heart developed by Christianity. From the Christian concept of repentance the moderns have derived the habit of continually retreating into themselves.

In order to reveal this entirely interior existence, there must be a great variety in detail so as to indicate the infinite nuances of the soul's workings. If, in our time, the fine arts were restricted to the simplicity of the Ancients, we would not achieve the primitive strength which is characteristic of them, and we would lose the intimate and varied emotions to which our soul is susceptible. Simplicity in art, with the moderns, would easily become coldness and abstraction, whereas the simplicity of the Ancients was full of life. Honor and love, courage and pity, are the sentiments which marked Christianity in the age of chivalry. Such states of mind can only make themselves evident through danger, daring, love, misfortune—in short, romantic concerns, which continually vary the situation. Thus, the sources of the effects of art are different, in many respects, in classical and romantic poetry. The one is ruled by Fate; the other by Providence. Fate does not take man's feelings into account; Providence only judges actions according to those feelings. How entirely different is the nature of the world created by poetry when, on the one hand, it is necessary to color the work with a blind and deaf Destiny always in conflict with mortals; and, on the other hand, an intelligent order, presided over by a Supreme Being to whom we may appeal and who responds to us.

The poetry of the pagans was by necessity simple and direct, as are things which present externals. Christian poetry needs the myriad colors of the rainbow to keep from vanishing into the mists. The poetry of the Ancients is pure as art, that of the moderns makes tears flow: the issue is not, however, the difference between classical and romantic poetry, but between imitation on the one hand and inspiration on the other. Ancient literature in the modern period is transplanted literature: romantic or chivalrous literature is indigenous to us for it is our religion and institutions which have given it birth. The writers who have imitated the Ancients have submitted to the most rigid conventions of taste; for being able neither to draw from their own nature nor from their own recollections, they had to conform to laws by which ancient masterpieces could be adapted to modern tastes, even though the political and religious contexts of these masterpieces were different. However accomplished these imitations of the classics may be, they are rarely popular, because they do not, in our time, relate to anything native to us.

French poetry, being the most "classical" of all modern poetry, is the only modern poetry not familiar to the people. The stanzas of Tasso are sung by the gondoliers of Venice; Spaniards and Portuguese of all classes know the verses of Calderón and Camoëns by heart. Shakespeare is as much admired by the common folk of England as by the upper classes. Poems of Goethe and Bürger are set to music and can be heard from the banks of the Rhine to the Baltic. Our French poets are admired by the cultivated classes of France and the rest of Europe, but they are completely unknown to the common people, and to the middle class, even of the cities. The reason for this is that the arts in France are not, as in other countries, native to the country where their beauties are displayed.

Some French critics have maintained that the literture of the Germanic peoples is still in the infancy of art. This opinion is false; the most knowledgeable critics of the languages and works of the Ancients are certainly not ignorant of the advantages and the disadvantages of the type of literature they adopt or of that which they reject. Their character, their habits and their reflections have caused them to prefer that literature whose basis is the memories of chivalry and the marvels of the Middle Ages rather than that literature based on Greek mythology. Romantic literature is the only literature capable of further development. It is the only literature which may grow and flourish for its roots are in our own soil; it breathes our religion; it summons up our history; its origins are venerable, but not ancient.

Classical poetry must go beyond the limits of paganism to reach us. Germanic poetry is the Christian era of the fine arts: it uses our own impressions to move us. The genius which inspires German poetry appeals directly to our hearts and seems to evoke our life itself, the most powerful and terrifying phantom of all.

Chapter XV. "The Art of Drama"

The theatre exercises a powerful influence over men. A tragedy which elevates the soul, a comedy which depicts manners and characters, almost have the effect of a real event. In order to obtain a great success on the stage, it is necessary to analyze one's audience and the various factors on which its opinion is based. Knowledge of men is as important as imagination in a dramatist. The dramatist must achieve feelings of general interest, without losing sight of the particular relationships which move an audience. A play is literature in action; the genius required in playwriting is rare because it is made up of an astonishing union of sensitivity to events and poetic inspiration. Nothing, therefore, would be more absurd than wanting to impose the same dramatic formulas on all cultures. Very important modifications are unavoidable when it is a question of adapting a universal art to the tastes of individual nations.

From this arise the numerous diverse opinions concerning what constitutes dramatic talent: a consensus is easier to obtain in all the other branches of literature.

It cannot be denied, it seems to me, that French playwrights are the most skillful in creating theatrical effects; they are also pre-eminent in the tragic style and in plotting. The French also are superior to other nations through the dignity of the situations portrayed. But while acknowledging this double superiority, we admit to experiencing deeper emotions in less well made plays. In their conception, foreign plays are sometimes more striking and bold. Often they include a certain force which speaks more directly to our hearts and touches us more closely than feelings we have actually experienced.

Since the French are easily bored, they avoid excessive length in everything. The Germans, in going to the theatre, are usually giving up no more than a dull game of cards at low stakes, a mere way of killing time; they are delighted to be calmly settled in a theatre and allow the author all the time he cares to take to develop the plot and his characters: French impatience would not tolerate such pacing.

German plays ordinarily resemble the work of classical painters: the faces are beautiful, expressive, contemplative, but all the bodies are on the same plane, sometimes indistinct, sometimes placed next to one another as in a bas-relief, rather than being grouped in a pleasing composition. The French think, with reason, that the theatre, like painting, must submit to the laws of perspective. If the Germans were more skillful in the art of drama they would also be skillful in other things, but they are not even competent in a simple conversation. Their thought is penetrating in a direct way; beautiful abstractions are accessible to them but relative beauties that are dependent on a knowledge of cause and effect and on speed of execution are not ordinarily within the realm of their capabilities.

It is singular that of these two peoples, it is the French who demand the most unrelenting gravity of tone in tragedy; but it is precisely because the French are more receptive to banter that they avoid giving occasions for it. Nothing, on the other hand, upsets the imperturbable seriousness of the Germans. They always judge a play as a whole, and they restrain both their criticism and their applause until it is over. The reactions of the French are much more spontaneous. It would be fruitless to inform them that a comic scene is destined to counterbalance a tragic situation: they would mock the former without waiting for the latter. For the French each detail must be as interesting as the whole: they demand from each moment the pleasure they expect to recieve from the fine arts.

The difference between the French and German theatre can be explained by the different characters of the two nations. In addition to these natural differences there are systematized opinions whose origins should be examined. What I have already said about classical and romantic poetry applies to plays as well. Tragedies based on mythology are of a completely different nature than historical tragedies. Subjects drawn from myth were so well known, the interest they inspired was so universal, that it was enough merely to mention them to make an impression on the imagination. What is eminently poetic in Greek tragedy—the intervention of the gods and the action of fate—results in its simple movement. Specific motives, character development, a diversity of facts, all become less necessary when the event is explained by a supernatural power: the miraculous simplifies everything. The action of Greek tragedy is amazingly uncomplicated. The majority of events have been predicted and have even been announced at the very start. A Greek tragedy is a religious ceremony: the performance is given to honor the gods, and hymns, interrupted by dialogues and narrations, portrayed the gods—sometimes beneficent, sometimes terrifying—but with destiny always reigning over human life. When the same subjects were transferred to the French theatre, our greatest poets gave them more variety, multiplied the incidents, contrived dramatic surprises and increased suspense. This was, in effect, necessary to replace in some way the national and religious interests which the Greeks brought to the performances of these plays, but which the French audience did not feel. Not content with bringing the Greek plays to life, we colored the characters with our manners and feelings, our contemporary politics, and our gallantry. This is the reason that so many foreigners do not feel the admiration that these masterpieces inspire in the French. In effect, when one hears them in another language, they are stripped of the wonderful beauty of style, and one is surprised at how little emotion they arouse and at the inconsistencies to be found in them. For is it not correct to term an inconsistency that which is neither in accord with the period, nor with the national customs of the characters being represented? And are these plays not ridiculous in those details which do not resemble us?

These plays with Greek subjects lose nothing through the severity of our dramatic rules. But if, like the English, we want to enjoy the pleasure of having an historical theatre—to be interested in our past and to be moved by our religion—how would it be possible to conform rigidly on the one hand to the three unities and on the other hand to the elevated style which is the norm in our tragedies?

The question of the three unities is so hackneyed that it hardly bears mention. Of the three unities only the unity of action is important; the others should not be considered except as subordinate to it. But if the truth of the action is lost through unthinking necessity, not to change the locale and to limit duration to twenty-four hours, then to impose this necessity is to subject the dramatist to a type of restriction found in acrostics. This type of restraint sacrifices the content of art to its form.

Of our great poets, Voltaire most frequently dealt with modern topics. To move us, he looked for subjects from the age of chivalry and Christianity. And, in my opinion, if one is honest, one must admit that *Alzire*, *Zaïre*, and *Tancred* cause more tears to flow than all the Greek and Roman masterpieces of our theatre.[12] De Belloy, a much inferior writer, has, however, succeeded in reviving our national past on the stage.[13] And, though he did not write well, his plays arouse an interest similar to what the Greeks must have felt witnessing the dramatization of events from their own history. The advantage genius can derive from this fact is manifest. But there are almost no events dating from our time whose action can be confined to the same day or the same place. The diversity of events of a more complicated social system, the subtleties of feeling inspired by a gentler religion, and, finally, the realism of manners to be observed in recent contemporary portraits, require a great latitude in dramatic composition.

One can cite a recent example of the cost of conforming to our dramatic orthodoxy when treating a subject taken from modern history. Raynouard's *Templars* is certainly one of the most praiseworthy plays to appear in quite some time.[14] What, however, is more strange than the author's need to show the Templars accused, judged, condemned, and executed in the space of twenty-four hours? Revolutionary tribunals acted swiftly, but, no matter how cruel their determinations, they would never succeed in moving as rapidly as a French tragedy! I could illustrate the disadvantages of the unity of time with equal ease in almost all our tragedies drawn from modern history. By preference I have chosen the most notable of these plays to make the disadvantages all the more conspicuous.

One of the most sublime statements heard on the stage is found in this noble tragedy. In the final scene we hear the Templars singing psalms on their pyre; a messenger is sent to bring them the royal pardon.

But time had run out, their songs had ended.

This is how the poet lets us know that these courageous martyrs had, indeed, died. In what pagan tragedy could one find the expression of such a sentiment? And why should the French, in their theatre, be deprived of all that is truly sympathetic to them, their ancestors, and their faith?

The French consider the unity of time and place to be an indispensable condition for theatrical illusion. Foreigners create this illusion in the delineation of character, in appropriate language, and in the exact observation of the manners of the age and country they have chosen to portray. It is necessary to reach an agreement concerning the word "illusion" in the arts: since we allow ourselves to believe that actors separated from us by only a few boards are Greek heroes, dead 3,000 years, it is surely clear that what is called illusion is not imagining that what is seen truly exists. A tragedy can only seem true to us through the emotion it arouses in us. If, by the nature of the circumstances represented, a change of place and the supposed prolongation of time increase the effect of the emotion, then the illusion itself becomes stronger.

A criticism has been made that Voltaire's most beautiful tragedies, *Zaïre* and *Tancred*, are based on misunderstandings. But, when the developments are supposed to occur in such a limited time-span, how can a writer not have recourse to the devices of intrigue? The art of drama thus becomes a *tour de force*. And to successfully depict great events within so many limitations, one must have the skill of those mountebanks who, as the spectator watches, make off with the very objects the audience has entrusted to them.

Historical subjects lend themselves even less to the conditions imposed on our writers than do invented subjects: the protocol of tragedy which is maintained in our theatre is often in opposition to the innovations which would be appropriate to plays drawn from modern history.

There is a simplicity of language, a naïveté of feeling, in chivalric manners that is full of charm. But neither this charm, nor the pathos which results from the contrast of ordinary circumstances with strong emotions can be permitted in our tragedies: elevated situations are the rule. Nevertheless, the picturesque interest of the Middle Ages is a result of the diversity of scenes and characters which produce such affecting responses to the poetry of the troubadours.

The pomp of alexandrine verse is an even greater obstacle than is the habit of conventional good taste to any change in the form and content of French tragedies. You cannot say, in alexandrine verse, that you are arriving or leaving, sleeping or lying awake, without having to search for a poetic locution. Any number of emotions and effects are thus banished from the stage, not by the rules of tragedy, but by the very exigencies of the versification. Racine, in the scene between Joas and Athalia, is the only French writer who ever toyed with these difficulties: he knew how to invest the child's language with a simplicity as noble as it was natural. But this admirable effort of an unparalleled genius does not prevent the various demands of art from often being an obstacle to inspired inventions.

Benjamin Constant, in the justly admired preface to his tragedy *Wallstein*,[15] observed that the Germans portrayed characters in their plays, and the French, passions. In order to portray character it is by definition necessary to deviate from the majestic tone exclusively maintained in French tragedy. For it is impossible to illustrate the flaws and virtues of a man without presenting him in diverse aspects. The vulgar in nature is often mixed with the sublime and sometimes heightens its effects. Finally, an extended period of time is needed to represent the action of a character; in twenty-four hours only a catastrophe can be presented. It will perhaps be argued that catastrophes are better suited to the theatre than are detailed portraits; the majority of the audience are pleased more by the movement excited by strong passions than the attention demanded by the observation of the human heart. National taste alone can dictate one of these different dramatic systems. We must recognize, however, that if foreigners hold a different conception than do we of theatrical art, it is the result neither of their ignorance nor their barbarity, but the result of serious reflection which merits our consideration.

Shakespeare, whom some might term a barbarian, has perhaps too philosophic a nature, too subtle a perception, for the optic of the stage. He judges characters with the impartiality of a superior being, and sometimes represents them with an almost Machiavellian irony. His plays are so complex that the rapidity of theatrical action results in the loss of many of the ideas in his works: in this respect, his plays are better read. Because of this, the action is often slowed. The French are much more skillful in painting characters, as well as scenery, with the large brush strokes which achieve their effect at a distance. What, you say! Can Shakespeare be reproached for an excess of subtlety in his perceptions, he who allows such terrifying situations in his plays? Shakespeare often combines contrary virtues and vices. He is sometimes within and sometimes outside the domain of art. The knowledge he possesses is that of the human heart, rather than that of the theatre.

In serious drama, comic operas, and in comedies, the French manifest a wit and charm that is unique. From one end of Europe to another, hardly any of those types of drama is performed that is not a translation from the French. It is not the same with tragedy. As French tragedies are more or less confined to the same circle, due to the strict rules to which they are subject, the perfection of style is indispensable to the admiration which they are calculated to inspire. In France, were you to risk any sort of innovation in tragedy, you would be immediately accused of writing melodramas. But is it not important to know why melodramas are so popular? In England, the plays of Shakespeare attract all classes of people equally. In France, the most beautiful tragedies do not interest the lower classes. Under the pretext of being too pure in taste and too delicate in feeling, art is divided: bad plays contain touching situations poorly expressed, and good plays admirably portray situations that do not affect us because they are too dignified. We possess few tragedies which are capable of exciting the imagination of people of all classes.

These observations are certainly not meant as criticisms of our great writers. There are scenes in foreign plays which produce more vivid impressions, but nothing can compare to the powerful and skillfully constructed unity of our dramatic masterpieces. The question is whether by limiting oneself, as is now the case, to the imitation of these master-pieces, we will ever produce any new ones. Nothing in life should be static, and art is petrified when it no longer changes. Twenty years of revolution have given the imagination other needs than those felt when Crébillon's novels portrayed love and the society of the period. Greek subjects have been exhausted. Lemercier alone, in his *Agamemnon*, has been able to reap more glory from an ancient subject.[16] Historical tragedy is, however, the natural trend of the age.

Tragedy is all in the events which concern nations. The immense drama which mankind has been performing for six thousand years would furnish innumerable subjects for the theatre if more freedom were al-lowed the art of drama. Rules are only guidebooks to genius: they only teach us the route followed by Corneille, Racine, and Voltaire. But if we reach the same goal, why quibble about the route? And isn't the goal to move the soul while ennobling it?

Curiosity is one of the great motivating forces in the theatre but the interest aroused by profound feelings is the only inexhaustible force. We are interested in poetry which reveals man to man; we like to see how beings like ourselves struggle with suffering, succumb to it, triumph over it, rise and fall at the hand of fate. There are situations in some of our tragedies that are as violent as those in English or German tragedies, but we do not represent these situations in all their force: sometimes artificiality weakens the effect, or rather, obliterates it. We rarely depart from conventional characterizations, which depict in similar fashion, ancient and modern manners, crime and virtue, murder and gallantry. This characterization is well constructed and artfully presented, but in the long run it is tiresome, and genius will invariably be gripped by the need to investigate more complex subjects.

It would be desirable to be able to escape the circle drawn around art by metre and rhyme; one must be bolder and more knowledgable con-cerning history. For if we cling exclusively to the ever more pallid copies of the same masterpieces, our stage will end up being inhabited only by heroic marionettes, sacrificing love to duty, preferring death to slavery, inspired by antitheses in their actions as in their words, but without any resemblance to the astonishing creature called man and the irrevocable destiny which alternately beckons to him and pursues him.

The defects of the German theatre are obvious. The flaws which can be attributed to a lack of worldliness are the first to be noticed by a superficial observer, in art as in society. But in order to appreciate its heart-felt beauties, we must bring to the examination of the works before us a simplicity which is completely in harmony with a lofty superiority. Mockery is often only a vulgar reaction translated into impertinence.

Being capable of admiring true greatness despite errors of taste, as amidst the inconsequential in life, is the only faculty which does honor to a person of judgement.

In commenting on a theatre based on principles so different from our own, I certainly do not maintain that these are better principles or that they should be adopted in France: but foreign models can generate new ideas. And when we perceive the sterility that menaces our literture, it is difficult for me not to want our writers to extend the limits of their profession: would they not do well in turn to become conquerors in the empire of the imagination? It can hardly cost the French anything to follow such advice.

From Chapter XVIII. "Wallstein *and* Maria Stuart"

. . . . . .

A very talented writer has revised Schiller's trilogy in line with the French concept of form and regularity. The praise and criticism generated by this work provide the opportunity for us to complete our presentation of the differences characteristic of the French and German systems of drama. The French writer has been reproached for writing verse that was not sufficiently poetic. Mythological subjects allow for brilliant imagery and lyrical inspiration. But how could the poetry of Theramenes' narration be introduced in a subject drawn from modern history? All the pomp of the Ancients is appropriate to the family of Minos or Agamemnon; it would only be a ridiculous affectation in plays of another sort. There are moments in historical tragedies when the exaltation of the soul naturally leads to a more elevated poetry: such, for example, is the vision of Wallstein, his speech after the revolt, his monologue before his death, etc. However, the context and the development of the play, in German as in French, necessitate a simple style in which the purity of language, but rarely its magnificence, is felt. We French want to see the effect with each verse rather than only in the scene as a whole. This is not compatible with reality. Nothing is easier than composing what are called "brilliant verses": there are formulas just for that. What is difficult is to subordinate each detail to the whole, and to maintain each detail in the whole; as it were the reflection of the whole in each part. French vivacity has given the action of plays a rapid and very agreeable movement, but it is detrimental to the beauty of art when it requires immediate successes at the expense of the general impression.

In conjunction with this impatience which tolerates no delay, we find a singular patience for all that decorum requires. These same Frenchmen who are irritated by the least slowness endure whatever is expected of them through respect for convention. They endure any type of boredom which is part of the traditional ceremony of art. For example, narrated expositions are indispensable in French tragedy, yet they are certainly much less interesting than enacted exposition. I have heard that the Italian audience once demanded during the narration of a battle that the backdrop be raised so they could see the battle themselves. One very often feels the same emotion during the performance of a tragedy; one would like to witness what is being described. The author of the French *Wallstein* was obliged to incorporate in his play the exposition which was handled so originally in the prologue set in the camp. The dignity of the first scenes is in perfect accord with the imposing tone of French tragedy, but there is a kind of animation in the irregularity of the German original which can never be improved upon.

The French author has also been reproached for dividing the interest between the love of Alfred (Piccolomini) for Thécla and the conspiracy of Wallstein. In France a play must be devoted completely to love or to politics. The combining of subjects is not well received. And recently, when the subject has been affairs of state, it has been difficult to imagine how the mind can encompass additional matters. Nevertheless, the grand *tableau* of the Wallstein conspiracy is only completed by the inclusion of the misfortunes it brings upon his family. It is worth keeping in mind how much public events can affect private emotions. The habit of presenting politics as a separate world from which feelings are excluded is immoral, insensitive, and dramatically ineffective.

A circumstantial detail in the French play has been the subject of criticism. No one has denied the beauty of Alfred's (Max Piccolomini) farewell to Wallstein and Thécla, but the fact that, in a tragedy, this moment was accompanied by music caused a scandal. It is easy enough to eliminate the music, but why should we be deprived of the effect it produces? When the military music, a call to arms, is heard, the spectator shares the emotion it arouses in the lovers, threatened with eternal separation. The music throws the situation into relief. A new art strengthens the initial impression of another art. Sounds and words move by turns our imaginations and our hearts.

Two scenes completely new to our stage also astonished French readers: after Alfred has killed himself, Thécla asks the Saxon officer, who brings the news, all the details of the horrible death; and, her soul overflowing with grief, announces her resolution to live and die near the tomb of her lover. Each expression, each word in these two scenes, is marked by a profound sensibility, but it has been argued that dramatic interest cannot exist without uncertainty. In all genres the French hasten to be done with what is irreparable. The Germans, on the contrary, are much more curious about what the characters feel than about what happens to them. The Germans don't fear lingering over a situation that is resolved as an action but which is characterized by a continuing reaction. More poetry, more sensibility, more precision in language is needed in order to move an audience when action—which usually arouses an ever-increasing anxiety—is at rest. We hardly notice the words when the facts themselves hold us in suspense. But when all is still, except grief, when there is no more external change, and interest is focused only on what passes in the soul, a nuance of feeling, a word out of place, disconcert like a false note in a simple and melancholy tune. No sound, then, escapes; everything is addressed directly to the heart.

Finally, the most universally repeated criticism of the French *Wallstein* is that the character of Wallstein himself is superstitious, inconstant, irresolute, and inconsistent with the heroic model demanded by this type of role. The French are deprived of an infinite source of effects and emotions by reducing tragic characters, like the notes of music, or the colors of a prism, to a few, unvarying, dominant traits: each character must conform to one of the principal recognized types. It could be said that with the French logic is the basis of the arts and that "undulating" nature, described by Montaigne, is excluded from our tragedies. In our tragedies only completely good or completely evil emotions are allowed, yet there is nothing that is not mixed in the human soul.

One reacts to a tragic character in France the way one reacts to a minister of state; one complains about what he does or doesn't do as if one were judging him with a newspaper in hand. Inconstancy of passion is allowed on the French stage, but not inconstancy of character. Passion is more or less understood by everyone. Its disorders are expected and its very contradictions can, to some degree, be anticipated. But character always has something of the unexpected and can never be encompassed by a single rule. Sometimes character is directed toward its goal, sometimes it deviates from this goal. In France, when you say of a character: "He doesn't know what he wants," you are no longer interested in him. Yet it is precisely the man who doesn't know what he wants in whom nature is present with a truly tragic force and independence.

Shakespeare's characters arouse completely different impressions in the audience at various times in the course of the same play. Richard II, in the first three acts of the tragedy bearing his name, inspires aversion and contempt. But when he is overtaken by misfortune, when he is forced in full parliament to cede his throne to his enemy, his situation and his courage move us to tears. We admire the nobility of character which appears in adversity. The crown still seems to hover over the head of he who has lost it. By a few phrases, Shakespeare can take control of his audience's emotions and move it from hatred to pity. The endless diversity of the human heart incessantly renews the sources open to talent.

In reality, we can admit that men are inconsistent and capricious and that often the finest qualities are intermixed with miserable flaws. But such characters are not appropriate to the theatre: dramatic art requires rapid action and, in this framework, men can only be drawn with vivid strokes and in striking situations. Does it therefore follow that we must be limited to those characters, resolute in their wickedness or in their goodness, which constitute the unvarying elements in the majority of our tragedies? What influence would the theatre be able to exercise over the values of the audience if nothing but a conventional nature is displayed! It is true that on this imaginary terrain virtue always triumphs and vice is always punished. But how would that ever apply to what occurs in life, since the men portrayed on the stage are not men as in life?

I would be curious to see the play *Wallstein* performed in our theatre, even more so if the French author had not submitted so rigorously to the conventions of French regularity. But to correctly assess it we would need to bring to the arts a youthful spirit which seeks new pleasures. To champion only the accepted masterpieces is an excellent regimen for taste, but not for talent. Talent needs unexpected impressions to motivate it; the works we have known by heart from childhood become habit and no longer excite our imagination.

. . . . . .

Chapter XXVII. "Declamation"

Because the art of declamation leaves no monument more substantial than fleeting memories, there has been little reflection on its composition. Nothing is more easy than the mediocre exercise of this art. We are not, however, incorrect in asserting that at its best it excites a great deal of enthusiasm. And far from depreciating this impression as evanescent, I believe that we can assign it characteristic causes. Rarely in life does one succeed in penetrating the innermost feelings of men; the workings of the heart are exaggerated, altered, contained or concealed by affectation and duplicity, coldness and modesty. A great actor displays the signs of emotional truth in characterization. He shows us the exact signs of true inclinations and feelings.

So many individuals live their lives without being conscious of the passions and their power, that often the theatre reveals man to man, and impresses him with a reverent fear of the soul's torments. In fact, words cannot paint such emotion with as much force as intonation, gesture, or expression! The words indicate less than the intonation; the intonation less than the facial expression; the inexpressible is precisely what a sublime actor reveals to us.

The same differences which are found in the French and German systems of tragedy are also found in their manners of declamation. The Germans imitate nature as closely as possible. Their only affectation is simplicity, which can indeed be an affectation in the fine arts. At times, German actors profoundly move the spectator, but at other times, they leave the spectator cold. In the latter instance they rely on the spectator's patience and their trust is not misplaced. The English have more majesty than the Germans in the recitation of verse, but they do not possess the ingrained pomp that the French, and French tragedies, demand of actors. Our style cannot accept a middle ground; the so-called "natural" itself is a product of artifice. Second-rate actors in Germany are cold and composed; they are often wanting in tragic effect; but they are almost never ridiculous. It is the same on the German stage as in German society, there are people who sometimes bore you, and that is that. In the French theatre, one becomes impatient when one is not moved. Bombast and artificiality are so repellent in tragedy that there is no parody, however vulgar, which is not preferable to the insipid impression made by affectation.

One would think that more attention would be paid to the accessories of art, stage machinery and settings, in Germany than in France, since German tragedies more often have recourse to these means. Iffland was able to accomplish all that could be desired in this area in Berlin.[17] But in Vienna, the barest requirements for actually staging a tragedy are neglected. French actors have infinitely better developed memories than do German actors. In Vienna, the prompter spoke each word of the parts in advance of the majority of the actors. I have seen him follow Othello from wing to wing in order to supply the actor with the lines he required while stabbing Desdemona.

Production in Weimar is infinitely better organized in all respects. The prince, an enlightened man, and the genius and connoisseur who is his administrator, were able to blend taste and elegance with the boldness that allows experimentation.[18]

In this theatre, as in other German theatres, actors play both comedy and tragedy. It has been argued that this diversity prevents their becoming superior in either genre. Nevertheless, the greatest geniuses of the theatre, Garrick and Talma, were equally adept in both genres.[19] A flexible voice which equally well conveys diverse feelings seems to me to be the hallmark of a natural talent. And in fiction, as in reality, melancholy and gaiety are perhaps both derived from the same source. Moreover, in Germany, pathos and humor alternate or intermingle in tragedy so that it is necessary for actors to be capable of expressing both. Iffland, the best German actor, sets the standard with a well-deserved reputation. I have not seen good actors in the roles of high comedy— marquis, fop, etc.—in Germany. The charm of this type of role is found in what the Italians call *disinvoltura*, which could be translated as disinterestedness. The German habit of giving everything importance is precisely what is most in opposition to this sort of frivolity. But it is impossible to surpass Iffland's acting in originality, comic spirit, and the art of character delineation. I don't believe that we have ever seen on the French stage a more varied or original talent than his. Nor have we seen an actor who risks the natural depiction of defects and foolishness in such a striking way. There are traditional types in comedy: miserly fathers, libertine sons, knavish servants, duped guardians; but Iffland's roles, as he conceives them, cannot be categorized by these types. Each of his roles must be identified by the character's name, for each is an individual, each differs remarkably one from the other, and in each Iffland seems to be completely at ease.

His manner of playing tragedy is also, in my opinion, very effective. The calm and simplicity of his declamation in the role of Wallstein is unforgettable. The impression he produces is gradual: at first it seems that his apparent coldness will never stir our emotions; but emotion grows, with an always more rapid progression, as the play proceeds; and the least word has a great effect when the prevailing tone is that of noble tranquillity. Each nuance is thus set in relief and the shadings of character are always preserved even in the midst of passion.

Iffland, who is as skilled a theoretician as a performer, has published several remarkably perceptive essays on declamation.[20] He begins with a sketch of the different periods in the history of the German theatre: rigid and formal imitation of the French; the tearful commonplaces of the sentimental drama which all but destroyed the art of speaking verse; finally, the return to poetry and the imagination, now the prevailing taste in Germany. There is not an intonation, not a gesture, whose cause cannot be found by the philosopher and artist Iffland.

A character in one of his plays furnished the possibility for the subtlest observations on comic acting: the character is that of an old man who suddenly abandons his usual feelings and habits to assume the costume and opinions of the younger generation. The character of this man is not bad in itself, but vanity leads him astray as if he were truly perverse. He had allowed his daughter to marry reasonably, if not remarkably; suddenly he advises her to divorce. Graciously smiling, a cane in his hand, balancing on one foot and then the other, he suggests that his child break the most sacred of bonds. With notable shrewdness, Iffland makes us aware of old age despite a forced elegance, and of restraint despite his apparent carelessness.

Considering Franz Moor, the brother of Schiller's robber chief, Iffland examines the question of how the roles of villains should be played.[21] "It is necessary," he says, "that the actor exert all his effort to make manifest the reasons a character has become what he is, the circumstances that have corrupted his soul. In fact, an actor must be a semi-official defender of the character he represents." In effect, truth, even in villainy, can only be portrayed through the nuances which make it evident that a man only becomes wicked by degrees.

Iffland also remarks the prodigious sensation that a very famous old Geman actor, Ekhof, excited in the play *Emilia Galotti*.[22] Odoardo, when he learns from the prince's mistress that his daughter's honor is menaced, seeks to conceal from this woman, whom he does not respect, the indignation and sadness she has aroused in him. Unknowingly, his hands plucked the feathers from his hat with a convulsive movement whose effect was frightening. Ekhof's successors were careful to pluck the feath ers from the hat as he had done, but the feathers merely fell to the ground unnoticed as genuine emotion had not given to this trivial gesture that sublime truth which stirs the soul of an audience.

Iffland's theory of gesture is very ingenious. He mocks the arms-turning-like-windmills style which is only useful in declaiming moral phrases. He believes that ordinarily a limited number of gestures, kept close to the body, give a better indication of true feelings. But, in this system, as in many others, there are two very distinct classes of talent: one relies on poetic enthusiasm, the other is born of the spirit of observation. One or the other element should dominate, according to the nature of the play or of the role. Gestures inspired by gracefulness and a sense of the beautiful do not aid in the characterization of a specific role. Poetry expresses perfection in general rather than in a particular manner of being or feeling. The art of the tragic actor consists, then, in representing the image of poetic beauty in his attitudes without neglecting the distinguishing traits of the character he plays. The domain of the arts is always composed of the union of the ideal and the natural.

When I saw the play *24 February* acted by two famous poets, A. W. Schlegel and Werner, I was most surprised by their manner of declaiming.[23] They had rehearsed extensively, and one sensed that they would have been annoyed had applause begun at the first verse. The sense of the whole was always evident in their conception, and success in details, which could be detrimental to the whole, would have seemed a fault to them. Schlegel, by his style of acting in Werner's play, allowed me to discover all the interest of a role I had hardly noticed in reading. He portrayed the innocence of a guilty man, the unhappiness of an honest man who had committed a crime as an innocent child, and who, though at peace with his conscience, was unable to subdue his imagination. I judged the man acted out before me as one comprehends a character in life, according to movements, gestures, intonations—which betray him in spite of himself. In France, the majority of actors never appear unconscious of what they are doing; there is on the contrary, something studied in all the means they use and the effect is predictable.

Schroeder,[24] regarded by all Germans as an admirable actor, could not bear being told that he had played well such and such a moment, or had declaimed well such and such a verse. "Have I played the role well?" he would ask. "Have I been the character?" And, in fact, his talent seemed to change its nature each time he changed roles. In France, no one would dare recite tragic verse in the conversational tone he often used. There is a general tonality, an appropriate intonation required in speaking alexandrine verse and the most impassioned moments rest on this pedestal, which is a sort of given in the art. French actors ordinarily aim for applause at almost every verse and earn it. German actors claim their applause at the end of the play and rarely obtain it elsewhere.

The diversity of scenes and situations found in German plays necessitates much more variety in acting skills. Pantomime counts all the more, and the audience's patience permits a wealth of detail which renders pathos more natural. In France, the actor's art consists almost entirely of declamation; in Germany there are many more accessories to the principal art, and often words are hardly necessary to achieve the desired effect.

When Schroeder, playing King Lear in Germany, was brought sleeping on stage, it has been said that this sleep, of an unfortunate old man, drew tears even before he awoke and before his lamentations made known his woes. Nothing was as affecting as the strength given him by despair as he carried the corpse of his faithful daughter Cordelia, killed because of her refusal to abandon him. Buoyed by a final hesitation, he tried to see if Cordelia still breathed. He, so old, could not persuade himself that one so young could be dead. The impassioned grief of this battered old man aroused the most heart-rending emotions.

German actors can, however, be fairly reproached for rarely putting into practice a knowledge of the arts of design so widely disseminated in their country. Their attitudes are not beautiful, the excess of their simplicity often degenerates into awkwardness. They almost never equal French actors in nobility and elegance of demeanor and carriage. Nevertheless, for some time now, German actresses have studied the art of attitudes and have themselves perfected that gracefulness so necessary in the theatre. In Germany, there is no applause until the end of the acts, and rarely is the actor interrupted by noisy applause. The Germans consider it barbaric to disturb, with applause, the effect of the emotions which they prefer silently to absorb. But this presents a further difficulty for their actors—for great self restraint is required to forego, while performing, the public's encouragement. In so emotional a setting, spectators can experience a unique and powerful communion.

A great familiarity with the practice of his craft allows a good actor to utilize the same skills and create the same effects when repeating a performance without the intial stimulus of the audience; but his first inspiration almost always comes from the audience. A singular disparity merits consideration. In those fine arts in which composition is solitary and reflective, all naturalness is lost when the audience is taken into consideration. In those fine arts which involve improvisation, especially in declamation, the sound of applause stirs the soul like martial music. This intoxicating sound quickens the pulse and satisfies more than a cold vanity.

In France, when a man of genius appears, no matter what his career, he almost always achieves an unparalleled degree of perfection, for he joins that audacity which separates him from the common path to the delicacy of good taste, which is important to preserve when the originality of talent does not suffer from it. Thus, it seems to me that Talma can be cited as a model of boldness and reserve, of naturalness and dignity. He possesses all the secrets of the various arts; his attitudes recall the beauty of ancient statues; almost unconsciously, his costume, at all times, is draped as though he had the time to arrange it in the most becoming way. His expressions, his regard, reflect his study of painting. Sometimes he appears with his eyes half-opened, suddenly emotion brings to them bursts of light which seem to illuminate the whole stage. With the first word, the sound of his voice alone is arresting, even before the sense of the words has aroused emotion. When descriptive verses occur in tragedy, he illuminates the beauty of this type of poetry as if Pindar himself were reciting his odes. Others need time to arouse emotion and do well to take it, but in the voice of this man there is an undefinable magic which, from the first sounds, awakens all the sympathy in our hearts. The charm of music, of painting, of sculpture, of poetry, and, above all, of the soul's language, are his means of evoking in his listeners all the power of noble and terrible passions.

What a knowledge of the human heart is displayed in his conceptions of his roles! Through his intonations and expressions he becomes a second author. When Oedipus tells Jocasta how, unwittingly, he killed Laius, the narration begins "I was young and proud."[25] The majority of actors before Talma chose to stress the word "proud" and raised their heads to signal it. Talma, sensing that all of Oedipus' proud recollections have begun to be transformed into remorse, pronounces these words, which recall a confidence he no longer possesses, in a timid voice. Phorbas arrives from Corinth at the moment when Oedipus begins to harbor fears regarding his birth; the former requests a private interview with him. Actors before Talma hastened to turn to their retinue and dismiss them with a majestic gesture: Talma keeps his eyes fixed on Phorbas; he can't let him out of his sight, and, with a troubled gesture, dismisses his courtiers. He has yet to speak, but his distracted movements betray his soul's agitation. And when, in the last act, he cries out as he leaves Jocasta, "Yes, Laius is my father, and I am your son," we see before us the hell to which men are consigned by perfidious destiny.

Talma as Ladislas in Rotrou's *Venceslas*, 1809-1810. (Author's collection.)

In *Andromache*,[26] when the enraged Hermione accuses Orestes of having killed Pyrrhus without her consent, Orestes replies: "And haven't you yourself so often commanded his death?" It is said that Lekain recited this verse stressing each word as if to remind Hermione of all the circumstances of the order he had received from her. That would be appropriate before one's judge, but in terms of the woman one loves, the unique and overwhelming emotion is that of discovering her to be unjust and cruel. That is how Talma conceives the situation: a cry escapes from Orestes' heart; he pronounces the first words with force and those that follow with an ever-increasing weakness; his arms fall; his face, in an instant, becomes as pale as death. The emotion aroused in the audience becomes proportionally greater as he seems to lose the power of expressing himself.

The manner in which Talma recites the monologue which follows is sublime. The sort of innocence that returns to Orestes' soul, tearing it apart, when he speaks the verse, "To my shame, I slay a king whom I revere," inspires a pity which even Racine's genius could not have anticipated completely. Almost all great actors have attempted Orestes' mad scene; but it is in that scene especially that nobility in expression and gesture add singularly to the effect of despair. The force of grief is all the more terrible when it is manifest in the very calm and dignity of a noble nature.

In plays drawn from Roman history Talma displays a completely different, but no less remarkable, talent. One understands Tacitus better after having seen Talma play Nero. Talma exhibits a spirit of great cunning in Nero, for it is only through sagacity that an honest man perceives the symptoms of crime. Nevertheless, it seems to me that he produces even greater effect in the roles which cause us to abandon ourselves while listening to him: he has done Bayard, in de Belloy's play, the service of ridding him of the bluster deemed appropriate to the character by other actors. Thanks to Talma, this Gascon hero has become as simple in tragedy as he was in history. In this role, Talma's costume, his simple and restrained gestures, recall the statues of knights to be seen in old churches. We are astonished that a man who successfully embodies a feeling for ancient art can also create a character out of the Middle Ages.

Talma occasionally plays the role of Pharon in Ducis' tragedy on an Arab subject, *Abufar*. A wealth of ravishing verses give this tragedy much charm. There is an admirable evocation of the colors of the Orient, the dreamy melancholia of the Asiatic south, the melancholy of countries where heat consumes, rather than embellishes, nature. The same Talma— Greek, Roman, and medieval knight—is an Arab from the desert, full of energy and love. His glances are guarded, as though to avoid the intense rays of the sun. In his gestures there is an admirable alternation between indolence and impetuousity. Sometimes he seems overwhelmed by fate; at other times he seems even more powerful than nature and seems to triumph over her. The passion which devours him, whose object is a woman he believes to be his sister, is locked in his breast. His hesitant movements seem to indicate that he wishes to flee. His hands repulse an image he believes to be ever at his side. And, when he at last presses Salema to his breast, saying to her simply, "I am cold," he is at once able to express the thrill he feels and the devouring ardor he seeks to conceal.

A great many flaws can be found in Ducis' French adaptation of Shakespeare's plays, but it would be unjust not to recognize in them beauties of the first order. Ducis' genius resides in depicting emotions, and it is there that he is effective. Talma acts in his plays as a friend of that admirable talent of this noble old man. The witches' scene in *Macbeth* becomes a narrative in the French play. One must see Talma attempt to render something of the vulgar and bizarre witches' speech while maintaining in this imitation all the dignity required in the theatre:

> With incomprehensible words, these monstrous beings
> Called one by one, applauded themselves,
> Approached, pointing at me with a wild laugh,
> Their mysterious fingers poised on their mouths.
> I spoke to them, and they suddenly disappeared in the shadows.
> One with a knife, the other with a scepter in hand,
> Another's livid body was encircled by a snake,
> All three took rapid flight towards this palace.
> And all three in the air, fleeing me,
> Left me the following words of farewell: *You will be king.*

The deep and mysterious voice of the actor pronouncing these lines, the way he placed his finger to his lips, like the representation of Silence, his expression, which altered to express the recollection of something horrible and repugnant, all combined to create a new species of marvel on our stage, one of which no previous tradition could have given an idea.

Not too long ago, *Othello* failed on the French stage. Apparently Orosmane prevents us from completely understanding *Othello*! But when Talma acts in this play, the fifth act moves us as though the murder were taking place before our very eyes. I have seen Talma, at home, declaim the last scene with his wife, whose voice and appearance are so well suited to the role of Desdemona. It was enough for him to pass his hand through his hair and to wrinkle his brow to become the Moor of Venice. He inspired terror in those near him as if he had suspended all the theatre's illusions.

Hamlet is his greatest triumph among tragedies based on foreign plays. On the French stage, the ghost of Hamlet's father does not appear. The appearance of the ghost is sensed entirely in Talma's expression, and it is certainly no less terrifying. When, in the midst of a calm and melancholy encounter, he suddenly sees the ghost, we follow all its movements in those eyes which contemplate it. We cannot doubt the presence of the ghost when such an expression testifies to it.

When Hamlet appears on stage alone in the third act, he recites in beautiful French verse the famous "To be or not to be" soliloquy:

> Death is sleep, it is perhaps an awakening,
> Perhaps—Ah! It is the word which freezes, terrifed,
> Man, beside the casket, halted by his doubt;
> Before this vast abyss, he leaps back,
> Recovering his existence and gripping the earth.[27]

Talma used no gesture. He only shook his head from time to time to question heaven and earth concerning death! Immobile, his whole being was absorbed in the dignity of meditation. One witnessed a man, among two thousand silent men, question the idea of mortal fate! In a few years all that is would no longer be, but other men in turn will experience the same uncertainties and will plunge into the same abyss without knowledge of its depths.

When Hamlet seeks to make his mother swear, on the urn containing her husband's ashes, that she had no part in his murder, she hesitates, troubled, and concludes by confessing her guilt. Hamlet draws the dagger with which his father has commanded him to kill his mother, but at the moment of striking her, tenderness and pity overwhelm him, and turning to his father's ghost cries out: "Mercy, mercy my father," In his intonation, every emotion seems to escape from his heart. And, flinging himself at his mother's feet, he pronounces these ineffably piteous lines:

> Your crime is horrible, execrable, odious;
> But it is no greater than Heaven's benevolence.

Finally, we cannot speak of Talma without recalling *Manlius*.[28] This play is barely theatrical: it is the subject of Otway's *Venice Preserv'd* transposed to an event in Roman history. Manlius conspires against the Roman senate. He confesses his secret to his friend of fifteen years, Servilius. He confides in him despite the doubts of his fellow conspirators, who are wary of Servilius' weakness and his love for his wife, the daughter of a consul. What the conspirators had feared occurs. Servilius is unable to conceal from his wife the danger to her father's life; she immediately reveals it to her parent. Manlius is arrested, his plot discovered, and he is condemned by the senate to be thrown from the Tarpeian Rock.

Before Talma, the passionate friendship of Manlius for Servilius was hardly perceived in this poorly written play. When a note from the

conspirator Rutilius announces the betrayal of the plot by Servilius, Manlius comes, this note in hand, to confront his friend, already devoured
by remorse, and, showing him the accusing lines, asks: "What do you
say to this?" I ask all who have heard this, can the expression and intonation ever express at the same time such different emotions? This
rage tempered by a heart-felt pity, this indignation alternately strengthened and weakened by friendship, can only be understood in this voice
which passes from soul to soul without the intermediary of words! Manlius draws his dagger to stab Servilius, his hand seeks his heart and
trembles on finding it. The memory of the many years Servilius had
been dear to him rises like a veil of tears between his vengeance and his
friend.

We have yet to mention the fifth act, where Talma is perhaps more
admirable than in the fourth. Servilius has braved every consideration
to expiate his treachery and save Manlius. In his heart he is resolved, if
his friend dies, to share his fate. Manlius' grief is tempered by Servilius'
regret. Nevertheless, Manlius dares not tell Servilius that he forgives
him, but privately takes Servilius' hand and places it on his heart. His
involuntary gestures seek out the guilty friend he wishes to embrace
before parting forever. Nothing, or almost nothing, in the text, indicated
this subtle emotion of the sensitive soul, respecting an old affection
despite the treachery that destroyed it. The roles of Pierre and Jaffier
in the English play powerfully illustrate this situation. Talma is able to
give the tragedy of Manlius the power it lacks. Nothing does more honor
to his talent than the veracity with which he expresses what is indestructible in friendship. Passion may despise the object of its love, but
when the bonds are those of a sacred relationship, it seems that even
crime is unable to destroy them. One awaits remorse as one awaits a
return after a long absence.

In speaking in some detail about Talma, I don't believe that I have
digressed from my subject. This artist gives as much as is possible to
French tragedy of what, justly or unjustly, the Germans accuse it of
lacking: originality and naturalness. He knows how to characterize foreign manners in the diverse plays in which he acts, and no actor hazards
greater effects by simlple means. In his declamation Shakespeare and
Racine are artistically joined. Why won't dramatists also attempt to unite
in their compositions what the actor has so well combined in his acting?

Notes

1. *King John*: IV 1. 41-58; and *Richard III*: IV 3. 1-22.
2. The death of Katherine of Aragon in *Henry VIII*. [Madame de Staël's note.]
3. The Duke of Clarence in *Richard III*. [Madame de Staël's note.]

4. Cardinal Wolsey in *Henry VIII*. [Madame de Staël's note.]

5. *Charles IX* was the first tragedy to portray a guilty king of France while the monarchy still existed. *Charles IX, or The School for Kings*, by Marie-Joseph Chénier, was first produced in 1789.

6. Although *Hamlet*, of all Shakespeare's great tragedies, is the one possessing the most revolting errors of taste, it is one of the most beautiful situations to be found in the theatre. Hamlet's folly is caused by the discovery of a great crime: the purity of his soul had not permitted him to suspect it. But his faculties alter through the knowledge that a heinous act has been committed, that his father has been the victim, and that his mother rewarded the guilty party by marrying him. He does not speak a word that does not attest to his contempt for the human race. He thinks more often of suicide than of revenge. It is a noble idea for the poet to have portrayed the virtuous man unable to bear living when he is surrounded by baseness and carrying in his breast the anxiety of a criminal when sorrow commands him to a just vengeance! [Madame de Staël's note.]

7. A term used by Diderot, Beaumarchais, and other eighteenth-century writers to label that genre which developed serious themes in middle-class settings.

8. Ducis, in several scenes in almost all his works; Chénier in the fourth act of *Charles IX*; Arnault in the fifth act of *The Venetians*, introduced into the French theatre a very remarkable new kind of effect of the sort more readily associated with the genius of Northern poets than with that of French poets. [Madame de Staël's note.]

Jean-François Ducis made neo-classical adaptations of several of Shakespeare's plays in the late eighteenth century. Antoine-Vincent Arnault's *Venetians* was produced in 1798.

9. *Fénelon, or The Nuns of Cambrai*, a tragedy by Marie-Joseph Chénier, produced in 1794.

10. The French public is slow in accepting innovations in genre in the theatre. Proud, with reason, of the masterpieces it possesses, the French public thinks it a regression in art to diverge from the path traced by Racine. However, I don't think it impossible to succeed in a new way by skillfully introducing some effects not yet risked on the French stage. But for such an enterprise to be successful, it must be guided by the surest of taste. A general knowledge of literary precepts is sufficient to prevent error when submitting to given rules. But when one wants to triumph over the natural aversion of the French audience for what they call the English or German mode, one must be scrupulously on guard for all the nuances subject to condemnation by delicacy of taste. One must be bold in conception, but prudent in execution, and, in this respect, follow in literature a principle that would be equally valid in politics: the more dangerous a project, the more careful the attention paid to details. [Madame de Staël's note.]

11. August Wilhelm Schlegel's *Lectures on Dramatic Art and Literature* (1808), and his *Lectures on the Beautiful in Art and Literature* (1801–1803) were the most important of Madame de Staël's sources for these ideas.

12. Voltaire wrote the most successful French tragedies of the eighteenth century. *Alzire* (1736) deals with the Spaniards in Peru; *Zaïre* (1732) is in part inspired by *Othello* and is set in the Middle East during the Crusades; *Tancred* (1760) helped initiate a vogue for plays dealing with French national history.

13. Dormont de Belloy, author of the historical tragedies *The Siege of Calais*

(1765) and *Gaston and Bayard* (1771). The latter was successfully revived by Talma.

14. François Raynouard's *Templars* was a great success at the Comédie-Française in 1805.

15. Constant's adaptation of Schiller's *Wallenstein* trilogy was published in 1809. It reduces Schiller's trilogy to five-act neo-classical form. Constant's spelling will be used here as Madame de Staël's references are to his version of the plays.

16. Népomucène Lemercier's *Agamemnon* (1791) had a minor success and remained in the repertory throughout the Empire.

17. August Wilhelm Iffland (1759–1814), actor and playwright. He was the leading actor in Berlin from 1796 until his death. He staged the plays of Goethe, Schiller, and Shakespeare as well as those of Kotzebue.

18. Goethe held the post of Director of the Weimar Court Theatre from 1791 to 1817. For a history of his work there see Marvin Carlson, *Goethe and the Weimar Theatre* (Ithaca, N.Y.: Cornell University Press, 1978). Madame de Staël visited Weimar in the winter of 1803–1804.

19. David Garrick (1717–1779) was one of the greatest English actors of the eighteenth century. He was the leading actor and manager at Drury Lane Theatre from 1747 to 1776. He adapted and wrote plays and is credited with reforms in the acting style and innovations in stagecraft. François Joseph Talma (1763–1826) was France's greatest actor during the Empire and the Restoration. Like Garrick, he was able to introduce reforms in the direction of realism within the neo-classical tradition.

20. Iffland's writings on acting, variously published before his death, were collected in *The Theory of Acting* (1815).

21. Schiller's Storm and Stress drama *The Robbers* was published in 1782 and was first produced by Iffland at Mannheim in 1782.

22. Konrad Ekhof (1720–1778) had been a member of the Hamburg National Theatre in 1767 when Lessing served as its dramaturg. He created the role of Emilia's father in Lessing's tragedy in 1772.

23. Zacharias Werner's fate-tragedy *24 February* was premiered at Weimar in 1810. Madame de Staël is referring to an amateur performance of the play given at her house at Coppet in September 1809.

24. Friedrich Ludwig Schroeder (1744–1816) helped establish a national tradition of acting in Germany in the late eighteenth century. He also helped popularize Shakespeare with German audiences.

25. In Voltaire's version of *Oedipus*.

26. By Racine.

27. Talma was appearing in Jean-François Ducis' adaptation of *Hamlet* (1769). I have translated Ducis' lines, which Madame de Staël cites, as they are rather different from the "To sleep, perchance to dream" section of Hamlet's soliloquy.

28. Antoine de Lafosse's *Manlius Capitolinus* (1698) was revived by Talma with great success in 1806.

2

BENJAMIN CONSTANT

Benjamin Constant de Rebecque (1767–1830) was born at Lausanne to a family of Swiss Protestant exiles. His rather erratic education included studies in both Germany and Scotland, which helped familiarize him with the languages of the two literary traditions that were to play an important role in the development of French romanticism. Unfortunately, as a student, Constant developed an addiction to gambling and a taste for dissipation which were to plague his adult years.

The most critical event in his life seems to have been his meeting and subsequent affair with Madame de Staël in 1794. Under her influence, which was to last until 1811, he entered the worlds of politics and literature. In 1800 he served as a Tribune under the Directory. He followed Madame de Staël into exile and continued to support the liberal cause during the Empire. During the Hundred Days, Napoleon, in a conciliatory gesture towards the liberals, asked Constant to draft a constitution. From 1819 to 1824 and from 1827 until his death, Constant served in the Chamber of Deputies. His major political writings were published in the Course of Constitutional Politics *in 1818–1819. Constant's political career and writings, as well as his massive work on the history of religion, have, however, suffered through comparison with the lasting success of his literary and autobiographical work.*

The major portion of Constant's literary work was undertaken while in exile. Adolphe *(published in 1816) justifiably holds an important position in the history of the French novel. Other writings from the 1806–1811 period include* The Red Notebook *and* Cécile *(both posthumously published) and* Wallstein *(1809), an adaptation of Schiller's* Wallenstein *trilogy. This last work was suggested by Madame de Staël when Constant accompanied her on her first trip to Germany in 1804. She was, at the time of the writing of* Wallstein, *at work on her own* Germany.

When Constant published his Literary and Political Miscellany *(Paris: Pichon and Didier, 1829), he revised the preface to* Wallstein, *thus returning to print an important early statement of some of the romantic attitudes toward drama. This essay and the "Reflections on Tragedy" published in the* Revue de Paris *in 1829, and here translated, establish Constant as a brilliant, though hardly influential, critic. The latter essay, which dates from the climactic period of the romantic battle in France, provides a fine and restrained statement of the liberal attitude toward drama and reform in the theatre.*

A *Literary and Political Miscellany* (1829)

Chapter V. *"On the Thirty Years' War: Schiller's Tragedy,* Wallstein, *and the German Theatre"*

This is a revision of "Some Reflections on the German Theatre," published as a preface to Constant's Wallstein *(Paris and Geneva: Paschaud, 1809). I use Constant's spelling for the name of the title character and his spellings for the names of other characters as he is referring to his adaptation of Schiller's play, except when he obviously refers to Schiller's play in the first part of the essay.*

The Thirty Years' War is one of the most remarkable periods in modern history. This war broke out in a Bohemian city, but spread rapidly throughout the major portion of Europe. The religious attitudes which lay behind it changed shape in the course of the war. Luther's sect almost everywhere replaced that of John Hus. But the memory of the terrible torture inflicted on the latter continued to influence the attitude of the reformers even after they had cast off his doctrine.

The need for religious freedom was the driving force behind the masses in the Thirty Years' War. The desire to preserve their political independence was the princes' motive. After a long and terrible struggle these two goals were achieved. The peace of 1648 guaranteed the Protestants the right to practice their religion and the petty princes of Germany the enjoyment and extension of their rights. The influence of the Thirty Years' War is still felt in our time.

The Treaty of Westphalia provided the German empire with a very complicated constitution. But, by dividing this massive area into a group of small, individual sovereignties, this constitution earned, with few exceptions, a century and a half of civil liberty and a peaceful and moderate administration for the German nation. The single fact that thirty million subjects were dispersed among a fairly large number of independent princes, whose apparently unrestricted authority was, in fact, limited by the small size of their domains, resulted in, for these thirty millions, an ordinarily peaceful existence, a fairly substantial security, an almost complete freedom of opinion, and, for the enlightened members of society, the possibility of devoting themselves to the cultivation of letters, to the perfection of the arts, and to the search for truth.

Given the influence of the Thirty Years' War, it is not surprising that it has been one of the favorite subjects for the studies of German historians and poets. In many diverse forms, they have taken pleasure in informing the current generation of their ancestors' vigor. And the current generation, which calmly reaps the benefits of a strength which they have lost, contemplates with curiosity, in history and on the stage, the men of the past whose force, determination, energy and courage, which, in the eyes of a weakened people, colors the German histories with the charm of the marvelous.

The Thirty Years' War continues to be interesting from another point of view.

No doubt since this war there have been several monarchs who waged war and won fame through military exploits, but the military spirit, as such, has increasingly become alien to the spirit of the people. The military spirit can only exist when social conditions are appropriate for its birth, that is to say, when there is a very large number of men who have been wrenched from their natural situation by need, anxiety, a lack of security, the hope and possibility of success, and the habit of aggression. These men, then, love war for its own sake and when they don't find it in one place, they seek it in another.

In our time, military power is always subordinate to political authority. The generals are obeyed only by the soldiers they command, by virtue of the power they have received from a higher authority. They are not the leaders of their own troops. These troops are not paid by the generals and ready to follow them without the consent of any monarch. At the beginning of and up to the middle of the seventeenth century, on the contrary, there were men who had no other authority than their sense of their own skill and courage. They kept in their pay battalions of men who were united under their personal colors, soldiers whom they controlled through the unique power of their personal genius. Sometimes they sold themselves, with their small armies, to the rulers who would have them; sometimes, weapons in hand, they tried to become rulers themselves. Such a man was Count Mansfeld, still less famed for his handful of victories than for the skill he ceaselessly deployed in adversity. Such were Christian of Brunswick and Bernard of Weimar, even though they issued from the most illustrious royal families of Germany. Finally, such a man was Wallenstein, Duke of Friedland.

It is true that this Wallenstein never bore arms except for the House of Austria, but the army he commanded belonged to him, was assembled in his name, paid at his order with the contributions raised on his personal authority in Germany. Like a potentate, he negotiated from the very center of his camp with the monarchs who were enemies of the Emperor. In the end, he sought to insure, as a right, the independence he enjoyed in fact. And, if he failed in this enterprise, his fall must not be attributed to the insufficiency of means at his disposal, but to the errors he committed through an odd mixture of superstition and uncertainty in his character. The way of life led by those seventeenth-century generals gave their character an originality which we can no longer envisage.

Originality is always the result of independence. As authority becomes centralized, individuals disappear. All the stones cut for a pyramid's construction and shaped to the place they were to fill have a uniform exterior. Individuality disappears in a man, in proportion as he ceases to be an end and becomes a means to an end: yet individuality alone can arouse interest especially in foreign nations; for the French, as I remarked earlier, do without it much more easily than do the Germans and the English.

You see then, without difficulty, why the German poets who wanted to place their own history on the stage have chosen, by preference, those periods when individuals were most self-sufficient and gave into their natural character with the least reserve. In this way, Goethe, the author of *Werther*, depicted in *Goetz von Berlichingen*[1] the struggle of the dying chivalric tradition with the Empire. Similarly, Schiller wanted to describe in *Wallenstein* the final throes of the military spirit and that independent, almost savage, life in the camps which civilization has replaced with uniformity, obedience, and discipline, even in the military camps.

Schiller wrote three plays dealing with the conspiracy and death of Wallenstein. The first is *Wallenstein's Camp*; the second is *The Piccolomini*; the third is *The Death of Wallenstein*.[2]

The idea of writing three plays which succeed each other and form a larger whole is borrowed from the Greeks, who called this form a "trilogy." Aeschylus has left us two such works, *Prometheus* and the three tragedies concerned with the House of Atreus. The *Prometheus*, as you know, was divided into three parts, each a separate play. In the first play, Prometheus was portrayed as the benefactor of mankind, bringing fire from heaven and teaching the structures of social life. In the second play, the only one which has come down to us, Prometheus is punished by the gods, jealous of the services he has rendered man. The third play would show Prometheus freed by Hercules and reconciled to Jupiter.

In the three tragedies dealing with the House of Atreus, the first deals with the death of Agamemnon, the second with Clytemnestra's punishment, and the third with Orestes' absolution by the Aereopagus. You can see that in the Greek drama each of the plays in a trilogy had its particular action which was brought to completion in the play itself. Schiller wished to more closely link the three plays in his *Wallenstein* trilogy. The action doesn't begin until the second play and does not end until the third. *Wallenstein's Camp* is a sort of a prologue without any action. It displays the camp life of the soldiers: some sing, others drink, others return enriched with booty plundered from the peasants. They relate their exploits; they discuss their leader and the freedoms and rewards he lavishes upon them. The scenes follow one another without being linked, but this incoherence is natural: it is a living portrait with neither past nor future. The genius of Wallenstein, however, presides over this apparent disorder: all thoughts are focused upon him, all are disturbed by rumors of the court's displeasure, and all swear their loyalty to their general and protector. We perceive all the symptoms of a burgeoning insurrection, awaiting but Wallenstein's signal to explode. At the same time, we distinguish the hidden motives which modify the loyalty of each individual; the fears, suspicions, personal ambitions, which intermingle with the general emotions. We see this armed force as susceptible as all popular uprisings, carried away by their own enthusiasms, unsettled by mistrust, forcing themselves to reason, and failing to reason, by habit. We see them defying authority, yet making it a point of honor to obey their leader. We see them at once insulting religion while avidly giving themselves over to any superstitious tradition. They are proud of their strength and always contemptuous of any profession other than the military, with courage as a virtue and the pleasure of the moment as a goal.

It would be impossible to transfer to our stage this singular production of the genius, the exactitude, and, I would say, the erudition of the Germans; for erudition is needed to unite all the traits which characterized seventeenth-century armies and which are no longer found in today's armies. Today, in the barracks as in the city, everything is predictable and regimented. Discipline has replaced high spirits. If there are occasional disorders, they are exceptions, which an attempt has been made to prevent. During the Thirty Years' War, on the contrary, these disorders were the norm, and the enjoyment of a crude and licentious freedom was the compensation for danger and fatigue.

The second play is called *The Piccolomini*. The action begins in this play, but the play ends before the action is completed. The plot is formed, the characters are developed, the last scene of the fifth act arrives and the curtain falls. The poet has placed the dénouement in the third play, *The Death of Wallenstein*. In reality then, the first two plays are expository: they are an exposition of more than 4,000 lines.

It would not seem possible to perform these three Schiller plays separately, yet this is done in Germany. Thus the Germans will sometimes tolerate a play without an action, *Wallenstein's Camp*; sometimes an action without a dénouement, *The Piccolomini*; and sometimes a dénouement without an exposition, *The Death of Wallenstein*.

Several attempts have been made to adapt these three plays for the French stage; these attempts have been unsuccessful. My imitation, *Wallstein*, the most faithful of all, was the object of much criticism. Free today of the vanity which animates an author during the period of first publication of a work, I recognize that several of these criticisms were justified.

In various ways I had destroyed the dramatic effect of the play by condemning myself to maintaining all our own theatre's rules.

Following Schiller's example, I had set myself the task of depicting Wallstein very nearly as he was, truly ambitious, but also superstitious, subject to anxiety, unreliable, jealous of foreign successes in his own country—even when these successes favored his own enterprises. He often acted against his own interests, allowing himself to be swept away by his character.

I had not even wanted to suppress his penchant for astrology, although given the attitudes of our times, the attempt to color this superstition with tragic overtones might seem risky. In France, we rarely consider superstition except in its ridiculous aspects. Nevertheless, superstition is deely rooted in mankind, and even philosophy is superficial and even presumptuous when it stubbornly refuses to take it into account. Nature has placed mankind in isolation. He alone has been destined to cultivate and populate the earth, having only arid and fixed relations with all that is not his kind. These relationships are determined by utility. A great correspondence exists between all moral and physical beings. I believe there is no person who, letting his gaze wander across a limitless horizon, walking on a wave-lashed shore, or looking up to the starry night sky, has not experienced an emotion he would find difficult to analyze or define. It is as though voices are heard from the heavens, are hurled from the rocky peaks, echo in the streams of the storm-tossed forests, or cry out from the depths of abysses. There seems to be something ineffably prophetic in the ominous flight of a raven; in the funereal cries of nocturnal birds; in the distant roars of savage beasts. Everything that has not been civilized, everything that has not submitted to man's artificial domination, touches his heart. Only those things he has made for his own use are silent, because they are dead. But even these objects, when time has erased their usefulness, re-assume a mystic life. Denied destruction, they are put back in touch with nature. Modern buildings are silent, while ruins speak.

The entire universe speaks to man in an ineffable language which makes itself heard in his soul, in a part of his being of which he is unaware, but which possesses both sensation and thought. Nothing is simpler than imagining that this effort of nature to penetrate our being is not without a mysterious significance. What is the reason for this intimate disturbance which seems to reveal to us what ordinary life hides? Doubtless, it cannot be explained by reason. When reason analyzes it, it vanishes. But it is because of this very thing, that it is essentially a matter for poetry. Consecrated by poetry, it finds chords in all hearts which respond to it. Fate written in the stars, forebodings, dreams, omens, those shadows of the future which hover about us, often no less lugubrious than the ghosts of the past, are found in all nations, in all periods, and in all beliefs. Who is the man who, when animated by great self-interest, does not, trembling, lend an ear to what he believes to be the voice of destiny? Every man, in the sanctuary of his mind, accounts for this voice as he can. Each man is silent, like all men, for there are no words to make universal what is always personal.

I had thought it necessary, therefore, to preserve in Wallstein's character a superstition which he shared with almost all the notable men of his age.

But, in deference to our conventions, I placed the revelation of my hero's superstition in a narration rather than depicting it in the theatre itself, from accidental circumstances.

Thus, in Schiller's play, while undressing for bed, Wallstein sees the chain on which the Order of the Golden Fleece is hung suddenly break. This chain was the first gift given Wallstein by the Emperor—then the Archduke—during the war of the Frioul, when both men, at the beginning of their careers, were united by a seemingly permanent affection. Wallstein holds in his hands the shattered links; he recalls the whole history of his youth; memories mixed with remorse besiege him; he feels a vague fear; for so long had his prosperity seemed to him dependent on the preservation of this first token of a now broken friendship. He contemplates the fragments sadly; finally casting them aside with an effort. "My career," he cries, "has changed course: this talisman's power has ended."

The spectator, aware of the danger threatening the hero, is profoundly moved by this omen (misunderstood by Wallstein) and by the words which escape him (uncomprehendingly). This effect is a result of man's inner disposition which, for all emotions—fear, tenderness, or pity—always reverts to what we call superstition through a mysterious and inescapable force. Many men regard this only as a puerile weakness. I am tempted, I admit, to respect everything that has its source in nature.

Furthermore, I had misunderstood an essential difference between our character and that of our neighbors across the Rhine. We have a need for unity which makes us reject everything in the character of our tragic figures which hinders the unique effect we wish to produce. We suppress everything in our heroes' past not directly related to the principal event.

What does Racine tell us about Phaedra? We see her love for Hippolytus, but nothing of her character independent of this passion. What does the same poet show us of Orestes? His love for Hermione. The transports of this prince are derived only from the cruelties of his mistress. At every point he seems ready to weaken; were Hermione to give him the least hope. This matricide seems to have completely forgotten his crime. He is concerned only with his passion. After the murder, he speaks of his innocence, which weighs upon him. And if, after he has killed Pyrrhus, he is pursued by the Furies, it is because Racine found the subject for a superb scene in the mythological tradition, but one which is not related to his subject as depicted.

This is not meant to be a criticism. *Andromache* is one of the most perfect plays written in any language. Racine, having adopted the French system, had to divert the attention of the spectator, as much as he could, from the memory of Clytemnestra's murder. This memory is incompatible with a love like that of Orestes for Hermione. A son still dripping with his mother's blood, yet thinking only of his mistress, would be revolting. Racine sensed this and, in order to more surely avoid the pitfall, imagined that Orestes had fled to Tauris to be freed through death of his unhappy passion.

The result is that the French limit themselves to depicting an event or an emotion, even in their tragedies based on tradition and history. In their tragedies, the Germans paint an entire life and a complete character.

When I say that they paint an entire life, I don't mean that their plays encompass the entire life of their heroes, but that they omit no important event in this life. And the combination of what happens on stage and what the spectator learns through narration or allusion forms a complete and scrupulously exact picture.

The same is true of character. The Germans omit nothing of what constitutes the individuality of their characters. They offer us characters with their weaknesses, their inconsistencies, and with the fluctuating mobility of human nature, which forms real beings.

The isolation in which the French system places the act which constitutes the subject of the tragedy and the passion which motivates the action has indisputable advantages.

By freeing the action you have chosen from all anterior acts, you focus interest more directly on the unique object. The poet has more control over the hero who, perhaps, has slightly less realistic coloring. This is because art can never entirely take the place of truth and because the spectator, even when he is ignorant of the liberties taken by the author, is aware—through who knows what instinct—that he is not seeing an historical personage, but an artificially created hero, an invention of the imagination.

More consistently tragic effects are obtained through the painting of a passion rather than a complete, individualized character, because individualized characters, by definition contradictory, prevent the unity of impression. But truth is perhaps the greatest loser. We ask what the heroes we see would be without the power of the passion which motivates them, and we find that very little reality would remain in their character. Moreover, there is much less variety among those passions suitable for tragedy than in individual characters created by nature. Characters are infinite in number; the number of theatrical passions is very small. No doubt Racine's admirable genius, which triumphs over all obstacles, finds diversity in this very uniformity. Phaedra's jealousy is different from Hermione's, and Hermione's love differs from that of Roxane. The diversity, however, still seems to me to be in the passion, rather than the individual character.

There is very little difference between the characters of Aménaïde and Alzire.[3] The character of Polyphontes[4] will suffice for almost any tyrant on our stage, while the character of Shakespeare's Richard III is suitable only for Richard III. Polyphontes possesses only general traits, artfully drawn, but which don't make him a distinct, individual person. He is ambitious, and his ambition is seconded by cruelty and hypocrisy. In addition to these vices, necessary to his role, Richard III encompasses many elements which are unique to him: his disaffection from nature, which, by giving him a hideous and deformed shape, seems to have condemned him to a life without love; his efforts to overcome an obstacle which thwarts him; his flirtatiousness with women; his amazement at his successes with them; the comtempt he feels toward such easily seduced creatures; and his display of this contempt. All these factors make him a singular being. Polyphontes is a type; Richard III is an individual.

Another drawback to my imitation of *Wallstein* was the too frequent allusion to specific events relating to the Thirty Years' War.

This war was waged in Germany, and everything pertaining to it is of national interest to the Germans and familiar in Germany. The names Wallstein, Tilly, Bernard von Weymar, Oxenstiern, and Mansfeld, evoke memories for the Germans which do not exist for us. The superstitious persecutions of Ferdinand II left deep marks in Bohemia and Hungary, and his barbarous orders to his generals remain engraved in blood on the walls of Magdebourg. The result for Schiller was the possibility of a myriad of rapid allusions which his compatriots would have no difficulty understanding. In France there is a certain neglect of the study of foreign history, a characteristic almost completely antithetical to the writing of historical tragedies of the sort found in the literature of our neighbors. Even tragedies which have subjects drawn from our own national annals are characterized by a good deal of obscurity.

The author of *The Templars*[5] had to accompany his work with explanatory notes, while Schiller, when presenting a French subject to the German audience in *The Maid of Orleans*,[6] was certain of being met with spectators knowledgeable enough to forego commentary. The most successful French tragedies are either entirely original, for they require few preconceptions, or are drawn from Greek mythology or Roman history as the study of these subjects is part of our early education.

By sometimes imitating the familiar style which iambic, or unrhymed, verse makes possible for German writers of tragedy, I had eliminated in my tragedy the poetic pomp to which the French ear is accustomed. The language of German tragedy is not subject to refined or restrictive rules as is ours. The pomp which is inseparable from our alexandrine verse requires a certain lofty nobility of expression. In developing their characters, German authors can use a variety of secondary circumstances, which would be impossible to place on our stage without distracting from the requisite dignity. Yet these small details, scattered through a portrait, give it life and truth. In Goethe's *Goetz von Berlichingen*, the hero, a soldier, offers his men a last supper to encourage them during the siege of his castle by the Imperial army. Toward the end of the meal, he asks his wife for wine. Following the custom of the times, she is both mistress and housekeeper of the castle. She replies in a whisper that only a single jug of wine remains which she had intended for him. There is no poetic device which would permit us to bring this detail into our theatre: the pomposity of our language would only spoil the naturalness of the situation and what is touching in German would only be ridiculous in French. Nevertheless, it seems to me that, our customs to the contrary, it is easy to admit that this detail taken from everyday life is better suited to illuminate the hero's situation than the most pathetic description would be. He is an aged and renowned soldier, proud of his hereditary rights and splendors, who, not long before was the lord of many vassals, and now, confined to a last stronghold, battles with a few intrepid and faithful friends the horrors of poverty and the vengeance of the Emperor. In Kotzebue's *Gustaf Vasa*,[7] Sweden's tyrant Christiern is shown trembling in his palace, which is surrounded by an angry mob. He mistrusts his own guards, his most loyal subjects, and forces an aged servant, who remains with him, to taste all his food. This touch, expressed without tragic pomp in the simplest dialogue, characterizes, in my opinion, the concomitant cowardice, defiance, and abasement of the near-defeated tyrant more successfully than could any poetic effect.

Schiller shows us the denunciation of Joan of Arc as a witch by her father during the festivities surrounding the coronation of Charles VII, whom she had restored to France's throne. She is forced to flee. She seeks asylum far from those who threaten her and from the court which has abandoned her. After a long and arduous journey she stops at a cottage; she is overwhelmed by fatigue and consumed by thirst; a sympathetic peasant offers her milk. At the moment she brings it to her lips, a child, who has been watching her attentively, snatches it, and cries: "It is the witch of Orleans!" This tableau always arouses a general shudder in the audience, but it would be impossible to present on the French stage. The audience is struck simultaneously by the idea of the proscription which pursues the liberator of a great empire into the most obscure locales and by the frame of mind which makes the proscription both inevitable and cruel. In this way, the important things, the period and the situation, are brought to mind in a single image by purely accidental circumstances.

In restricting the number of characters[8]* in my play, I had sacrificed, without any compensation, another advantage possessed by Schiller. Subordinate characters which are not directly linked to the plot allow the Germans a type of effect unknown in our theatre. In our tragedies, everything transpires directly between the hero and the audience. Confidants are always carefully kept in the background. They are present to listen, and sometimes to reply. On occasion, they narrate the hero's death, which he cannot relate himself. But there is nothing from the moral sphere in their entire existence. All reflection, all judgement, and all dialogue between them is strictly forbidden. For them to excite the least interest would counter the theory of subordination in the theatre. In German tragedies, independent of the heroes and their confidants, who, as we have just seen, are merely machines—their necessity making us forgive their improbability—there exists, on a second plane, a second sort of roles which are, in a way, spectators themselves. They watch the principal action, which has a very indirect effect upon them. The impression made by the situation of the principal characters on these secondary characters often seems to me to add to the general effect made on the audience. Thus we can say that the audience's opinion is anticipated and directed by an intermediary audience which is closer to the action, but no less impartial.

If I am not mistaken, the effect of the chorus in ancient Greek tragedy must have been very nearly like this. The chorus brought a perspective to the feelings and actions of the kings and heroes whose crimes and misfortunes they contemplated. By means of their judgement, they established a moral correspondence between the stage and the spectators. The latter must have derived pleasure in seeing the emotions they felt described and defined in harmonious language.

I have only seen one play in which an attempt was made to introduce the chorus of the Ancients: it was Schiller's *Bride of Messina*. I went to see it full of prejudices against such imitations of the Ancients. Nevertheless, I experienced a type of satisfaction which I had never previously imagined. This was derived from those general maxims expressed by the people, but which acquired more truth and warmth from the fact they appeared to be suggested to them by the conduct of their leaders and by the misfortunes which seemed to reflect upon them. The public opinion was personified, in a way, and sought my own thoughts, in order to present them to me with more precision, elegance, and force. This was the wisdom of the poet, who understood what I must feel and gave shape to what, in me, was but a vague, indeterminate dream.

The introduction of the chorus in tragedy, however, was not successful in Germany. It has probably been abandoned because of the difficulty of its staging. Highly trained actors are needed, if a group of them, speaking and gesturing in unison, are not to produce a confusion bordering on the ridiculous.[9]* Moreover, Schiller had altered the nature of the ancient chorus in his experiments. He had not dared to leave the chorus as detached from the action as it was in the best of the ancient tragedies—those of Sophocles—for I am not speaking here of Euripides' choruses. This unquestionably admirable poet was, through his defects as well as his virtues, the first to rob Greek tragedy of the noble simplicity that had distinguished it. He possessed talent in emotionalism and irony, but was pretentious, declamatory, and extravagant in his effects. In order to conform to the taste of his time, Schiller had thought it necessary to divide the chorus into two halves, each of which was made up of partisans of the two heroes who, in his play, quarreled over a lady's hand. Through this awkward arrangement he had stripped the chorus of the impartiality which gives weight and solemnity to its words.

The chorus must never be anything more than a mouthpiece of the people taken as a whole. Everything the chorus says should be a kind of somber and imposing echo of the general response. Impassioned statements are not appropriate to the chorus. And, as soon as you imagine the chorus taking part in the play's action, its rationale is altered and its effect is ruined.

But, if the Germans have rejected the introduction of the chorus in their tragedies, they have replaced it, in many respects, as we have noted, with a variety of subordinate characters who are introduced on stage in a natural, albeit accidental manner. To prove this point, we need only examine what Schiller did in his *William Tell* and ask ourselves what a Greek poet would have done with the same subject. Tell, escaping from Gessler, scaled the summit of a rocky crag which looked out upon the route Gessler would have to travel. The Swiss peasant waits for his enemy, the crossbow and arrows which, after having served paternal love, must now serve his vengeance. In a monologue, he reflects on the tranquillity and innocence of his earlier life. He is astonished to see himself wrenched by tyranny from the obscure and comfortable existence which he had laid out for himself. He recoils when confronted with the act he feels he must commit. His hands, still pure, tremble at the thought of being stained, even with the blood of a guilty man. It is necessary, however, to save his own life, that of his son, and those of his loved ones. Without doubt, in a Greek tragedy, at this point the chorus would have taken the stage to synthesize into general truths the feelings which flood the spectator's mind. Not possessing this resource, Schiller compensates for it by introducing a country wedding party, which passes on the road near the spot where Tell is hidden. We hear music; the contrast between this joyous group and William Tell's situation instantly brings to the mind of the audience all of the reflections the chorus would have expressed. William Tell belongs to the same class as these other men, strolling so free from care. He is poor, unknown, hard-working, and innocent like them. Like them, he seemed to have nothing to fear from a power placed so far above him; yet his obscurity did not serve as an asylum. The Greek chorus would have developed this truth in sententious and poetic language, German tragic practice throws it into relief no less forcefully through the appearance of a troop of characters unrelated to the plot and who have no ulterior relation to it.

At other times, these secondary characters provide a lively and profound way of developing the principal characters. Werner, who is known even in France through the deserved success of his tragedy *Luther*,[10] joined in the highest degree two apparently irreconcilable qualities: intelligent and often amusing observation of the human heart and an enthusiastic and dreamy melancholy. In *Atilla*,[11] Werner paints a picture of Valentinian's court giving itself over to dancing, concerts, and every other pleasure while the Scourge of God is at Rome's gates. We see the young Emperor and his favorites with no care other than to ignore the bothersome news which would interrupt their amusements. They hold truth to be an indication of malice and foresight to be an act of sedition. They consider faithful subjects only those men who deny the facts that would inconvenience them. They seem to think that they can deny reality by not listening to those who report it. Such heedlessness placed before the spectator has a much greater effect than a simple narration.

And, from *Wallstein*, we will draw two other examples. Tersky, Wallstein's brother-in-law and confidant, has the generals sign, en masse, after a banquet, a pledge of loyalty to Wallstein in disregard of the court's wishes. Tersky achieves his end, reminding them of all the benefits they have recieved from their leader. By itself, the enumeration of these rewards provides an incisive picture of the nature of this group—its lack of discipline, its willful, anarchic, military character. This scene possesses a remarkable originality and much accurate detail, but can only be rendered in language that our tragic scene rejects.

Later in the play, Buttler gathers the common soldiers together to enlist them in Wallstein's assassination. And if the scenes dealing with Banquo's assassins in Shakespeare are striking in their brevity and vigor, those of Wallstein's assassins have another kind of merit. Schiller is masterful in developing the motives open to them and in orchestrating the effects that these motives produce in them. We see the struggle in the hearts of these savage men between loyalty and greed. We see the cleverness employed by the man who wishes to corrupt them as he adjusts his arguments to their gross intelligence, making them regard crime as a duty and gratitude as a crime. We see them eagerly seize upon any justification for their determination to slay their general. We perceive the need, even in such debased souls, to create an illusion and decieve their own conscience by disguising the crime they are about to commit with the appearance of justice. And finally, we see the arguments which convince them and which, in so many different circumstances, will convince so many men who think themselves honest to commit an act their conscience condemns—because, if they do not do it, others will. All of this is both dramatically and morally very effective. But the language of the assassins is vulgar, as is their status and are their feelings. It would be a betrayal of decorum in character to give them an elevated vocabulary and, in this case, a noble tone of dialogue would be inappropriate. I had worked especially hard to throw into relief the principal idea, the decisive consideration which silences all objections and overrides all scruples. After giving an account of his efforts to win over his accomplices, Buttler concludes with the following verses:

> When I told them others were willing;
> Others were already soliciting my favor in selecting them,
> That the prize was near, that tonight, others
> Would reap the fruits of their loyalty,
> Each one eyed the man beside him;
> Their eyes gleamed with hope, envy, and greed;
> Their brows tinted with a hectic flush;
> They repeated softly: Others are willing.

But I soon sensed that I was descending to an improbability which no detail would save. In seeking to include Isolan in the projected assassination, Buttler was unable, without seeming absurd, to complacently expound on the greed and baseness characteristic of those he had chosen to realize his plan.

The obligation to narrate what could be put into action in other nations' theatres is a stumbling block for French writers. These narrations are almost never placed in a natural way. Neither his situation nor his interest require a character to narrate in this manner. Moreover, the poet invariably finds himself forced to seek details that are as pompous as they are undramatic. The inconvenience of Theramenes' superb narration in *Phaedra* has been noted a thousand times. Unable, like Euripides, to offer the audience Hippolytus' body, torn, bloodied, broken by his fall, in the final convulsion of pain and death, Racine was forced to narrate this death. This necessity forced him to contradict both probability and nature in the recitation of a terrible event through a profusion of poetic details inappropriate in a friend and which a father should not hear.

My respect for our habits and customs caused me to commit an even more serious error. The character Thécla, Wallstein's daughter, excites a universal enthusiasm in Germany. It is difficult to read Schiller's work in the original language without sharing that enthusiasm. But I had feared that in France, this character would not obtain the pubilc's favor. The admiration she arouses in Germany relates to the German attitude toward love; this attitude is very different from ours. We only consider love as a passion, similar in nature to all other human passions, that is to say, having the effect of leading our reason astray, with the realisation of pleasure as a goal. The Germans see in love something religious, sacred, an emanation from the Divinity, a fulfillment of man's destiny on this earth, a mysterious and all-powerful bond between two souls which exist only for each other. From the former point of view, love is common to man and animals; from the latter it is common to men and God. The result is that many things which seem improper to us because we only perceive the consequences of passion in them seem legitimate and even respectable to the Germans, because they believe them to be reflections of the action of celestial feelings. There is truth in both these points of view. But love will, of necessity, have a different position, depending on which point of view is adopted. When love is only a passion, as in the French theatre, it can only attract attention through its violence and frenzy. Sensual ecstasy, jealous rages, the struggle between desire and remorse, such is tragic love in France. But, on the contrary, when love is, as in German poetry, a ray of divine light which warms and purifies the heart, it possesses at once more calm and more strength. At the moment of its appearance, one senses that it dominates everything around it. It may have to combat circumstances, but not duties; for it is, itself, the first among duties, and it insures the fulfillment of other duties. Love cannot lead to guilty actions, it cannot lower itself to criminal acts, it cannot even employ guile, for this would contradict its nature, and it would cease to be itself. Love cannot give way before obstacles, it cannot die, for its essence is immortal. Love can only withdraw into the heart of its creator.

This is the way that Thécla's love is presented in Schiller's play. Thécla is not an ordinary girl. She is divided between her inclinations for a young man and her submission to her father. She disguises or conceals the feelings which dominate her until she has obtained the consent of her father, who has the right to dispose of her hand. She is frightened of the obstacles which threaten her happiness. Finally, she experiences herself an uncertainty—of which the audience receives an impression— as to the consequences of her love and the steps to be taken if her hopes are deceived. Thécla's love has raised her above common nature. Her love has become her entire existence and has set the course of her destiny. She is calm because her resolution cannot be shaken; she is confident because she cannot be deceived about the nature of her lover's feelings; she is dignified because one senses something of the irrevocable in her, and she is frank because her love is not part of her life, it is her entire life. In Schiller's play, Thécla is placed on an entirely different plane from that of the rest of the characters. She is a divine being, so to speak, who soars above the crowd of ambitious men, traitors, and savage warriors pitted against each other by powerful and practical interests.

You feel that this luminous, almost supernatural, being has descended from ethereal regions and must soon return to them. Her voice sounds sweetly above the clash of arms. The delicacy of her form contrasts with those of armour-clad men. Her purity of soul stands out in contrast to their greedy scheming. Her celestial calm contrasts with the agitation of the men. This arouses in the audience an emotion at once loyal and melancholy, of a sort no ordinary tragedy can make them feel.

None of the female characters portrayed in the French theatre can give the idea of this emotion. Alzire, Aménaïde, Adélaide du Guesclin,[12] our passionate heroines, possess a certain masculinity. You feel that they are strong enough to combat events, men, and unhappiness. There is no perceptible disproportion between their fate and their inherent strength. Monime, Bérénice, Esther, Atalide,[13] our tender heroines, are utterly sweet and charming, but they are weak and timid women who can be overcome by events. The sacrifice of their feelings is not presented as an impossibility. Bérénice resigns herself to living without Titus; Monime resigns herself to marriage with Mithridates; Atalide resigns herself to seeing Bajazet marry Roxane; Esther does not love Assuérus. Voltaire's heroines struggle against obstacles while Racine's heroines succumb to them, because both the former and the latter are equal in nature to what surrounds them. Thécla can neither struggle nor succumb; she loves and she waits. Her fate is determined and she cannot change it.

Nor can she overwhelm this fate by arguing her position among men: she has no arms against them; her strength is internal. In this way, her feelings free her from the decorum demanded by the morality we are accustomed to seeing depicted in our theatre.

Thécla assumes none of the disguises we impose on our heroines. She places no veil over her profound, exclusive and pure love. She freely proclaims it to her lover. "Where on earth would truth exist," she says to him, "if you did not hear it from me?" She does not state that she has made her hopes dependent on her father's consent. We foresee that if he refuses, she will not believe herself guilty in resisting him. Her love possesses and consumes her entire being. She exists solely for the feeling that fills her soul. She is so far from considering her flight from her father's home a crime when she learns that her lover has been killed that she believes, on the contrary, to be fulfilling a duty. I had thought that the French audience would have been incapable of tolerating this exaltation, this independence, in a girl. It is all the more foreign to us since there is no suggestion of frenzy or folly in her. I still believe that our audiences would be shocked by this disregard for all conventional ties, of this manner of viewing as secondary customary duties, and of such a complete absence of the submissiveness they admire in Iphigenia. Such an enthusiasm cannot serve as the basis for a general system, but, in France, we appreciate only what can be given a universal application. The principal of utility dominates our literature as it does our life. The morality of the French theatre is much more rigorous than that of the German theatre. This is a result of the fact that the Germans take feeling as the basis for morality, while for us, the basis of morality is reason. A sincere, faultless, and unlimited emotion seems, to the Germans, not only to excuse what it inspires, but to ennoble it, and, if I dare employ this expression, to sanctify it. Such a point of view is manifest in their institutions and their customs as in their literature. We have infinitely more strict principles, and, in theory, we never deviate from them. A feeling which disregards duty appears all the more guilty to us. We would pardon more readily self-interest because self-interest always employs more artfulness and respect for convention in its transgressions. Feeling braves opinion, and angers it. Self-interest seeks to deceive opinion by humoring it. And opinion accepts this sort of homage from self-interest even when the deception is discovered. I had reduced Thécla to French proportions while forcing myself to preserve something of the German tonality. I had tried to retain the sweetness, the sensitivity, affection and melancholy in her character. But everything else in her character seemed to me to be in direct opposition to our customs, being too colored with what the French literati who know the German term the "German mysticism." Without depriving Thécla of her foreignness, too vague and dreamy to please our French classicists, I had not, through this alteration, given her the requisite coloring of our Turkish, Greek, or Roman, but always Frenchified heroines. The result proved to me that I had been wrong.

Had I possessed more foresight or daring, I would have avoided the majority of the flaws I have just indicated in my own work. I should have foreseen that a political revolution would carry over into a literary revolution. I should have foreseen that a nation which had only momentarily renounced liberty in order to hurl herself into the perils of conquest would no longer be satisfied by the weak and imperfect emotions which had sufficed for spectators softened by the pleasures of a peaceful existence and a refined civilization.

What had deceived me was the general immobility fostered in everyone by the imperial regime, engraved, as it were, on all faces. Literature shared in this immobility. Bonaparte liked discipline in everything, in administration, in the army, and in writers, and the latters' submission was neither the least prompt nor the least eager. The weakness of the head of state, as fatal to France as to Bonaparte himself, was his desire to imitate Louis XIV, as if this were progress, rather than a regression. Among the literati who aspired to gain his favor, there was a compliance at once self-centered and vain: for, in obeying the new Louis XIV, they believed themselves the equals of the great writers who had flattered the original. Thus, the rules of drama, like court etiquette, seemed an obligatory part of the imperial procession.

Furthermore, from the beginning of our upheavals, there has always been, among the most politically revolutionary men, a tendency to proclaim their respect and affection for the most rigid doctrines of seventeenth-century literature and for the rules advocated by the spokesmen of the French Parnassus. You might say that by proving to be scrupulous and docile in their writing, they wished to atone for the vigor and energy of their other opinions and prove that their popular doctrines did not tarnish the purity of their taste. In that way, they believed they were rehabilitating themselves in the eyes of what was still called "good company"; a pretentious and formal coterie which preferred the disregard of duty to the disregard of forms. The Revolution had broken up the old coterie, but Napoleon labored to create a new one. It was all the more susceptible to both social and theatrical propriety as it possessed a neophyte's ardor and an awareness that it ran the risk of stumbling on the unknown ground where its master had placed it. As a consequence, all the writers during the Empire were classicists.

Chénier, the greatest talent of that period, when young and in the grip of his republicanism, even before the fall of the monarchy, had, as a dramatic author in *Charles IX*,[14] trampled underfoot the barriers that would have restrained him. At the end of his short career, Chénier himself had become the most zealous partisan of all the chains inherited from Aristotle and consecrated by Boileau.

These barriers have now been overthrown. Poetry has won its freedom. The scope of our theatre has been enlarged. And the rules, which in the past were rigorous laws in whose light critics judged authors, are now only traditions to be judged by authors.

The victory has been won. It has perhaps been too successful at the moment for the best interest of art. The maxim that it is better to strike hard rather than justly was invented in France. The result is that our authors often strike so hard that they no longer strike with any justice at all. Their exclusive aim is to make an impression. And when, with reason, they shake off certain rules, they frequently commit the error of disassociating themselves from truth, nature, and taste.

As it is much easier to make an impression with fortuitous occurrences, a multiplicity of actors, scene changes, and even ghosts, marvels, and scaffolds, than with situations, feelings, and characters, it is to be feared that—our young authors rushing along this path impetuously—our stage will no longer be the setting for anything but scaffolds, battles, feasts, apparitions, and a succession of dazzling sets.

The German character possesses a scrupulousness, a candor, and a consistency which always keeps imagination within certain limits. German writers have a literary conscience which generates a need in them as much for historical accuracy and moral probability as for public approbation. In their hearts they possess a natural and profound sensibility which takes pleasure in the depiction of true feelings. They derive such enjoyment from this that they are much more concerned with what they feel than with the impression they produce.

Consequently, no matter how numerous their external devices seem, these are all merely accessories. But in France, where one never loses sight of the public, where one speaks, writes, and acts only for others, the accessories could easily become the most important things.

This certainly does not mean that I advocate a puerile respect for superannuated rules. The rule of the unities of time and place is particularly absurd. It makes of all our tragedies plays of intrigue. It forces conspirators to plot the tyrant's death within his own palace. It prevents Coriolanus from leaving the Roman forum to go to the Volscian camp, where, however, he must place himself at the head of the enemies of his ungrateful country.

The unities of time and place circumscribe our tragedies in a space which makes their composition difficult, their course rapid, and their action both fatiguing and improbable.

The unities of time and place often compel the poet to neglect, in his events and characters, the truth of gradation and delicacy of nuance.

This flaw dominates all of Voltaire's tragedies. We constantly find gaps in them; transitions that are too brusque. We feel that nature does not move so quickly and does not cast off intermediate steps in this way.

Therefore it is incontestable that our writers must free themselves from this bondage in their new system of writing tragedy. It is only necessary for them to guard against too frequent and too brusque scene changes. However adroitly these changes are managed, they draw the spectator's attention to the scene change and thus divert a part of his attention from the main interest. After each new set appears he is obliged to recapture the illusion from which he has been distracted. The same thing occurs when a too considerable lapse of time occurs between the acts. In both these cases, the poet reappears, so to speak, in front of his characters, and there is a kind of implied prologue or preface which is detrimental to the effect of continuity.

But these inevitable inconveniences, in literature as in politics, will not last long; wherever freedom reigns reason is not long in regaining authority. Rigid souls cry in vain that innovation corrupts the public theatre; public taste is not corrupted; it approves the truthful and the natural; it rejects the falsification of truth and the alienation from nature through exaggeration. The people have an admirable instinct. This instinct has already outlined the necessary limits for the reconciliation of order and liberty in our political needs. This instinct aids religion in placing it in its proper sphere between unbelief and fanaticism. The same instinct will exercise its influence on literature and will restrain writers without imprisoning them.

"Reflections on Tragedy" (1829)

The complete title of these articles is "Reflections on Tragedy, Occasioned by a German Tragedy by Robert Entitled Of the Power of Prejudices." *These two articles were written by Constant while at Baden in 1829. They were first published in the* Revue de Paris, *7 (1829), 5–21 and 126–40, and were not reprinted until 1957, when they were included in the Bibliothèque de la Pléiade edition of Constant's* Oeuvres. *The play that inspired these articles was written by Louis Robert (1778–1832) and was published in 1819 as* Die Macht der Verhältniss *("The Power of Circumstances"). There is no record of publication of the French translation to which Constant refers.*

My translation of "Reflections on Tragedy" first appeared in Educational Theatre Journal, *23 (October 1971), 317–34. It is reprinted here by permission of* Educational Theatre Journal.

Fifty years ago, Diderot wrote:

To be precise, it is no longer character which ought to be put on the stage, but rank or station. Up to the present character has always been the principal object in comedy and station has been no more than an accessory. Today social function needs to become the principal object and character need be no more than accessory. Plot used to be derived from character; in general, circumstances are sought which throw characters into relief, and these circumstances are then linked together. It is social station, its duties, its advantages, its difficulties, which ought to serve as a basis for the work. The duties of station, their advantages, their inconveniences, their dangers, have not yet been portrayed in the theatre. But every day these advantages, these inconveniences, these dangers, show us men in very difficult situations. Every day new social functions are created. Perhaps nothing is less known to us than social station, and nothing should interest us more.[15]

I certainly don't offer Diderot as a model to follow in dramatic compostion, either for the theory or the execution. His manner is turgid and full of a false exaltation to which he abandoned himself both by inclination and calculation. Diderot was, it should be remembered, one of the encyclopedists, men who were honorable and effective adversaries of an absurd and loathsome government. They were men who considered even literature as a means of fighting that regime. Their goal in art was completely different from that of perfection which they sacrificed to their central idea.

The Father and *The Bastard* are the defective and ridiculously declamatory works of a man whose talent lay in other areas. The sections of doctrine that I have just cited only treat from the most superficial and narrow point of view a question which, examined in depth, would take on a different sort of importance. Diderot's words, taken literally, merely introduce us into a lower sphere. By selecting as a basis for dramatic motivation, the duties, the difficulties, in short the particulars of a social situation, by painting these in the prince, the diplomat, the magistrate, the soldier, the merchant, one might create several more or less interesting portraits of manners; but this is hardly a revolution worthy of being announced with so much pomposity.

Behind Diderot's thesis, I see a larger one and I want to try to develop it.

I warn my reader at the outset that Diderot applied his system particularly to comedy, and, in fact, within the limits he circumscribed it, it is only applicable—and barely so—to comedy. On the contrary, I will apply my thesis specifically to tragedy.

Three things may serve as a basis for tragic compositions: the painting of passions, the development of character, and the action of society, such as it is constituted in each epoch, and such as it affects passion and character.

Phaedra, *Andromache*, and *Mérope* are tragedies wherein passion alone rules. There is no individualization in characters. What Phaedra would be without her incestuous desire, Andromache and Mérope without their maternal devotion, is unknown. Orestes is composed of mythological reminiscences rather than traits having to do with a character. These characters are, in a way, personifications of passion. Remove the passion, and nothing remains.

In several Shakespearean tragedies, and in the best, *Richard III* and *Hamlet*, character dominates. Passion is destined to show only how it acts under the rule of character, how it can briefly modify character, only to see character soon re-appear. The same is true in many German plays. In *Wallenstein, Egmont, William Tell, Tasso*—although in the latter, the action of society—the painful pressure it exerts on excitable sensibilities—already makes itself felt. One can find the germ of tragedy of character in several of Voltaire's plays, and, in an epoch further from us, in *Britannicus*. One can imagine what Mahomet would be independent of his love for Palmyre, Orasmane, when the attractions of Zaïre do not influence him, and one discerns the young tyrant in Nero possessed of his desire for Junie.[16]

As for tragedies which would be based on the action of society in conflict with the individual, opposing obstacles not only to his passions, but to his nature, or breaking not only his character, his personal inclinations, but the movements which are inherent to all human beings, I know of none which fulfill the idea that I have conceived.

Without a doubt, properly speaking, even in dramatic works devoted to the painting of passions or to the developing of character, the action of society always occupies a large place.

What, after all, is dramatic composition but the portrait of the moral force of man combatting an obstacle? One can give diverse names to this moral force without regard to the cause which set it in motion. Thus, one names it alternately love, ambition, vengeance, patriotism, religion, virtue; but it is always the inner force struggling with an exterior obstacle. In the same way, one can label diversely the obstacle which this moral force tries to resist: one can call the obstacle despotism, religious oppression, laws, institutions, prejudices, customs: it doesn't matter; it is always society weighing down upon, enchaining, the individual.

It seems to me, however, that up to now, dramatists writing tragedy have only considered the action of society as a framework, as one of the stage properties, and have voluntarily turned away from it, in order to devote themselves fully to the painting of passions or character.

Let us consider whether they were right and whether character and passions offer a large and varied enough canvas for tragedy in our time.

Passions, at least those which are liable to inspire a lively interest and profound emotion in the theatre, are limited in number. In truth, they are limited to one—love; because ambition, patriotism, and vengeance are contained more precisely in the category of character. All the nuances, all the effects of love, its fears, its violence, its despairs, its rages, its crimes, have been inimitably described by Racine and with success by other poets: Colardeau in *Caliste*, Ducis in *Abufar*.[17] Isn't the well a bit dry? Isn't the circle already circumscribed? I know that Boileau stated: "The sensitive painting of love is the surest road to the heart."[18]

I doubt, however, that today such methods are the most efficient means of making the most delicate and resonant chords of the soul vibrate.

At this point, I do not plan to compose either madrigals or epigrams. Nor do I want to appear to be slandering progress—which, in fact, pleases me—in noting the inevitable results of civilization. I shall, nevertheless, try to formulate my idea. Everyone knows what love is as far as its physical nature is concerned. But certain situations, a certain state of society, can encircle this physical need with magic, which makes of it a most irresistible and exalted passion.

Imagine a situation where communication between the sexes is infrequent, where women only leave their retreats as from a mysterious sanctuary, or where perils surround the conquest of women. Imagine a situation where the absence of all national concerns, of all political careers, condemns men to an idleness at the heart of which self-love seeks an occasion to shine. Such a woman can become for such a man the unique and sacred object of desire, of protective impulse, and, in that way, of an exclusive adoration. Or, in the converse hypothesis, such a woman presents to the vanity of such a man, a victory of the sort it desires. In proportion, however, as communications with women are less difficult, as they are more frequently in the company of men, as fewer dangers surround their weaknesses, and as masculine life becomes filled with more serious concerns, then the need for the ardor of passion or for the excitation of vanity abates. The security which is established removes the obstacles presented to seduction, and love, real or feigned, loses a degree of its importance. Love continues to exist, however, because of its physical basis in nature, and because its prestige is transmitted to the imagination by tradition and literature.

But each day these traditions disappear. Books less in accord with actuality are losing their power. Who reads nowadays *Great Cyrus* or *Clélie*?[19] And yet their ten 800-page volumes are scarcely sufficient for minds that are curious about the refinements of love.

Who, now, would write: "In order to appear pleasing in her beautiful eyes, I have warred with kings as I would with gods"?[20]

And nevertheless, this bragging passion of a nobleman of the Fronde was already far from the love described in *Amadis*.[21] Who, in the end, admires Count Valmont,[22] the vanquisher of a credulous heart and a barbarous hero of fatuity? Who, given our present ideas, would want to be such a man? Who would buy success at the expense of pain?

Cooled by innumerable facilities, subordinated by calculation in real life, that which remains of love no longer decides—with a few minor exceptions, most of the time unhappy and discouraging—the whole of any destiny. Love has been put in its place in France, at last, even by the young: how many of our young people would sacrifice their background or their future to a marriage based on love?

I am so little disposed to reproach civilization for this weakening of a formerly extravagant passion that I actually take pleasure in recognizing that morality gains from it. Since the imagination is no longer exalted, each person is content with his wife by virtue of proximity. Sometimes habit and especially identification of interests also produce a moral inclination. Vice becomes a superfluity, a fatigue, a deterrent to regular and lucrative occupations. One is faithful to the bonds of matrimony through reasons of proximity. One is moral because one's energy is employed elsewhere.

Tragedies based on love, then, no longer seem to me to be of the nature to encounter a numerous public whose emotions they would satisfy. I have come across exceptions, but they become rarer every day and the appropriate audience for this genre of tragedy will have to be mostly composed of eigtheen-year-old young men and girls of fifteen. Such conditions do not go unnoticed: consequently we see none of our poets choosing love as the principal motivation of tragedy.

Voltaire, France's Euripides, informed (like the Greek Euripides) by an admirable sagacity that he ought no longer to base tragedy on passion alone, sought material in philosophy. He borrowed from philosophy, a novelty at that time, means of success which were all the more infallible in his day, firstly, since they rested on that new-born party spirit which was in the first strength of its youth, and secondly, since its enemies were odious and absurd. But these means were harmful in respect to art; they gave art a goal other than itself; they made of poetry an instrument, they assigned it a secondary rank; it followed that, although thanks to the prodigious mobility that sometimes transported Voltaire into the souls of heroes, he remained a poet. In several sections of his tragedies, he was often, like the Greek poet to whom we have already compared him, only a harmonious and clever rhoretician. His characters are destined only to herald or discredit one or another doctrine; one forgets their difficulties in order to hear their axioms. One judges these axioms with regard to an ensemble of opinions external to the situation which serves as a pretext for dogmatic exposition.

This criticism will probably be a eulogy in the eyes of those who prefer that all work have a moral aim, yet the poetic painting of passions proves nothing in favor of a doctrine.

Phaedra, in its Greek elements, excepting the slight distortion in the presentation of Hippolytus and the awkward introduction of Aricia, is certainly the most perfect of our tragedies in the genre of the passions. Yet it embodies no precept intended to improve the spectator. I won't speak of the rather inappropriate verses directed against flatterers, a tribute paid by Racine to the growing opposition to the Court. Thus considered, these verses are a strength which honor the man, but disserve the poet. The tragic movement of the play is interrupted and generalities are substituted for emotions which should be directed toward the particular. This exception aside, nothing is sententious in the language of Phaedra; she thinks only of herself, her love, her sadness, her remorse, and never considers re-forming them into maxims. Almost all the tragedies of Voltaire, on the other hand, have a moral goal. Alzire preaches tolerance, Zaïre religious tolerance, Oedipus defiance of sacerdotal frauds, Mahomet horror of hypocrisy. However, what is colder than Zaïre remarking to her confidant that belief depends on chance, or Alzire discoursing on suicide? And so it is in Euripides, when Orestes, stained with his mother's blood, declaims for thirty lines on the influence of education.

I repeat, Voltaire's talent and mobility, which enabled him to identify with his characters, frequently saved him from this use of self-imposed defects. Nature had endowed him, as it had the third Greek tragedian, with that rare and happy flexibility which raises his works, in steps, to the most sublime and rending pathos. That is what constitutes in his work a merit which exceeds its shortcomings. Had he been able to remain faithful to his theory, his plays would be rhetorical works, and one would always see the schoolmaster behind his heroes.

I don't blame these faults in him; circumstances were pressing; it was necessary to use any means to destroy those institutions both vicious and criminal with respect to our species, those prejudices both stupid and barbarous. A tragedy, an amalgamation of philosophy and passion in Voltaire's hands, was a battering ram which his strong arm directed against the crumbling towers of the *ancien régime*. That regime is fallen; we have finished with it; neither the gentry nor the assassins, the Lombardemonts, the Jefferies, or the Dominicans will resurrect it. Let us then leave the instruments of war sleeping on the debris of battered towers, and let us concern ourselves with tragedy, without wanting, henceforth, to draw from it effects foreign to its nature and prejudicial to its perfections; because passion impregnated with doctrine and serving philosophy is a courtesan in the realm of art.

I have said that passions without individuality are no longer sufficient as motivation for tragedy. Let us next examine character.

Character, firstly, although more diversified than passion, is not, for tragedy, an inexhaustible mine. The poet needs contrasting traits and bold colors. All that is undefined, uncertain, inconsequential, mixed, is unsuitable for him. An audience demands a unity, a consistency—to take this word in its English sense—a coherence in character which nature has refused to provide. There are few truly suitable character types for tragedy, and, secondly, in order to adapt them, they must necessarily be stripped of a portion of their truth. Paint a tyrant with touches of humanity, a hero with weaknesses that are not precisely those of a violent passion; you will mislead the audience. Regard Félix in *Polyeuctes*,[23] he is a character of a sort we meet often enough in life. He has generous leanings, *pitiable ones, even base ones*. Nothing is more true than this portrait, but nothing is less tragic. We turn away from him with a sort of disgust. When we go to the theatre, we want to see men better than our friends. Doubtless you can present the criminal tortured by remorse after a crime; remorse is a presumed result of crime. You can even, before an offense is committed, show its future perpetrator preyed upon by incertitude and recoiling from his action; again, it is a given, a struggle foreseen and admitted in advance. But this is not what concerns us. I want to speak of those individual, almost fortuitous weaknesses, that is to say, those of which the cause lies in the nature of the individual, and which it is necessary to take, if one is to be faithful, as a particularity which is forced on the individual. Thus, in *Wallenstein*, the faith in astrology which defers rashness and negates calculation; in *Egmont* the movement toward pleasure, the lightness which distracts from political interests and dangers; these individual traits upset the unity of the character, and make him a fluctuating being in whom variations deviate slightly from the conventional line. These things, at least for we French, weaken sympathy and replace it with impatience. The spectator does not want to be deceived in his expectations: he becomes angry with the dramatic character as with a real person who doesn't produce what was promised.

Voltaire eluded this danger in his *Mahomet*, where there is, as I have said, not only a passion, but a character. This character has neither variations nor subtleties. He does not fluctuate in the manner of real characters. The prophet is not tempted to stop in mid-stream as is Wallenstein. He is not moved to tenderness as is the Duke of Friedland toward Max Piccolomini. He wants to possess Palmyre, that is has passion; he wants to subjugate or destroy whomever resists him, that is his character. Character and passion are all of a piece.

I recall that when I finished an imitation of *Wallenstein*, a friend, who had listened with attentive good will to my reading of it, said to me:

It is imperative that a large and unique idea dominate your play. Wallenstein must conspire against the House of Austria in order to establish a just system of political and religious liberty. Suppress these moments of loyalty to Ferdinand, who, being intolerant and superstitious, does not merit your hero's affection; or if he feels these relapses, let them serve to show with what stoicism he sacrifices his memories of a friendship to the cause of a humanity he wants to free. Suppress these prejudices about legitimacy, which, in the enlightened spirit of Wallenstein, as he must be drawn to interest us, cannot be on an equal plane with the welfare of the human race. Suppress above all this belief in astrology which degrades Wallenstein, renders him ridiculous, and prevents us from identifying with the destiny of a man which can be changed by a cloud or a moonbeam.

"All that you say is very fine," I answered, "Wallenstein will doubtless be a very handsome and well sustained character such as the eighteenth century created or such as the nineteenth century will perhaps see; but will this be the seventeenth-century man? Will this be Wallenstein?"

This alternative, either to suppress in the characters all which doesn't serve the action; to make, for example, all tyrants a Polyphontes,[24] or to preserve individual traits at the risk of destroying unity and disorienting the audience; this alternative from which I say our poets cannot escape without sacrificing interest or renouncing truth, greatly restricts their art. And characters of the sort demanded on the French stage are, or will become, like passions, insufficient for dramatic compositions.

Let us turn to the third motivation of tragedy, which has hardly yet been tried: the action of society on passions and character.

When a man, weak, blind, without intelligence to guide him, and without weapons for his defense, is, without knowing it, thrown into this labyrinth called the world, the world surrounds him with a group of situations, laws, institutions, public and private relations. This complex set of situations places on him a chain of which he is not aware, which weighs down upon him like a pre-existing burden. He has only been granted the possibility of struggling against this burden, when he feels it and learns to recognize it, with marked inequality and great danger.

It is evident that this action of society is the most important aspect of human life. Everything derives from it; to it everything leads; one must submit to this predestined, unauthorized, unknown thing under the penalty of being broken. This action of society determines the manner in which the moral force of man acts and makes itself evident. As a result, Diderot's statement concerning the diverse social stations—in a very narrow sense and uniquely applicable to comedy—ought to be said in truth of the action of society taken as a whole. Passion and character are secondary; the action of society is the principal factor.

This is not a simple re-arrangement of words, one of those verbal subtleties with the aid of which old ideas are refreshed; it is a principal that, in the future, will always crucially influence dramatic success.

Were you to choose a state in which the human species could never, in reality, exist, or were you to choose an action of society which could, in no instance, affect the individual, than all the talent you might bring to the painting of a moral force in conflict with this state or this social action would be of little use. Beautiful passages will obtain fleeting applause, sublime or harmonious poetry will momentarily captivate rapt ears, but there will be nothing lasting in the emotions because you will have placed the man in none of the situations in which the social order might place him, situations which he might fear or desire.

This is not to say that one must be limited to the depiction of contemporary society. It is peculiar to art that it transports man into foreign situations. But again, it is necessary that these situations be related in some manner to those situations common to all men. Corneille, for example, did not paint the state of society exactly as it was when he wrote; but republicanism and the troubles of Rome were not completely alien to the social state which had replaced the League and been perpetuated under the Fronde.[25]

Today, you will invariably fail if you base a tragedy on the fatality of the ancients. Why did Racine not fail? Racine presented the French public their fatality escorted by the pomp of Greek mythology, which was offered for the first time in the theatre in harmonious verse and in majestic forms. Although fatality as conceived by the ancients had no rapport with modern beliefs, the enthusiasm for antiquity's treasures, recently in vogue, had passed from the erudite class to the elegant one. It was, in a way, an ideal social order which momentarily eclipsed the material social order. Look, however, at the obstacles Racine met. Read Madame de Sévigné's judgements of him, which are certainly representative of a large portion of the public which held no sympathy for Greek theology. For what was Phaedra reproached in a famous sonnet so much in vogue? For speaking verse of which "no one understood anything." In fact, many of the people understood nothing of that magnificent exposition of a system that had little affinity with the habitual order of their ideas. Greek mythology, however, was identified with the ideas of the court and its pageants. Louis XIV delighted in seeing Olympian gods and goddesses dancing ballets in his honor. Deprived at the same time of this artificial support and all natural links with our religious concepts, this mythology is not only foreign to us, it is dead to us. Its prestige is dissipated and the admiration which *Phaedra* and *Iphigenia* excite in us, owes, in one aspect, to the unique talent of an inimitable poet and, in the other part, to the fact that this admiration is traditional. The subject is a hindrance, rather than an aid, to interest.

There exist sufficient resources for drama in our present social structure, in those which have preceded it, in those of neighboring countries, and in the action which society used to, and continues to, exercise in opposition to our inherent needs. I don't want to enumerate them here. What would be nothing but a presentation of facts would be taken for a social satire. There are things which, in a given society, are indispensable, but which have an odious aspect. For example, to pit two against one is, in the eyes of natural sentiment, cowardice. Society pits a million against one in the name of justice. It is necessary for the maintenance of order; it would be unfortunate in many cases if it were otherwise. But one imagines, if one chooses a social structure which imposes injustice or oppressive laws on the individual, that this union of so many forces for the purpose of assuring obedience to the laws, this conspiracy of so many heads for the purpose of making one head fall, this cooperation of so many hatchet-bearing arms against two weaponless, chained hands, this society which takes away a life which it would not be able to give, which cannot create a single being, but which can destroy hundreds of lives, and which does destroy them, possessing a sword as logic, its humanity replaced by the rack and the wheel, one imagines that such conditions will form a tableau capable of interesting and even more, moving. It is worth noting that emotions of this sort are excited specifically by our best tragedies. The character Britannicus in actuality scarcely interests us at all. What produces the great effect in the play which bears his name are the discourses of Agrippina, of Narcissus, all of which present the social order which weighed down Rome. The two lines of verse

> And those who possess a great familiarity with the court
> Model their masks after the features of Ceasar.
>
> (II. 1635–36)

make us indignant, make us tremble, as we remember a truth common to all ages, while the loves of Junie leave us rather cold.

Here results a precept which it is essential not to overlook. The attention of the audience must be directed even more, toward the action of society, than on the character or passions of those oppressed by that society. One can doubt that only passion or character are needed for interest, but there is a measure, a proportion, which must be divined by genius rather than defined by words. If you concern yourself too exclusively with the portrayal of passion or the development of character, or, at the least, if you don't continually lead thought from the individual to the social state, you will hinder the effect; you will return to the genre of dramatic composition worn out by your predecessors. The whole must be presented, at the same time, as strongly as the isolated figure who must dominate the foreground. If this isolated individual shines in colors so brilliant that the whole is thrown into an obscure and confused background, then attention would be attached only to the individual. The impression of the whole would be weakened.

Now let us take up some examples; they will clarify my ideas. Let us transport ourselves into one of those happy countries far from Europe, but which believe themselves to be as civilized as Europe because they have their vices, and where the social structure allows slavery, where one race pretends to be the proprietors of the other race and calculates what is to be gained from the sufferings, tortures, agonies, and death of the proscribed race. Locate in the heart of this social state one of its victims who is struggling to destroy the state, either in order to free his companions from misery or because a love which this state proclaims to be guilty pushes the daring man to break the barriers which separate him from his beloved; you will certainly have tragic effects; but these effects will be even more tragic if you will observe more scrupulously the rule which I have proposed. Not only the individual, but the action of society must be presented, these institutions of torture, this bloody rule, these judges, these merciless masters, all this arsenal of public force crushing one single unfortunate man because his color is different; these merchants talking of beings who are their equals as though these beings were rotted cargo; the corruption spreads at once through the ferocious race and the debased one; human nature is degraded equally by tyranny and by servitude; these slaves who are the accomplices of their masters and are their scourge; these informers, murdered in the end by the whip and chain, and who betray their brothers; pity abjured or rather unknown by the naïveté of barbarity; everything which is horrible in cannibals; everything which is hypocritical in civilization. Whatever the dénouement may be, either that the oppressors perish in flames or that the oppressed succumb—reprisals having been foregone—the tableau of such a society, and it exists, of such an action of society, and it occurs, would penetrate more directly to the soul than would the depiction of a passion or the exclusive painting of a character.

This example doesn't suffice? Let us take a state and the action of a society of another area.

A harmless population is gathered together on a barren plain or in a valley which is hidden from view by mountains and forests. Women, children, and old men press against one another as if for protection. Their quiet courage is mingled with uneasiness. They know the danger, but their beliefs demand that they brave it. They pray and they tremble. A man at their center is more especially destined to torture if he is discovered. Words believed to be from God fall from his lips. Hymns rise to heaven. Suddenly, the pious sanctuary is surrounded. Soldiers appear, led by courtiers. They must momentarily leave the palace festivals to preside over a massacre. Fugitives are pursued. Each victim is an homage which the zealous servants want to place at the feet of their king; because honors are their rewards, the possessions of the proscribed are their wages; they buy them, or the king bestows them, and they are shared. The old men are put in irons, the dying are executed, the women are beaten with pikes, the children are jailed to be converted by their fathers' executioners, the pastor is sent to the galleys, or to the gallows, if he doesn't apostatize; were he to resist, he would perish on the wheel.

One chats about it occasionally at court, distractedly, as of the Turkish war, less than of the stay of the Stuarts at St. Germain, and throughout the love affairs, the festivities and amusements, each person recounts the gift given him by the king, and the monarch, between adultery and devotion, between his concubines and his confessors, applauds himself for having established purity of religion in his kingdom. There you have, I believe, a social situation which can furnish a tragedy. But here an observation, already made, must be repeated. The subject of *The Honest Criminal*[26] is almost identical to what I have described but the author wanted to concentrate the interest on the hero. He combined philosophy and filial piety. He painted neither an epoch, nor a society, but only an individual's devotion. Even were it possessed with talent, the play by Fenouillet de Falbaire would today have less success than *The Barricades* or *The Jacquerie*.[27] The masses feel that they have come into their own right; they want to see themselves on the stage, themselves or their ancestors. Individuals are only a pretext, an occasion, an accessory.

In order to illustrate my thought even better, I shall choose a final example, more startling perhaps than the preceding ones, because it is a fact, and one to which I add neither a word nor a circumstance of my own invention; and in order not to be suspected of any hostile intention, I shall transcribe the fact in the very terms of the memoirs of the period.

This essay was originally published in two consecutive issues of the Revue de Paris in 1829. The following paragraph began the second section, hence the assumption that time had elapsed between this and the previous paragraph.

I promised an example which would illustrate my thought and which, not being of my invention, would free me from suspicions of hostile intent. I have taken it from the most brilliant epoch of the old monarchy, from the middle of Louis-le-Grand's reign, so majestic, so full of elegance and nobility; a type of absolute monarchy which (according to the enemies of our present institutions) is worthy of imitation and envy.

At Saint-Germain there was a great hunting party. The Count de Guiche, the Count (afterwards the Duke) du Lude-Vardes, M. de Lausun, who told me the story, and I don't know how many others, strayed from the main group, and found themselves lost in the dead of night. They spied a light ahead and made their way to the door of a kind of chateau. They asked for hospitality. Their host preceded them and had dinner prepared which they greatly needed. The host was polite and respectful, neither too ceremonious nor too officious; with the bearing and manners of the best society. They learned that his name was Fargues and that the house was called Courson and that he had been in retirement and had not left his home for several years. After they had eaten well,

Fargues did not keep them from their beds. They found everything in order, they each had their own room, and Fargues's servants waited upon them properly. They were very tired and slept for a long time. When they had dressed, they found an excellent breakfast waiting for them, and after leaving the table, found their horses ready, as thoroughly refreshed as were their masters. These gentlemen were the flower of the court, and of gallantry, and all were influential with the king. They told him of their adventures, the marvels of their reception, and greatly praised their host, his fare, and his household. The king asked his name. When he had heard it, he said, "What, Fargues, is he so close!" And the gentlemen began to praise him again, but the king said nothing. Passing by the apartment of the Queen-Mother, he spoke to her of this adventure.

Fargues had been seriously involved in the movements directed against the Court and Cardinal Mazarin; but he had been protected by his party, and finally included in the amnesty. Mazarin was dead, there was no longer any question of past events; but as he had been deeply implicated, he feared that some charge might be brought against him, which was why he had lived for so long in such retirement and such peace with his neighbors, and (having faith in the amnesty) in such security. The king and his mother, who had only pardoned Fargues under duress, called for the First President Lamoignon and charged him with the task of secretly inquiring into the conduct and life of Fargues, and to examine carefully if there might be any way of punishing his past insolence and of making him repent of living so near the court in such opulence and tranquillity.

Lamoignon, a good and greedy courtier, resolved to completely satisfy them, and to profit by it. He made his inquiries and took into account so many things, and did it so well, that he found a way of implicating Fargues in a murder committed in Paris at the height of the troubles. He quietly issued a warrant for Fargues and one morning had him seized by the hussars and conducted to the prison of the Conciergerie. Fargues, who was sure that since the amnesty he had done nothing reprehensible, was completely astonished; he was even more astonished when, during the interrogation, he learned what it was about. He defended himself very well against the accusations and further alleged that the murder in question, having been committed at the height of the disturbances and revolt in Paris, had occurred before the amnesty, and that the amnesty had erased the memory of all that had occurred in those troubled times. The distinguished courtiers who had been so well received at this unfortunate man's house made all sorts of efforts in the presence of the king, but all were useless. Fargues was promptly beheaded, and his property was given to the First President as recompense; it brought much to his position and became the inheritance of his second son. Basville was scarcely one league from Courson.[28]

A tragedy written on this subject, presenting the image of a social state consistent with so execrable and base a tyranny, would produce, in my opinion, an enormous effect; but in order that this effect not be mixed, and thus weakened, it would be necessary to seek it in the situation itself and to only surround the victim with the interest that would result from his situation. If one substituted for the Louis XIV pursuing with a ferocious and ignoble tenacity the unfortunate man who had lived in peace under the faith of the amnesty a tyrant who was in love with the wife of this amnestied man and, thus, one established the conflict between conjugal love and adulterous passion, one would have a play of intrigue in which there would be romance and passion but there would be nothing new and probably, nothing profound, because it would be constructed from the pieces of *Mithridates, Andromache, Britannicus,* and *The Orphan of China.* Even if one imagined the addition of only one detail to the portrait, of making one of the guests who were so well received by Fargues denounce him to please the despot, this would upset the entire effect. Imagination would be directed against the individual rather than the entire regime.

Paint, on the other hand, the state and the action of society. Show the heinous powers, the official servility, and the infamous zeal of Louis XIV, who was the veritable author of the death of an unfortunate man, who for years had been protected by the laws. Paint the greedy and abominable Lamoignon. Paint the evasion of a bloody and perfidious legislature which weakened itself and became a sword rather than a shield. Paint an indifferent France and her corrupt magistrates. Paint that court whose more reasonable members were silent. Paint the flower of that court, the favorites, so high in the esteem of the king, who plead, we are told, for the man they have caused to be discovered, but who do not think of separating themselves from such a king soiled by such a crime. Stained with innocent blood, they continue to serve their master, to flatter him, to adorn his festivals, to squander their lives for his ambition. And, as a last touch, paint Saint-Simon himself, a man of integrity, but nevertheless one on whom had been engraved the imprint of the epoch and of the court. Paint a Saint-Simon who only reports the fact in passing, as an historical and curious anecdote, hardly thinking to stigmatize, by means of a fugitive word—if not an energetic reproof and an indelible word—the homicidal prince and his infamous mother.

The social order, the action of society on the individual, in diverse phases and in diverse epochs, this network of institutions and conventions, which envelops us from our birth and is not broken until our death, these are the tragic motivations which one needs to know how to manipulate. They are entirely equal to the fatality of the ancients; their weight composes all that was invincible and oppressive in that fatality; the habits which it engenders—insolence, frivolous harshness, obstinate negligence—all possess that heart-rending and hopeless aspect of fatality; if you represent this truth, this state of things, a modern man will quake with the recognition that it is inescapable, as those in ancient times quaked before the mysterious and somber power which permitted no escape; our public will be more moved by this combat of the individual against the social order that robs or pinions him than by Oedipus pursued by Destiny or by Orestes pursued by the Furies.

Do not, however, believe that I only consider the social order, the action of society, in an unfavorable light. It seems to me possible to present them from the opposite point of view and to excite dramatic interest in the highest degree. Take the English social order with the accession of James II. Show the people who had been made indignant by Charles II's licentious court, who had tired of his duplicity, and were happy with the demonstrations of sincerity squandered on them by his successor. Let your exposition be the hope of a majestic and noble future, let it show the public gratitude for a monarch who seems to be associated with the efforts and progress of a free and generous nation. Let this exposition be short because the representation of happiness must not be prolonged, lest it become monotonous. Pass next into the palace; show the dissatisfied courtiers, their ambitions deceived, their vanities bruised, their cupidity irritated by unaccustomed obstacles; their mixture of false pride and their true baseness; show the prince beset by their clamorings, appalled by their laws, regretting in secret the epoch when absolute power held the throne, when that immense power commanded suppliant nations without restraints, when the masses gave themselves blindly, when the will of a single person towered above all wills, ordering by means of a gesture and certain of being obeyed; show theocracy playing its part, not that theocracy proportioned to the needs of ignorant tribes and which was a relative good without becoming an absolute evil, but that hypocritical theocracy, aping conviction, parodying fanaticism, faking conscience; absolving the violation of promises, offering to legitimize tyranny in order afterwards to seize it and make a slave of its agents; a theocracy more contemptible still in its impostures than execrable in its furors. Around this deceived and dominated monarch bring together all that is impure in the court, all the assassins, the traitors, the casuists, all the foxes with hopes of becoming tigers; let this rebellious and servile rabble drive the unhappy prince to risking, without knowing it, the chances of secret conspiracy or an overt rebellion; let him seek devotion in treason and fidelity in perjury, since he has been abused by demonstrations which were lies and by the appearance of courage which only accompanies danger in order to belie it; let him believe that he finds supporters where there are only accomplices as ready to desert even before defeat as they are to plunder after victory; let arise among the defenders of the people one of those imposing figures whose type has been handed down to us by antiquity and which has been viewed only once in our time. Find incidents which will aid the development of popular movements, an action wherein cross the duplicity of the courtiers, the incertitude of timid men, the apostasy of the weak, the audacity of the seditious, the credulous generosity of the young, and the faint-hearted hesitation of the old; let the increasing perils and events be prepared with art, and the scene with well-drawn characters and passions, and you will have powerful and serious tragic images, you will have perfected the social order, you will show society invested with its rights weighing down on the rebels and their insurrection. On the one hand there will be the ferocity of several hired assassins, the rapacity of several marauders; on the other hand will be the development of all faculties, the accomplishment of all hopes, the future of the human race; the struggle it seems to me will be both beautiful and impressive. Whatever catastrophe the author may choose, it will be all the more instructive if instruction is not the end but the effect of the painting. If the plot remains faithful to history, the joy will be great, but not unlimited; James II, a fugitive, will generate some interest since it is his courtiers who are truly guilty. Would you prefer a happier ending? Let the prince become enlightened; the conpirators will bite the dust, and the people will praise the liberating king. Would you rather have it a hundred times more disastrous? Substitute the triumph of Don Miguel for the reversal of James II; the spectator will leave indignant and will count on human and divine justice.

But even in this example, I took as a main character a king who conspires: in general, the genre of tragedy which has concerned me here is of a lower degree, it sets aside purple robes and golden crowns. Kings are no longer obligatory as heroes on our stage. On the contrary, the lower the condition, the more difficult and dangerous the position, the more numerous the obstacles to be vanquished, the more the efforts and the effects result in tragedy. If you give to an author who is less cold than Saurin the subject of the slave Spartacus or the patrician Manlius, Spartacus will hold much more interest than Manlius.[29] The abyss is deeper, the combat more desperate. A single restriction would be necessary; that the condition be such that nothing abject, narrow, or ignoble be involved, as emotion then would be misled or destroyed.

In taking societies' actions on man as the principal motivation, tragedy must renounce the unities of time and place. The representation of passion is compatible with these unities. Passion is swift, and pacing it, from its beginning to its peak, it is possible to precipitate events in such a way that the catastrophe is accomplished without too much improbability in a space that is twenty feet square and in a period of twenty-four hours.

Character is less compatible with so restricted a period and so confined a space. The great merit of dramas which rest on the description of character is their truth, their exactitude, and their gradation. I have shown above that the individuality of a character can be foreign to the action, properly speaking, and even sometimes contrary to the action. Such is the superstition of Wallenstein, such is Richard III's anger at Nature which has made him deformed and at the men who are repulsed by this deformity; such is, in Hamlet—which I should have mentioned earlier as the play is the ideal tragedy of character—that melancholy, which is half philosophic and half dream-like, which is more affected by the miseries of the human condition than by its own misfortune. But it is always necessary for this individuality to be explained, so that it is not seemingly inconsistent, a mere caprice on the part of the author. It is necessary that it occur frequently enough to prove that it is inherent and indestructible. The individuality of Richard manifests itself at councils, in his denunciation of Hastings's sorcery, in his fury against his nephews, at his loves, which are masked with irony and ferocity. Wallenstein's ferocity directs his plans for the marriage of his daughter, directs his plot against Ferdinand, and explains his obstinate confidence in Piccolomini, and leads him to be heedless an hour before his assassination, as he believes the stars to have announced the peril past. The individuality of Hamlet does not abandon him either in the execution of his father's revenge or in his love affair with Ophelia. We would not know him completely without his encounters with the soldiers, without his conversations with the actors during which his ironic contempt for life is so energetically revealed, when one sees that everything in life seems to him to be a theatre game without truth or continuity; and the grave-digger scene, so faulted by his ignorant critics, completes the portrait. One needs time, continuity, progression, and also truth in the events, so that the character is thus developed, is presented in all its facets, and so the spectator is penetrated by this individuality. If you accumulate these things in one place, in one day, nothing is probable, nothing is explained, suggested, or completed. The character does not have sufficient latitude to make himself known. The spectator lacks the time needed for careful observation and is left breathless by following an intrigue which moves by fits and starts and in which everything is accumulated without preparation; from this results a fatigue, a preoccupation which disorients and distracts the spectator. We feel this fatigue at the performance of several of Voltaire's tragedies, and even more at those of his imitators.

If the unities of time and place falsify tragedy based on the development of character, they are even more destructive to tragedy based on the pressures of the social order, offered in all its complexity. It is evident that a long enough time and a variety of locales are indispensable if a complex social order is to be presented in its entirety. The author often has need of more secondary characters. The spectator must learn what the social state is in itself; independent of the hero; because it does not press down solely upon the hero, but on all that encircles him, on all who co-exist with him. When the audience is penetrated with this impression—which, in a manner of speaking, is abstract—of the empire that social order holds over all things, then the audience sees with more emotion the character in whom it should be interested, and who is crushed by the weight of society.

In order to put his *Joan of Arc* in accord with, and then, in conflict with, the social order of her time, in order to make this social order known in its essential parts, in that superstition that is at once credulous and defiant, which is spread throughout every class, and which is sometimes prostrate before the supernatural as before a divine gift, and sometimes labelling the supernatural as anathema, as an infernal art—to do this, Schiller was not content to limit himself to the family of the heroine. He needed persons who were extraneous to the main action, children, villagers, spread among diverse locales, who only appear in a specific episodic scene in order to represent that superstition, which is, in its rapid variations, alternately adoring and threatening to the virgin of Vaucouleurs. When Goethe, in his *Goetz von Berlichingen*, wanted to steep us in the social order of a century in which imperial power pressed the great lords, and they in turn, pressed the people, and in which this double pressure provoked resistance by opposites, resulting in total anarchy; it was not sufficient for him to paint only Goetz and his vassals, but the emperor's lieutenants and his guards. Goethe needed a thousand different tableaux in which the hero took no part; the peasant revolt, Miltenburg in flames; the Bohemians, themselves social pariahs who drag behind the regular armies; and rebel bands who are enemies as well as slaves; and the toys of both sides, the earnest spies and treacherous guides who dig in the ashes after the fire, living from the plunder of the pillage. To circumscribe such tableaux in the unities is to reduce to a miniature a Gérard painting, inspired in the grandiose and multiple nature of its figures. Yet the comparison is not exact, because in miniature the proportions are preserved and the details can be distinct, while in tragedy it is impossible for the characters and episodes not to involve a shocking disproportion and a fatiguing confusion.

But if a tragedy must renounce the unities of time and place it must take up local color all the more. Local color is the element which essentially characterizes the social state whose portrayal is the goal of dramatic writing. Local color has a charm and a particular interest. This charm was not felt in earlier periods. Corneille offers only a few traces of it in *Horace*, *Nicomedes*, and *Cinna*. Certainly there is no local color in his *Oedipus*, in which Philoctete compares the evils of absence to those of the plague. What makes *The Cid* noteworthy is the profound and noble nature of its emotions, the son sacrificing his love for his father's honor; not at all its local color. The swaggerings of a Castilian hero are generically false, purely conventional, and artificially exalted. The criticism of such conventions was anticipated in *Don Quixote* and the parody of them has existed since *Gaston and Bayard*. Racine's genius had discovered the need for local color. Several passages in *Phaedra*, several sections in *Britannicus*, entire scenes in *Athalia* offer examples. But always present was Louis XIV and his court; the allusions and the flattery. All truth disappeared under the obligatory, feigned veneer. As for Voltaire, there are happy borrowings from Sophocles in his *Oedipus*, several republican speeches in *Brutus* and *Cataline* and there is the faithful representation of the character of Cicero, who remains easy enough to paint as he is a modern type. All these give to the three plays tints of the epoch and the country. In all the others, amid the incontestable riches of an immortal talent, there is only France and the eighteenth century. With the imitators of Voltaire's school there is not a vestige of local color. Their heroes, who are well disciplined, either strongly sentimental or strangely Machiavellian, kill themselves because they must, like Greeks and Romans, but thinking and speaking all the while like well-educated Frenchmen. Local color is nevertheless the basis for all truth; without it nothing in the future will succeed.

If I wanted to digress from my topic, I would apply this precept to history. I would say that a failure in the presentation of local color pursues us painfully as we read the much-praised Hume, the so-ludicrous Robinson, or Gibbon, so richly erudite, but so monotonous in his antitheses. These historians, and others more recent, do not present, like the master Voltaire, the color of either the time or the places which they describe. The events pertain to the past, the actors belong to our own era. We may be thankful that Guizot, de Barante, and Thierry have founded another school.

The reflections you have just been reading were suggested to me in part by the soon to be published translation of a German tragedy.[30] The author, Mr. Robert, is known in Germany by other literary works which have given him a place among the most distinguished writers of his country. However, I will not analyze this tragedy; I shall limit myself to transcribing several passages from a letter addressed to me by Mr. Robert. "Forms," he wrote, "continue to command, after what was the basis, the reality, the intimate conviction have completely changed, and their change is recognized as necessary and reasonable. I have placed all my characters in *countersense* to these forms, that is to say, the conventions, the prejudices, and the proprieties. Only heroes can break this yoke; rather than painting a hero, I wanted to show the position power holds in the social order."

The central character in Robert's tragedy is a man oppressed by prejudices and institutions. The author had the fortunate idea of representing him, at the same time, as the conscientious defender of these institutions and prejudices, an ingenious way of showing how inexorable they are. Moreover, experience has already convinced us of this in France. Who does not know the naïve exclamation of a woman of the court who is eager to praise the devotion of a commoner for the cause of the nobles and who recognizes in this commoner even more merit since he is a *nobody?*

One thing, however, renders difficult the transplantation of Robert's play in our theatre. The prejudice which forms the core of the tragedy is not simply that of inequality of classes, a chimera to which the debris of a certain caste among us are still attached through their beliefs and regrets; it is a prejudice more insolent and more intolerable, which had already ceased to exist during the last years of the *ancien régime*, a prejudice which, when a nobleman was the offender in respect to an inferior, would forbid this inferior reparation. I believe, if I remember correctly, that a great lady made this reminiscence from an epoch which has slipped away from us, the episode of a novel written with spirit and grace. It was courageous in her position, as nothing could have irritated more heartily a generation in which equality had penetrated into all souls and circulated through all veins. But this idea, tolerated in a work one reads, which doesn't have to fear an explosion of public disapproval, would certainly excite unfortunate storms were it put on the stage. This aspect of German mores has become as repugnant to us as Turkish ribbon or Chinese bamboo. Therefore I believe Robert's drama, in its French translation, would be destined only to be read. It admirably presents great beauties of detail, well-drawn characters, the oppression of society, the sadness of the soul, and outraged moral disgust, which will surely in the public's eye, make up for those elements which seem an insult and a scandal.

The translator has made two changes—one is concerned with the title; the other with the dénouement.

The title which the translator has substituted for the original only renders half of the original thought; but this imperfection is excused by the impossibility of expressing in a single French word the meaning of *Verhältnisse*; which comprises all the rapports that exist between men. To entitle the play *Of the Forces of Affinity Among Men* would be to give it such a metaphysical title that it would seem to be an enigma. The words "good will" would have seemed too weak, and "conventions" would have been too obscure; "prejudices" was the least defective, and the translator can be excused for having chosen it.

I am less at ease with the change in the catastrophe. A father, who gives to his son, who has murdered his brother, the poison which will free him from the gallows, seemed too horrible to the French translator. It is, however, the prejudices, the proprieties of society such as it existed, which produced both the crime and the unhappiness. The father, fearing a misalliance, left his son to languish in a subordinate class. The other son, who saw his brother as a plebian, "a man of no consequence" as our great lords of the *ancien régime* used so aptly to remark, did not believe that they could be equals or that he should allow his brother the honor of a duel. From that arose righteous indignation, vengeance, and murder. In modifying the catastrophe, by preserving the life of one brother and giving honor to the other by means of the Imperial favors of a prince, the effect of the play is destroyed. The reader no longer knows what social state or what realm of opinion in which to locate himself. In my opinion, it would have been more valuable to leave the dénouement in its primitive severity. One might better judge the social order; one might more deeply pity its victim.

These observations are complimentary to the theory which I established twenty years ago in my Preface to *Wallstein*.

In this Preface I announced the abolition of the rules which then constrained our dramatic poets, and which prepared the way for the fall of tragedy in France; because as it is with actions so it is with art; when one condemns them to remain stationary, decadence is inevitable. Immobility in all things contradicts nature. I nevertheless expressed myself with discretion and reserve in that writing which I now permit myself to recall. I used to think that it was necessary to treat the past with politeness, firstly, since everything in the past is not bad, and secondly, since politeness more gently engages the past to withdraw. I have of late applied this principle to politics as well as literature; the honest partisans of abrupt reform have often imputed me with crime. I have no answer for them. Everyone expresses himself according to his own nature and education.

My observations, despite their politeness, have left a mark. I can affirm this without much presumption because they are still cited today as a means of refuting me. Writers who surpass me in the talent and interest in a cause which I have defended because it was good, but to which I could not attach so lively a passion, have completed my outlines and developed my insights. A woman, the most distinguished of women, making a marvelous use of what she knew and divining no less marvelously what she did not know, brought a kind of unexpected enlightenment to France through her work on Germany.[31] The theatrical revolution is in effect. It is contested because it is anarchic in its first stages; but this anarchy is a necessary transition between the past which is fleeting and the future which is arriving. The enemies of the revolution are given an apparent advantage. They hold up the bizarre and monstrous attempts which are created each day and demand if it were worth the pain of overturning the rules merely to throw us into such chaos. What does that prove? What has been newly made is often bad. And so it must be. The generation which marshalls itself because of its instincts beneath a new standard is divided in two unequal parts. One is composed of those whose genius—and they do possess genius—would be impeded by the rules: that is the smaller number; this small group occasionally loses its way in its liberty. The other part is composed of those who blame the rules for what they lack in genius: this is necessarily the majority. Slaves or freemen, nothing will help them. But genius will ripen before it is given liberty. I see it dawning in *Clara Gazul*, in *The Barricades*, in *The Jacquerie*, and in *The Assembly at Blois*. The literary revolution is decided. It will be accomplished. Even its opponents are yielding. They evade the rules which they defend; they torture the rules in order to escape them.[32]

Notes

1. Goethe published *Goetz von Berlichingen* in 1773 at the age of twenty-three.

2. Schiller's *Wallenstein Trilogy* was produced by Goethe at the Weimar Court Theatre in 1798–1799.

3. Aménaïde is the principal female role in Voltaire's *Tancred* (1760). Alzire is the title role in Voltaire's tragedy (1736).

4. Polyphontes, the King of Messina, in Voltaire's *Mérope* (1743).

5. By François Raynouard, produced at the Comédie-Française in 1805.

6. Schiller's play (1801) about Joan of Arc.

7. August Friedrich von Kotzebue was the most popular dramatist in Germany during the late eighteenth and early nineteenth centuries. *Gustaf Vasa* was published in 1800.

8. There are forty-eight characters in the German *Wallenstein*; there are only twelve in the French adaptation. [Constant's note.]

9. Schiller had introduced a chorus that speaks rather than sings. [Constant's note.]

10. Zacharias Werner's *Luther, or the Consecration of the Powers* (1807) was translated into French in 1823.

11. Werner's *Attila, King of the Huns*, a romantic tragedy, was published in 1808.

12. For Alzire and Aménaïde, see note 3. *Adélaïde du Guesclin* (1734) was written by Voltaire.

13. Heroines respectively in Racine's *Mithridates* (1673), *Bérénice* (1671), *Esther* (1689), and *Bajazet* (1672).

14. *Charles IX, or The School for Kings*, by Marie-Joseph Chénier, was first produced in 1789.

15. This is an abridgement of a section in the third "Interview" of the "Essay on Dramatic Poetry" appended to Diderot's play *The Bastard* (1757).

16. Nero, Junie, and Britannicus form the love triangle in Racine's *Britannicus* (1669). Palmyre and Mahomet are the central characters in Voltaire's *Mahomet* (1742). Mahomet is the cruel tyrant enamoured of Palmyre, one of two Christian children captured by his soldiers and reared as infidels. Orasmane and Zaïre are the central characters in Voltaire's *Zaïre* (1732).

17. *Caliste* (1760) by Charles-Preuve Colardeau; *Abufar* (1795) by Jean-François Ducis.

18. From *The Art of Poetry* (1764), canto III, lines 95–96.

19. *Artamène or Great Cyrus* (1649–1653), and *Clélie* (1654–1660) are novels by Madeleine de Scudéry.

20. Constant appears to be quoting from memory, imperfectly, lines from Pierre du Ryer's *Alcionée* (1640) II. v.

21. *Amadis de Gaule* (1508) is a celebrated novel in the chivalric tradition by Garcia Rodriguez.

22. Valmont is the protagonist of Laclos's novel *Les Liaisons Dangereuses* (1782).

23. Félix, in Corneille's *Polyeuctes* (1671). Through fear of the emperor, he has Polyeuctes, his daughter's husband, executed.

24. See note 4.

25. The League was formed in 1576 by Henry de Guise to defend the Roman Catholic religion from the Calvinists. It was ended in 1594 when King Henry IV adopted Catholicism. The Fronde was the name given to two revolts against the absolutism of the French crown; the first occurring in 1648; the second in 1651–1653.

26. Fenouillet de Falbaire, *The Honest Criminal* (1767).

27. See note 32.

28. This is an abridgement from the *Mémoires* of Saint-Simon (1675–1755).

29. Bernard-Joseph Saurin (1706–1781), *Spartacus* (1760).

30. See headnote, p. 94.

31. Madame de Staël.

32. *The Jacquerie* (1828), and *The Theatre of Clara Gazul* (1825), by Prosper Mérimée. The former consisted of scenes describing a peasant rebellion in France during the feudal period. The latter is a collection of satires and burlesques. *The Barricades* (1826), and *The Assembly at Blois* (1827), by Ludovic Vitet. These scenes from history form the first two parts of a trilogy entitled *The League*.

3

STENDHAL

The adult life of Henri Beyle (1783–1842) may be divided conveniently into three phases. During the Empire he served in Napoleon's army and held minor government posts. The Restoration brought his career in government to an end. He retired to Milan until his liberal politics led to his expulsion from that city, when he returned to Paris. During the Restoration he began his career as a writer and journalist. He reentered government service under the July Monarchy, serving most notably as the consul at Civita Vecchia, near Rome.

Beyle's early writing consists primarily of journalism and criticism and includes the Letters on Hayden and The Life of Mozart *(1815),* A History of Painting in Italy *(1817),* Rome, Naples and Florence in 1817 *(for which, for the first time, he employed the pseudonym Stendhal),* On Love *(1822),* Life of Rossini *(1823), and* Racine and Shakespeare *(1823–1825). His first full-length fiction,* Armance, *was published in 1827, but it was with* The Red and the Black, *published in 1831, that Beyle established his literary reputation. In the 1830s he published the* Italian Chronicles *and his masterpiece* The Charterhouse of Parma *(1839). During the last decade of his life he worked on the unfinished novels* Lucien Leuwen *and* Lamiel, *as well as the autobiographical works* Souvenirs of Egoism *and* The Life of Henry Brulard.

At the time of the writing of Racine and Shakespeare *Stendhal was a journalist who dabbled in the arts, having written on painting, music, and the theatre. He was a political liberal and a realist who is more appropriately placed in the tradition of Constant and in the company of such writers as Mérimée and Vitet in the liberal salons of the 1820s than among the radical young poets. Although he did not sympathize with the romantic poets, he did help introduce them to both modern Italian and English literary ideas.* Racine and Shakespeare *argues for liberalism in literature before the French romantics had grouped for battle and makes its plea in a tone free of the often frenetic rhetoric of those who would follow him.*

Racine and Shakespeare (1823)

This work was published in Paris in 1823 by Bossange, Delaunay and Mongie. Chapters 1 and 2 had appeared in the Paris Monthly Review *in October 1822 and January 1823, respectively.*

Chapter 1. "To write tragedies of interest to the public of 1830, ought one take Racine or Shakespeare as a model?"

France seems to be weary of this question, yet only one side of the argument has been given much attention. The press, absolutely opposed in political opinions. . .is in agreement on only one subject: to proclaim the French theatre not only the pre-eminent theatre in the world but also the only viable one. Even if lowly *romanticism*[1] were prepared to issue a statement, all the newspapers, regardless of their political affiliation, would be equally closed to it.

But this apparent disfavor doesn't frighten us at all because it is a matter of politics. We respond with a single fact:

What literary works have had the most success in France in the last ten years?

The novels of Walter Scott.

What are Walter Scott's novels?

Romantic tragedy interspersed with long descriptions.

You will object, citing as examples *The Sicilian Vespers, The Pariah, The Maccabees, Regulus.*[2]

These plays arouse much pleasure, but it is not a *dramatic pleasure*. The public, which, moreover, does not enjoy much freedom, likes to hear the recitation of noble sentiments expressed in beautiful verse.

But that is an *epic*, not a dramatic, pleasure. There is never that degree of illusion needed to express profound emotion. That is the reason, the secret reason, that the audience of young people at the Odéon—ignorant themselves of this reason, for, no matter what is said, at twenty they prefer entertainment to thought, which is well enough—proves to be so unexacting regarding the plot of plays which it applauds rapturously. What, for example, is more ridiculous than the plot of *The Pariah*? It does not bear examination. This was a generally accepted criticism, but it did not have an effect. Why? Because all the public wants is beautiful verse. At present in the French theatre the public expects to hear a series of exceedingly pompous odes which, moreover, forcefully express noble sentiments. It is enough that these odes be introduced by a few transitional lines. It is like the ballets at the Opéra; their action is expressly designed to introduce beautiful movement and to motivate, whether bad or good, agreeable dances.

I fearlessly address those misguided youths who thought themselves patriotic, defending the honor of their nation, by hissing Shakespeare because he was English.[3] Since I have great esteem for these diligent youths, the hope of France, I will use the severe language of truth with them.

The entire dispute between Racine and Shakespeare can be reduced to deciding if, by observing the two unities of *place* and *time*, one can write plays that will be of interest to nineteenth-century audiences, plays which will make these audiences tremble and weep, or, in other words, which will give them *dramatic* pleasure rather than the *epic* pleasure which makes us return to the fiftieth performance of *The Pariah* or *Regulus*.

I think that the observation of the two unities of *place* and *time* is a habit in France, a *deeply ingrained* habit, a habit we will be rid of with difficulty because Paris is the drawing room of Europe and sets the tone. But I do declare that these unities are not at all necessary to produce profound emotion and true dramatic effects.

Why, I will ask the partisans of *classicism*, do you require that the actions represented in a tragedy last no longer than twenty-four hours or thirty-six hours, and that the setting not change, or, at the least, as Voltaire says, that the scene changes not go beyond the various rooms of a single palace?

The ACADEMICIAN: Because it is not probable that an action which is represented in two hours encompasses a time span of a week or a month, nor that, in this space of a few moments, the actors go from Venice to Cyprus, as in Shakespeare's *Othello*, or from Scotland to the court of England, as in *Macbeth*.

The ROMANTIC: Not only is that improbable and impossible. It is equally impossible that the action encompasses twenty-four or thirty-six hours.[4*]

The ACADEMICIAN: God forbid that we are absurd enough to pretend that the fictional time must correspond exactly to the *physical* time of the representation. At that point the rules would truly be shackles for genius. In the arts of imitation it is necessary to be severe but not rigorous. The spectator can very well imagine that several hours pass in the interval of the entr'actes, especially since he is distracted by the orchestral music.

The ROMANTIC: Be careful of what you are saying, Sir. You give me an immense advantage. You admit, then, that the spectator can *imagine* that a greater time passes than the time during which he is seated in the theatre. But, tell me, will he be able to imagine that the time passed is double the actual time, triple, quadruple, and a hundred times greater? Where shall we stop?

The ACADEMICIAN: You are strange, you modern philosophers. You criticize poetics because, you say, it hampers genius. But now, for the sake of plausibility, you would have us apply the rule of the *unity of time* with the rigor and exactitude of mathematics. Isn't it sufficient for you that it is manifestly contrary to all probability that the spectator can imagine a year, a month, or even a week to have passed since he bought his ticket and entered the theatre?

The ROMANTIC: And who told you that the spectator cannot imagine that?

The ACADEMICIAN: Reason dictates . . .

The ROMANTIC: I beg your pardon. Reason would not be able to teach it to you. If experience had not taught you, how would you know that the spectator can imagine twenty-four hours to have passed when, in effect, he has only been seated in his box for two hours? How, but through experience, would you be able to know that the hours, which seem so long to a man who is bored, seem to fly by for the man who is amused? In a word, it is *experience* alone which must decide between you and me.

The ACADEMICIAN: Yes, it is experience.

The ROMANTIC: Well, then! Experience has already testified against you. In England, for two centuries, in Germany for fifty years, tragedies are presented in which the action lasts months and the audience's imagination accepts it readily.

The ACADEMICIAN: But you're talking about foreigners, and worse, Germans!

The ROMANTIC: We will speak another time of the incontestable superiority of the French in general, and the Parisians in particular, over all the other peoples of the world. To be fair, that sense of superiority is unconscious; you are despots spoiled by two centuries of flattery. Fate has decreed that it be you Parisians who determine the literary reputations of Europe. And so a woman of lively intelligence,[5] known for her *enthusiasm* for natural beauty, to please the Parisians cried out: "The most beautiful brook in the world is the brook of the rue du Bac." Well-mannered writers, not only in France, but of all Europe, have flattered you to obtain in exchange their dram of literary renown. And what you call *internal feeling, moral obviousness,* is nothing more than the moral obviousness of a spoiled child, in other words, *the habit of flattery.*

But let's return to our point. Would you deny that the inhabitants of London or Edinburgh, the countrymen of Fox and Sheridan,[6] certainly not complete fools, do not witness the representation of tragedies such as *Macbeth,* for example, without in any way being shocked? Well, this play, which is applauded countless times each year in England and America, begins with the assassination of a king and the flight of his sons, and ends with the return of these same princes at the head of an army assembled in England to dethrone the bloody Macbeth. This series of events necessarily demands a time span of several months.

The ACADEMICIAN: Ah! you will never persuade me that the English and Germans, foreigners though they may be, really imagine that whole months pass away while they are in the theatre.

The ROMANTIC: Similarly, you will never persuade me that the French audience believes twenty-four hours pass while they sit at a production of *Iphigenia in Aulis.*

The ACADEMICIAN (provoked): There is no comparison!

The ROMANTIC: Calm down. Please reflect on what you are saying. Try to push aside the veil which habit has thrown over actions which happen so quickly that you have almost lost the power to follow them with your eyes and see them *happening.* Let's come to an understanding about the word *illusion.* When we say that the spectator is able to imagine that the time necessary for the events represented on stage has elapsed, we do not mean that the illusion goes to the point of the spectator's believing all this time has really elapsed. The fact is that the spectator, caught up in the action, is not shocked by anything; he simply does not think about the time elapsed. Your Parisian spectator sees Agamemnon wake Arcas at seven sharp. He witnesses the arrival of Iphigenia. He sees her taken to the altar where the jesuitical Calchas waits. He would certainly be able to answer, were he to be asked, that several hours are necessary for all these events. However, if he takes out his watch during the argument between Achilles and Agamemnon, it reads a quarter past eight. Is there a spectator who would be surprised by this? Yet the play he applauded already has taken several hours.

Even your Parisian spectator is accustomed to see time move with a different rhythm on stage than in the auditorium. There is a fact you cannot deny.

It is clear that even in Paris, even at the Comédie-Française, the imagination of the spectator easily accepts the assumptions of the poet. Naturally the spectator pays no attention whatsoever to the gaps in time needed by the poet. No more than in sculpture does he presume to reproach Dupaty or Bosio the lack of movement in their figures. That is one of art's weaknesses: the spectator, when he is not a pedant, is concerned solely with the facts and the developing passions which are presented to him. Exactly the same thing occurs in the mind of the Parisian who applauds *Iphigenia in Aulis* and in that of the Scotsman caught up in the story of his ancient kings Macbeth and Duncan. The only difference is that the Parisian, the product of a proper upbringing, has acquired the habit of mocking the latter.

The ACADEMICIAN: In your opinion, then, the actual illusion would be the same for both of them?

The ROMANTIC: To have illusions, to be in the state of *illusion*, means to be deceived, according to the Academy's dictionary. An *illusion*, says Guizot, is the effect of a thing or idea which deceives through a deceptive appearance. Illusion, then, signifies the action of a man who believes a thing to exist when it does not, as in dreams, for example. Theatrical illusion is, then, the action of a man who believes the things which happen on the stage to be truly occurring. In the past year (August 1822) a guard in a Baltimore theatre, seeing Othello (in the tragedy of the same name) about to kill Desdemona, cried out: "I'll never let that god-damned nigger kill a white woman!" In the same breath he drew his gun and shot the actor playing Othello in the arm. One reads regularly of similar occurrences in the newspapers. Well, this soldier was possessed by an *illusion*, and believed the action which passed on the stage to be true. But an ordinary spectator, in the most intense moment of pleasure, when he *applauds* ecstatically Talma-Manlius, saying to his friend: "Do you recognize this writing?"[7] is not in a state of *complete illusion*. The very fact that he applauds indicates this, for he applauds Talma and not Manlius, the Roman. Manlius is not doing anything that merits applause, his action is very simple and completely in his own best interests.

The ACADEMICIAN: Pardon me, my friend, but what you are saying is a platitude.

The ROMANTIC: Pardon me, my friend, but what you are saying is the excuse of a man incapable of correct reasoning because of his long-standing habit of being satisfied with eloquent phrases.

It is impossible for you not to admit that the illusion one seeks in the theatre is not a perfect illusion. *Perfect* illusion was the state of the soldier on guard in the Baltimore theatre. It is impossible for you not to admit that the spectators are well aware of being in the theatre and that they are witnessing the presentation of a work of art and not a real event.

The ACADEMICIAN: Who pretends to deny that?

The ROMANTIC: You will, then, concede that the illusion is *imperfect*? Be careful.

Do you believe that from time to time, for example, two or three times in the act, and each time for the duration of a second or two, the illusion is complete?

The ACADEMICIAN: I am not sure. In order to answer you, I would need to return to the theatre several times and observe my reactions.

The ROMANTIC: Ah! That's a lovely reply, full of good faith. It is obvious that you are an academician and that you no longer need the approbation of your colleagues to be elected. A man whose reputation as a learned man of letters was still to be made would be wary of being so clear and of reasoning in such a precise manner. Watch yourself; if you continue to show such guilelessness, you will find us to be in agreement.

It seems to me that these moments of *perfect illusion* are more frequent than generally thought and especially than is conceded to be true in literary discussions. But these moments are of infinitely brief duration, a half-second, for example, or a quarter-second. Manlius is quickly forgotten in order to focus on Talma. These moments last longer for women—which is why they shed so many tears at a tragedy.

But let us enquire into which moments of tragedy the spectator can hope to encounter these marvelous moments of *perfect illusion*.

These moments are not met when the scene changes, nor when the poet causes twelve or fifteen days to elapse before the spectator's eyes, nor when the poet is obliged to insert a long narrative by one of his characters, for the sole reason to inform the spectator of a previous event (the knowledge of which is indispensable to him), nor when he produces three or four admirable lines, remarkable *as verse*.

These moments, so delightful and so rare, of *perfect illusion*, can only be encountered in the heart of an animated scene, when the actor's responses are rushed: for example, when Hermione says to Orestes, who has just assassinated Pyrrhus at her command: "Who told you to do it?"[8]

These moments of *perfect illusion* are never found at the instant when a murder is committed on stage, nor when guards appear to take a character away to prison. We cannot believe all such things to be true, and they never produce an illusion. These things function to prepare the way for scenes during which the spectators encounter these wonderful half-seconds. And I claim that these brief moments of *perfect illusion are more often found in Shakespeare's tragedies than in Racine's.*

All the pleasure you derive from a tragic performance depends on the frequency of these brief moments of illusion *and from the emotional state in which the spectator is left in the interval between them.*

One of the things most opposed to the creation of these moments of illusion is an admiration, however just it may be, for the beautiful verse of a tragedy.

It is even worse if one decides he wants to judge the *verse* of a tragedy. Well, that is precisely the frame of mind of the Parisian spectator when he first goes to see the much-lauded tragedy, *The Pariah*.

There you have the question of *romanticism* reduced to its ultimate terms. If you are prejudiced, or if you are insensitive, or if you are petrified by LaHarpe,[9] you will deny my brief moments of perfect illusion.

And I confess that I have no answer to that. Your feelings are not some material object that I could extract from your heart to place before your eyes and confound you.

I tell you that you ought to have such and such a feeling at this moment, all generally well-constituted men experience this feeling at this moment. You reply: Excuse me, but *that's not true*.

As for me, I have nothing to add I have reached the outer limits of what a logician can grasp of poetry.

The ACADEMICIAN: That is an abominably obscure metaphysic. Is it with that you plan to have Racine hissed?

The ROMANTIC: First, only charlatans claim to teach algebra effortlessly or pull a tooth painlessly. The question we are debating is one of the most complex faced by the human mind.

As for Racine, I am very glad you mentioned this great man. His name has been made an insult for us, for his greatness is immortal. He will always be one of the greatest geniuses to arouse the awe and admiration of men. Is Caesar less great a general because gunpowder was invented since his campaigns against our ancestors, the Gauls? All we claim is that if Caesar were to return to life, his first concern would be to have cannons in his army. Would you say that Catinat or Luxembourg were greater leaders than Caesar because they had a force of artillery and in three days captured sites that would have withstood Roman legions for months? It would have been good advice to have said to François I at Marignan: "Beware of using your artillery. Caesar did not have cannons. Do you think you are better than Caesar?"

If men of incontestable talent such as Chénier, Lemercier, and Delavigne had dared divest themselves of the rules whose absurdity has been well known since Racine, they would have given us better plays than *Tiberius*, *Agamemnon*, and *The Sicilian Vespers*. Isn't *Pinto* a hundred times better than *Clovis*, *Orovèse*, *Cyrus*, or any other highly conventional tragedy by Lemercier?[10]

Racine did not believe that tragedy could be written differently. If he were living today, and were he to dare to follow the new rules, he would do a hundred times better than *Iphigenia*. Instead of inspiring only admiration, a rather cool emotion, he would cause torrents of tears to be shed. What even moderately elightened man would not derive more pleasure from a production of Lebrun's *Mary Stuart*[11] at the Comédie-Française than from Racine's *Bajazet*? And yet Lebrun's verse is very weak; the enormous difference in the quantity of pleasure is due to the fact that Lebrun has dared to be semi-romantic.

The ACADEMICIAN: You have spoken at length. You have, perhaps, spoken well, but you have not convinced me at all.

Lith. de C. Motte, B. des marais

Mlle Duchesnois,
Rôle de Marie Stuart.

Miroir, (Journal)

Mlle Duchesnois in the Title Role of Pierre Lebrun's *Mary Stuart*, 1820. (Author's collection.)

The ROMANTIC: That's to be expected. But this somewhat long entr'acte is about to end. The curtain is going up. I sought to relieve the boredom by rousing your anger a bit. You must admit that I have succeeded.

Here ended the dialogue of the two adversaries, a scene I actually witnessed in the orchestra of the theatre in Chantereine Street.[12] I, alone, can name the interlocutors. The romantic was polite; he did not wish to anger his good-tempered senior. Otherwise he would have added: In order to be able to know his own heart, in order that the veil of habit be torn away, in order to be able to enter into the experience for the moments of *perfect illusion* we have described, one must be less than forty!

We all have habits. Disturb these habits and for a long time we will be sensitive only to our annoyance. Suppose that Talma appeared on stage and played Manlius in a powdered wig arranged in ringlets? We would laugh throughout the entire performance. Would he be less sublime in the fundamentals of his role? No, but we would not see this sublimity. Lekain would have produced exactly the same effect in 1760 had he appeared, without such a wig, to play this role of Manlius. The spectators would have been preoccupied throughout the production by the *shock to convention*. That is exactly Shakespeare's position in France now. He opposes a great many of those ridiculous habits that we have contracted in the assiduous reading of LaHarpe and other minor perfumed rhetoricians of the eighteenth century. What is worse, we are vain enough to maintain that these prejudices have their basis in reality.

Young people can still recover from this error based in vanity. Their souls are susceptible to lively impressions, pleasure can make them forget this false pride, and that is what it is impossible to ask a man older than forty. In Paris, men of that age have taken sides on every issue, even on issues of much greater importance than knowing if, in order to write intriguing tragedies in 1823 it is necessary to follow the method of Racine or of Shakespeare.

From Chapter 3. "What Romanticism is"

Romanticism is the art of presenting people with literary works which, given the current state of their social customs and beliefs, are susceptible of arousing the most possible pleasure.

Classicism, on the contrary, offers them that literature which gave the greatest possible pleasure to their great-grandfathers.

Sophocles and Euripides were eminently romantic. They offered tragedies to the Greeks assembled in the theatre at Athens which, considering Greek ethics, religion and presumptions concerning mankind, must have aroused in them the greatest possible satisfaction.

Classicism is the imitation of Sophocles and Euripides today and the pretense that these imitations will not cause a nineteenth-century Frenchman to yawn.[13]*

I do not hesitate to propose that Racine was romantic. He offered the aristocrats of Louis XIV's court a portrait of passions tempered by the highly developed notion of personal dignity then in fashion, a dignity which resulted in a duke of 1670 never failing to address his son as "Sir," even in the most tender effusions of paternal affection.

That is why Pylades in *Andromache* always calls Orestes "Milord." And yet what a friendship was that of Pylades and Orestes!

Such dignity is not to be found in the Greek plays. But it is because of that *dignity*, which we find cold today, that Racine was a romantic.

Shakespeare was romantic because he presented to the Englishman of the year 1590, first the bloody catastrophes brought on by civil war, and, as a respite from these sad spectacles, a multitude of subtle delineations of the workings of the heart and nuances of the most delicate passions. One hundred years of civil war and almost continuous social tumult, a multitude of betrayals, tortures, noble self-sacrifices, had prepared Elizabeth's subjects for that type of tragedy which had nothing of the artificial air of peaceful kingdoms. The Englishman of 1590, fortunately very ignorant, enjoyed, in the theatre, the image of the wars that the resolute character of his queen had only recently removed from his life. These same naïve details, which our alexandrine verse would reject with disdain, and which are so highly esteemed today in *Ivanhoe* and *Rob Roy*,[14] would have appeared to be lacking in dignity to the proud aristocrat of Louis XIV's time.

The details would have mortally terrified the sentimental and perfumed dolls who, in the time of Louis XV, could not see a spider without fainting. This is a statement barely worthy of repetition.

Courage is needed to be romantic, for *risks must be taken*.

The prudent *classicist*, on the contrary, never advances without the hidden support of some verse of Homer, or of a philosophical comment by Cicero from his treatise *De Senectute*.

It seems to me that a writer needs almost as much courage as a warrior; the one must no more think about journalists than the other of the hospital.

Lord Byron, the author of several sublime, but rather similar, heroic poems, and of many decidedly boring tragedies, is by no means the leader of the romantics.

If a man were to be found who might be the subject of the bickering of hack translators in Madrid, Stuttgart, Paris, and Vienna, one would be able to assert that this man had divined the moral tendencies of his epoch.

With us, the popular Pigault-Lebrun is much more romantic than the sensitive author of *Trilby*.[15]

What is romantic in tragedy at present is that the poet always gives a good role to the devil. He speaks eloquently and is much relished. The opposition is favored.

What is anti-romantic is Legouvé, in his tragedy *Henry IV*, unable to quote the best-known saying of this patriotic king: "I should like the poorest peasant of my kingdom, at least on Sundays, to have a chicken in the stewpot."[16]

This quintessentially French saying would have provided the most untalented of Shakespeare's imitators with a very effective scene. Racinian tragedy says, much more nobly:

> Lastly, I would wish, that on the Sabbath day
> The honest host of a humble cottage
> Would have, by my grace, on his lowly board,
> One of those delicacies once reserved for the rich.
>
> > (*The Death of Henry IV*, Act IV)[17]*

. . . . . .

The romantics do not advise anyone simply to copy Shakespeare's plays.

What needs to be imitated in this great man is his manner of studying the world in which he lives and the art of giving one's contemporaries exactly the type of tragedy they require but don't have the audacity to demand, so terrified are they by the great Racine's reputation.

As Fate would have it, the new French tragedy would closely resemble Shakespearean tragedy.

But this is only because our circumstances are the same as those of England in 1590. We, too, have factions, political imprisonments, and conspiracies. Anyone who laughs aloud in a salon while reading this brochure will be in prison within a week! Someone else, who jokes with him, will appoint the jury which will condemn him.

We would soon see the new French tragedy which I have the boldness to predict, if we were secure enough to freely concern ourselves with literature. I say secure for there is an especial evil in imaginations which live in fear. Our countryside and roads are astonishingly safe in comparison to those of England in 1590.

As we are much more cultivated than the audience of Shakespeare's day, our *new tragedy* will have more simplicity than theirs. Every time Shakespeare uses rhetoric it is to make comprehensible one or another situation in his play to a rough public which had more courage than polish.

Our new tragedy will resemble in many ways *Pinto*, Lemercier's masterpiece.

The French spirit will specifically reject the pompous German nonsense that many people today call *romantic*.

Schiller merely aped Shakespeare and his rhetoric; he did not have the sensibility to provide his compatriots with the tragedy demanded by their own culture.

I have forgotten to mention the *unity of place*. It will disappear with the overthrow of alexandrine verse. Picard's charming comedy *The Storyteller*,[18] which needed only the hand of a Beaumarchais or a Sheridan to be absolutely delightful, afforded the public the chance to see that there are agreeable subjects for which a change of set is indeed necessary.

We are almost as advanced in tragedy. We can question how it is that Emilia in *Cinna* comes to conspire in the Emperor's very apartment. How can we imagine *Sylla* played without set changes?[19]

If Chénier had lived, this man of spirit would have rid us of the *unity of place* in tragedy, and consequently, of *boring narrations*. It is the unity of place that always makes it impossible to treat great national subjects: *The Assassination of Monterau, The Assembly at Blois, The Death of Henry III*.

For *Henry III*, it is absolutely necessary to have on the one hand: Paris, the Duchess of Montpensier, the Jacobin cloister; on the other hand: Saint-Cloud, the irresolution, the weakness, the voluptuousness, and the sudden death which ends it all.

Racinian tragedy can never take more than thirty-six hours of an action; thus there is never any development of passions. What conspiracy has time to hatch, what popular movement can develop, in thirty-six hours?

It is interesting, it is *beautiful*, to see Othello, so in love in the first act, kill his wife in the fifth. If the change had occurred in thirty-six hours, it would be absurd and I would despise Othello.

Macbeth, an honest man in the first act, is led astray by his wife and kills his benefactor and his king, becoming a bloody monster. Either I am greatly deceived or these shifts in feeling of the human heart are the most magnificent things poetry can offer to us. They touch and instruct us at the same time.

Racine and Shakespeare, No. II (1825)

This work was published by Dupont and Roret in Paris in March 1825.

From Letter No. 2. "Response of the Romantic to the Classicist"

. . . . . .

I will not deny that, even today, one can create beautiful effects following the *classical* method, but they will be *boring*.

This is because they will, in part, be modeled on the needs of the Frenchman of 1670, and not on the moral requirements and dominant passions of the Frenchman of 1824. *Pinto* is the only play I have seen written for modern Frenchmen. Were the police to allow the production of *Pinto*, in less than six months the public would no longer be able to tolerate conspiracies in alexandrine verse. I advise the classicists to be fond of the police, otherwise they would be ingrates.

As for me, in my small circle and at an enormous distance from *Pinto* and all publicly accepted works, I would first state that, lacking a more serious occupation since 1814, I write as one smokes a cigar; to pass the time. A page that I enjoyed writing always has some value for me.

I appreciate, then, as much as I ought, and more than anyone else, all the distance which separates me from the writers who possess the admiration both of the public and the French Academy. Had Villemain or Jouy received the manuscript of *The Life of Rossini* in the mail, they would have considered it to be *written in a foreign language* and would have *translated* it into a good academic style in the manner of Villemain's *Preface* to the *Republic of Cicero* or of the letters to *Stephanus Ancestor*. This would have been advantageous to the bookseller (as there wold have been twenty-six reviews in the press) and he would now be occupied in the preparation of the book's sixth edition. But had I tried to write it in a lofty academic style, I would have been bored, and I admit it would have been the work of a stooge. To my mind, this ordered, formal style, full of piquant reversals—*precious*, if I must speak plainly—was marvelously appropriate for the Frenchman of 1785. Delille was the leader in this style. I have attempted in my own writing style to be suitable for the children of the Revolution, men who seek thought rather than beautiful phrases; men who, instead of reading Quintus-Curce and studying Tacitus, participated in the Moscow campaigns and witnessed at first hand the strange events of 1814.

I had heard, during that period, of a number of insignificant conspiracies. From then I have despised conspiracies in alexandrine verse and what I desire is *tragedy in prose*: a *Death of Henry III*, for example, in which the first four acts take place in Paris over a period of months (this much time is required for the seduction of Jacques Clément) and the last act takes place at Saint-Cloud. It would be all the more interesting to me, I admit, in comparison to Clytemnestra or Regulus making twenty-four line *tirades* in the *official* manner. The *tirade* is perhaps the most anti-romantic element in Racine's system. If it were absolutely necessary to choose, I would prefer to see the two unities retained than the *tirade*.

You defy me, sir, to reply to the simple question: what is romantic tragedy?

I reply boldly: it is tragedy in prose whose actions last several months and which takes place in diverse settings.

The poets who cannot understand this sort of complex argument, Viennet for example,[20] and the men who don't want to understand, loudly demand a *clear* idea. Well, it seems to me that nothing is more clear than this: *A romantic tragedy is written in prose; the succession of events it presents to the spectator lasts several months and takes place in several settings.* Heaven grant us soon a talented man to write such a tragedy! Let him write *The Death of Henry IV* or *Louis XIII at the Susa Pass.* We will see the brilliant Bassompierre say to this king, so French in both his bravery and his weakness: "Sire, the dancers are ready. At your majesty's command, the ball will commence." Our history, or rather our historical memoirs, for we have no history, are full of charming and artless anecdotes. Only romantic tragedy can portray them for us.[21]* Do you know what would happen to the ghost of *Henry IV*, a romantic tragedy in the manner of Shakespeare's *Richard III*? The whole world would immediately reach an agreement as to what the expression *romantique* means. And soon in the classical genre it would no longer be possible to stage anything but the plays of Racine, Corneille, and Voltaire. Yet Voltaire found it easier to write in a completely epic style in *Mahomet*, *Alzire*, etc., rather than to adhere to the noble and often touching simplicity of Racine.

. . . . . .

From Letter No. 3. "The Romantic to the Classicist"

. . . . . .

Romanticism applied to that intellectual pleasure with respect to which the true battle between the classicists and romantics takes place—between Racine and Shakespeare—results in a prose tragedy whose action lasts several months and occurs in various settings. It is possible, however, to conceive of a romantic tragedy the events of which, by chance, are confined within the walls of one palace and within thirty-six hours. If the diverse incidents of this tragedy resemble those revealed to us by history; if the language, instead of being epic and official, is simple, lively, brilliant, and natural, without *tirades*, then it will not be the assuredly very rare circumstance which has placed the events of this tragedy in one palace and within the time limits set by the Abbé d'Aubignac[22] which will prevent it from being a romantic tragedy. That is, it will offer the public the impressions it requires and consequently will earn the approbation of men who think for themselves. Shakespeare's *Tempest*, however mediocre it may be, is nevertheless a romantic play though its actions last only a few hours and take place within the confines of a small Mediterranean island.

You refute my theories, Sir, by recalling the success of several tragedies, Racinian imitations (*Clytemnestra*, *The Pariah*, etc.) that at present more or less correctly satisfy the conditions that the taste of the marquis of 1670 and the tone of Louis XIV's court imposed on Racine. I reply that such is the power exerted by the dramatic art on the human heart, that this art pleases, no matter how absurd are the rules to which the pitiable poets are obliged to submit. If Aristotle or the Abbé d'Aubignac had imposed a rule on French tragedy permitting characters to speak only in monosyllables; if every word with more than one syllable were banished from the French stage and French poetic style with the same severity as, for example, applies to the word "pistol"—very well, then, in spite of this absurd rule, tragedies written by geniuses would still please. Why? In spite of the rule of the monosyllable, no more extraordinary than many other rules, a genius would have found the secret of filling his play with a richness of thought and an abundance of feeling which would hold our attention from the start. The idiocy of the rule would have forced him to sacrifice some touching rejoinders and several emotions of an otherwise assured effect, but this would not affect the success of the tragedy *as long as the rule subsists*. It is at the moment when the rule finally falls under the tardy blows of good sense that the traditional poet runs a true risk. *With much less talent* will his successors be able to deal with the same subject better than he? Why? They will dare to employ the appropriate expression, unique, necessary and *indispensable* to the illustration of whatever emotion is in the soul or to the realization of whatever incident is in the plot. For example, how would you avoid having Othello pronounce the base word, "handkerchief," when he kills the woman he adores, simply because she has let his rival Cassio seize the fatal handkerchief which he had given her at the beginning of their courtship?

If the Abbé d'Aubignac had demanded that actors in *comedy* walk only on one foot, Marivaux's comedy *The False Confessions*, as played by Mlle. Mars, would still move us, despite this bizarre idea.[23]* Our grandfathers were moved by the Orestes of *Andromache* played in a full powdered wig, scarlet tights, and shoes adorned with rosettes of crimson ribbon.

Every absurdity which has become a convention in the imagination of a people is no longer an absurdity for them and is in almost no way prejudicial to their basic pleasure until that fatal moment when someone indiscreet appears and tells them that *what they admire is absurd*. At this moment many men, honest with themselves, who had believed their souls to be closed to poetry, breathe a sigh of relief: for, in liking it too much, they had thought not to like it. It is thus that a young man, endowed by the Lord with some delicacy of soul, believes himself, sincerely, to be insensible to love: when confronted by Fate in his situation as a sub-lieutenant in a garrison town where, in the society of a certain good woman, he witnesses the success of his comrades and the types of pleasures they pursue. Finally, one day, Fate presents him with a simple, natural, honest woman, worthy of being loved, and he feels that he has a heart. Many older men are classicists in good faith. To begin with, they do not understand the word *romantic*. On the authority of the *Associated Poets for Good Writing* they believe romantic all that is lugubrious and silly, like Satan's seduction of Eloa.[24] LaHarpe's contemporaries admired the ponderous and mournful tone that Talma too often assumes in the *tirade*. They call this lamentable and monotonous song the perfection of French tragedy. They maintain, and it is a poor argument, that the introduction of prose in tragedy, the freedom to encompass several months and wander several leagues, is not necessary to our pleasure. They argue that very moving masterpieces have been written and continue to be written which scrupulously follow the rules of the Abbé d'Aubignac. We reply that our tragedies would be more touching and they would treat a variety of great national subjects which Racine and Voltaire were forced to renounce. The appearance of art will change as soon as it is allowed to change the settings, and, for example, in the tragedy of *The Death of Henry III*, go from Paris to Saint-Cloud.

At present, since I have explained myself at length, it seems to me that I can state with the hope of being understood by everyone and the assurance of not being parodied, even by the celebrated Villemain, that romanticism in the tragic genre IS A TRAGEDY IN PROSE WHOSE ACTION LASTS SEVERAL MONTHS AND TAKES PLACE IN SEVERAL SETTINGS.

When the Romans built those monuments which, after so many centuries, still inspire admiration in us (the triumphal arch of Septimus Severus, Constantine's Arch, the arch of Titus, etc.), they depicted soldiers armed with helmets, shields and swords on the sides of these famous arches. Nothing was simpler, for these were the arms with which their soldiers had just conquered the Germans, the Parthians, the Jews, etc.

When Louis XIV had the triumphal arch known as the Porte-Saint-Martin erected, the bas-relief on the north side depicted French soldiers attacking the walls of a city. They were armed with helmets and shields and arrayed with coats of arms. Well, I ask you, were the soldiers of Turenne and the Grand Condé who won Louis XIV's battles armed with shields? What good is a shield against a cannonball? Was Turenne killed by a javelin?

The Roman artists were *romantics*; they depicted what was true for their time and, consequently, what was affecting to their countrymen.

Louis XIV's sculptors were *classicists*. They placed figures which resembled nothing seen in their time on the bas-relief of their triumphal arch, so worthy of the lowly name of Porte-Saint-Martin.

I ask the young writers who have not yet had their work received at the Comédie-Française, and who leave this discussion having carefully considered the issues: is it possible to accuse the romantics of not being able to explain themselves? After such a clear, palpable example—easily verifiable if you go to see Mazurier perform[25]—is it possible to accuse them of not giving a clear and lucid idea of what is romantic and what is classical in the arts? I do not ask, Sir, that you agree with me, but I want you to be willing to admit, that, good or bad, you understand my argument.

From Letter No. 6. "The Romantic to the Classicist"

When you mention *prose tragedy on national themes* to those men, full of positive ideas and with an unlimited respect for a good box office, who are at the head of our theatre administrations, you do not find them possessed, as are the writers of verse, of an ill-disguised hatred concealed beneath a benign Academic smile. Far from it. The actors and producers sense that one day (but perhaps in twelve or fifteen years; therein resides the whole question for them) romanticism will make a fortune for some lucky Parisian theatre.

A financial manager of one of the theatres to whom I was speaking about *romanticism* and its future triumph, said to me himself: "I understand your idea. The *historical novel* has been mocked for twenty years in Paris. The Academy has offered learned proof of the ridiculousness of this genre. We all believed it. Then Walter Scott appeared, *Waverly* in hand. Ballantyne, his publisher, has just died a millionaire. The only barrier that exists between the box office and a good take," continued the producer, "is the attitude of the Colleges of Law and Medicine and the liberal newspapers who guide the students. It would take a rather rich producer to buy the literary opinion of the *Constitutionalist* and two or three smaller newspapers. Until then, which of our theatres would you advise to stage a romantic drama in five acts and in prose titled *The Death of the Duke of Guise at Blois* or *Joan of Arc and the English* or *Clovis and the Priests*? In what theatre would such a tragedy be able to continue past its third act? The editors of the influential papers, who, for the most part, have verse plays of their own currently in the repertoire or in rehearsal, permit melodramas à la d'Arlincourt,[26] but will never allow *melodrama written in a reasonable style*. If this were not the case, do you think we would not have tried Schiller's *William Tell*? The police would censor a quarter of the text and one of our adaptors would eliminate another fourth, but what remained would play a hundred performances

if it were permitted three. But that is what the editors of the liberal papers
will never allow, and consequently that is the attitude of the School of
Law and Medicine."

"But, Sir, the large majority of young people in society have been
converted to romanticism by Cousin's eloquence. Everyone applauds the
solid theories of the *Globe*. . ."[27]

"Sir, your young society gentlemen don't go to the theatre to strike
the first blow. And in the theatre, as in politics, we despise philosophers
who do not strike the first blow."

This lively and frank conversation bothered me more than I admit;
more than all the Academy's wrath. The next day, I sent to the reading
rooms of the *rue* St. Jacques and the *rue* de l'Odéon and asked for a list
of the most circulated titles. Three or four copies of LaHarpe's *Course
in Literature*, not Molière or Racine, *Don Quixote*, etc., are worn out each
year by the law and medical students. Such is the mania for judging
profoundly rooted in the national character, so much does our quavering
vanity need ready-made ideas to carry into conversation.

If Professor Cousin were still offering his course, his seductive eloquence and his unlimited influence on the young would succeed in con-
verting the students of the Colleges of Law and Medicine. These young
people would take pride in parroting phrases other than those of
LaHarpe. But Cousin speaks too well ever to be allowed to continue to
speak.

As for the editors of the *Constitutional* and the fashionable newspapers,
very strong arguments would be needed in order to hope for their
change. Having success, for the most part, at their disposal, these gentlemen will always have the lucrative idea of writing good plays themselves
in the conventional genre, which is also the most rapidly written. Or, at
least, they will ally themselves with its authors.

It is therefore useful for several modest writers, who do not see in
themselves the talent necessary to create a tragedy, to devote a week or
two each year to publish a literary pamphlet destined to furnish the
young people of France with *ready-made* phrases.

If I were lucky enough to find a few felicitous phrases, worthy of
quotation, perhaps our so-independent young people would finally understand what *dramatic pleasure* is. It is a pleasure which you must seek
in the theatre, not the epic pleasure of hearing the recitation of beautiful
sonorous verse which, as Mr. Duviquet has said, "one knows by heart in
advance."[28]*

Unbeknownst to the world, romanticism has made immense progress
in a year. Noble souls, despairing of politics since the last election, have
thrown themselves into literature. They have brought reason to literature
to the consternation of men of letters.

The enemies of prose tragedy on national themes or of romanticism (for, like Auger,[29] *I have spoken only of theatre*) can be divided into the following four types:

1. The aged *classicist* rhetoricians, former rivals and colleagues of the LaHarpes, the Geoffroys, the Auberts;

2. The members of the French Academy, who, because of the splendor of their title, believe themselves obliged to present themselves as the worthy successors of those angry, impotent men who, in the past, criticized *The Cid*;

3. The authors who make money writing tragedy in verse and those who, in spite of hisses, obtain pensions through their tragedies.

The happiest of these poets, those whom the public applauds, being simultaneously liberal journalists, dispose of the fate of premières. They will never suffer the appearance of works more interesting than their own;

4. The least redoubtable enemies of prose tragedy on national themes (such as *Charles VII and the English*, *The Jacques Bonhommes*, *Bouchard and the Monks of Saint-Denis*, and *Charles IX*) is the clique of "Good Writing." Although powerful enemies of prose in their position as fabricators of verse for the use of the Hôtel de Rambouillet—and especially detesting a simple, correct prose without ambition, modeled on Voltaire—they cannot, without contradicting themselves, be in opposition to the appearance of a tragedy which draws its principal effects from the violent passions and terrifying customs of the Middle Ages. . . .

. . . . . .

Note to Letter No. 8. "The Romantic to the Classicist"

1. There should never be any combats on stage, nor any executions. Such things are epic, not dramatic. In the nineteenth century the spectator's heart is repulsed by the horrible. And when, in Shakespeare, an executioner is seen advancing to burn out the eyes of children, instead of arousing terror, there is laughter at the red-tipped broomsticks which represent hot iron rods.

2. The more ideas and incidents are romantic (drawn from current needs) the more necessary it is to respect language, *which is by nature conventional*, in expression, as in words. One should try to write like Pascal, Voltaire, and La Bruyère. The demands and exigencies of the pedants will appear as ridiculous in fifty years as Voiture and Balzac appear today.[30] See the Preface to the *History of the Dukes of Burgundy*.[31]

3. The passionate interest with which one follows the emotions of a character constitute *tragedy*: the simple curiosity which allows our attention to focus on a hundred diverse details is *comedy*. The interest inspired by Julie d'Etanges is tragic.[32] Shakespeare's *Coriolanus* belongs to the

world of comedy. The mixing of these two interests seems to me to be very difficult.

4. Unless one is trying to depict the successive changes wrought by time in the character of a man, one may find that in order to please in 1825, it is not necessary for the action of a tragedy to last several years. Besides, each poet will experiment. After these experiments, it is possible that a year will be found to be the appropriate median length for a tragedy. If the tragedy is extended much longer than that, the hero at the end would not be the man he was at the beginning. The Napoleon dressed in imperial robes in 1804 was no longer the young general of 1796 who wore the grey overcoat in which he is remembered by posterity.

5. We must steal the *art* from Shakespeare, understanding that this young wool-worker earned 50,000 francs per year stirring up the English of the year 1600, in whose hearts was fermenting all the black and empty horrors they saw in the Bible, the source of their Puritanism. A naïve and somewhat simple faith, an absolute devotion, a certain difficulty in being moved by and understanding trivial incidents—but in return, a great emotional constancy and a great fear of hell—separates the English of 1600 from the French of 1825. It is, however, the latter who must be pleased. These cultivated, violent, impressionable beings are always on guard, always the prey of a fleeting emotion, always incapable of a profound sentiment. They believe in nothing but fashion and simulate all convictions, not by reasoned hypocrisy, like the *cant* of the English upper classes, but only to play their role well in the eyes of their neighbors.

Major Bridgeworth in *Peveril of the Peak*,[33] whose father had seen Shakespeare, acts with a somber and morose sincerity, according to absurd principles. Our notions of morality are very highly developed but, on the contrary, one no longer finds unlimited self-sacrifice except in the speeches published in the *Monitor*. A Parisian only respects the opinion of everyday society, his devotion is limited to his mahogany furniture. In order to create romantic dramas (adapted to the needs of the epoch) it is necessary to deviate a great deal from Shakespeare's method and, for example, not fall into *tirades* with a people who grasp everything wonderfully well merely by nuance. It was necessary to explain things at length and through strong images to the English of 1600.

6. After having taken the *art* from Shakespeare, we should look to Grégoire de Tours, Froissart, Livy, the Bible, and the modern Hellenists for the subjects of tragedy. What subject is more beautiful or touching than the death of Jesus? Why were the manuscripts of Sophocles and Homer not discovered until the year 1600, after the Renaissance of the century of Pope Leo X?

Madame de Hausset, Saint-Simon, Gourville, Dangeau, Bézenval, the Congresses, the Fanar of Constantinople, the histories of the conclaves assembled by Gregorio Leti—will provide a hundred subjects for comedy.

7. We are told that *poetry is the ideal beauty of expression*. Given an idea, poetry is the *most beautiful* way of rendering it, the way to give it the most effect.

YES, for satire, for epigram, for satirical comedy, for epic poetry, for mythological tragedy like *Phaedra*, *Iphigenia*, etc.

NO, when it is a matter of that sort of tragedy which draws its effects from the exact representation of the movements of the soul and from the incidents of modern life. The idea or feeling *above all* must be clearly stated in drama; it is the opposite in the epic poem. "The table's full" cries Macbeth, trembling with horror at the sight of Banquo's ghost—a man he had killed but an hour earlier—taking the place at the royal board reserved for him, the King, Macbeth. What poetry, what metre, could add to the beauty of such a phrase?

It is a cry from the heart, and the cry from the heart does not admit inversion. Do we admire "Let's be friends, Cinna" or Hermione's asking of Pyrrhus "Who told you to do it?" because they are part of an alexandrine?

Note that exactly those words, and not others, are needed. When the length of the verse line does not admit the exact word used by a passionate man, what do our academic poets do? They betray the passion for the poetry. Few men, especially eighteen-year-olds, know the passions well enough to cry out: "You are neglecting the correct word. The word you are using is a cold synonym," especially when the most idiotic person in the audience knows very well what constitutes pretty verse. He knows even better which word is from the *noble language* (for in a monarchy all language is directed toward it) and which is not.

At this point, refinement in the French language has gone well beyond the natural: a king, arriving at his enemy's house at night, says "What time is it?" to his companion. Well, then! The author of *The Cid of Andalusia*[34] dared not write this response: "Sire, it is midnight." This daring author was courageous enough to compose the following lines:

> The tower of Saint-Marcos, near this residence,
> Has, as you were passing, sounded the twelfth hour.

I will develop later the theory which is here presented in the following simple statement: it is characteristic for poetry to domesticate the reasons for feeling one of nature's beauties through the use of ellipses, inversions, ellisions, etc., etc.—the brilliant privileges of poetry. But in drama the effect of what we hear pronounced in a scene is dependent on the preceding scenes. For example: "Do you recognize Rutilius' handwriting?"[35] Lord Byron approved of this distinction. The character is diminished to nothing more than a rhetorician *whom I mistrust* through my own limited experience of life if he seeks to add force to what he says by using poetic expression.

The first condition of drama is that the action occurs in a room from which one of the walls has been removed by the magic wand of Melpomene and replaced by the audience. In a moment of peril, what courtier would not reply clearly to his king who asks "What time is it?" From the moment there is an apparent concession to the audience there are no longer dramatic characters. I can see only rhapsodists reciting a more or less beautiful epic poem. In French the domain of *rhythm* or of verse begins only when inversion is allowed.

This note would become a volume if I were to try to answer all the absurdities ascribed each morning to the romantics by the pitiful versifiers, fearing for their position in the world. The classicists possess the theatres and all the literary posts underwritten by the government. Young men are not admitted to those positions which do become vacant except upon appointment by aged men *who work for the same party*. Fanaticism is a qualification. All the servile minds, all the petty ambitions of the professoriat, the Academy, the libraries, etc. *have a stake* in the publication each morning of classicist articles. And, unhappily, declamation is, in all the genres, the eloquence of that indifference which pretends to be a burning faith.

Moreover, it is fairly amusing that, at present, when literary reform is declared vanquished by all the newspapers, they believe themselves obliged however, to publish each morning some new *nonsense*, which, like *Lord Falstaff, a great judge in England*, amuses us for the rest of the day. Does not such conduct indicate the beginning of the end?

Notes

1. Stendhal uses *romanticisme* rather than the more common French form *romantisme*.

2. *The Sicilian Vespers* (1819), and *The Pariah* (1821), tragedies by Casimir Delavigne which were favorably received by the liberals. *The Maccabees* (1822), a tragedy by Alexandre Guiraud. *Regulus* (1822), a tragedy by Lucien Arnault. The first three plays were performed at the Odéon Theatre, which had reopened in 1819 and where innovation was more warmly received than at the Comédie-Française.

3. *Racine and Shakespeare* I was written in response to the hostile reception accorded a troupe of English actors in Paris in July 1822.

4. Dialogue reported by Ermès Visconti in the *Conciliatore*, Milan, 1818. [Stendhal's note.]

5. Madame de Staël.

6. Charles James Fox (1749–1806), a Whig orator sympathetic to the French Revolution. Richard Brinsley Sheridan (1751–1816) was a parliamentary orator, proprietor of Drury Lane Theatre, and author of *The Rivals* (1775), *The School for Scandal* (1777), and other plays.

7. Manlius, in Antoine de Lafosse's *Manlius Capitolanus*, was one of Talma's great roles.

8. In Racine, *Andromache*, act IV, scene 3.

9. Jean François de LaHarpe (1739–1803), playwright and critic during the late eighteenth century. His *Lycée, or Lectures on Ancient and Modern Literature* (1799–1804) was a popular source for neo-classical ideas during the Empire and Restoration.

10. *Agamemnon* (1797), *Clovis* (1801, performed 1820), *Isule and Orovese* (1802), and *Pinto* are tragedies by Népomucène Lemercier. *Cyrus* (1804), and *Tiberius* (published posthumously in 1819) are tragedies by Marie-Joseph Chénier.

11. Pierre Lebrun's *Mary Stuart*, adapted from Schiller, was produced at the Comédie-Française in 1820.

12. After the riots at the Porte-Saint-Martin Theatre in July and August 1822, the English troupe moved to a small theatre in Chantereine Street where they were able to perform through October.

13. See Metastasio's analysis of Greek theatre. [Stendhal's note.]
Metastasio's notes on Aristotle's *Poetics* were published in 1782.

14. Walter Scott's novels appeared in 1820 and 1822.

15. Guillaume Antoine Charles Pigault-Lebrun (1753–1835), comic playwright and popular novelist. Charles Nodier published *Trilby, A Scottish Tale* in 1822.

16. *The Death of Henry IV* (1806), by Gabriel Legouvé.

17. Everything can be said in English and Italian verse. Only alexandrine verse, conceived for a haughty court, contains all that is ridiculous. . . . I will add, as a digression, that the most passable tragedy now written is found in Italy. There is a charm and real love in the *Francesca da Rimini* of the unfortunate Pellico. It is the most Racinian of the plays I have seen. His *Eufemio di Messina* is very good. The *Carmagnola* and the *Adelchi* of Manzoni announce a great poet, if not a great tragic writer. We have produced nothing in thirty years in our comedy as true as the *Ajo nell'imbarazzo* by Count Giraud of Rome. [Stendhal's note.]

18. By Louis-Baptiste Picard (1769–1828), one of the most successful comic playwrights of the Empire and Restoration periods.

19. The first reference is to Corneille's *Cinna* (1640); the second to Etienne de Jouy's *Sylla* (1821).

20. Jean-Pons-Guillaume Viennet (1777–1868) was a prominent classicist.

21. Refer to the second volume of Froissart's *Chronicles*, published by Buchon, for the narrative of Edward III's siege of Calais and Eustache de Saint-Pierre's self-sacrifice. Immediately after this, read *The Siege of Calais*, a tragedy by de Belloy. If the Lord has given you the slightest sensitivity, you will passionately desire, like me, *national tragedy in prose*. If the *Pandora* had not spoiled this expression, I would say that it would be an eminently *French* genre, for no people has memoirs more piquant than ours from its *Middle Ages*. It is necessary only to imitate the *art* in Shakespeare, the manner of painting, not the subjects being painted. [Stendhal's note.]

22. In *The Whole Art of the Stage* (1657).

23. Anything ridiculous which goes unnoticed has no place in the arts. [Stendhal's note.]

24. The Associated Poets for Good Writing was founded in 1821 to combat political liberalism. It attracted the conservative young romantic poets. *Eloa* (1822), is a poem by Alfred de Vigny.

25. Mazurier was a dancer and lead comic at the Porte-Saint-Martin Theatre.

26. Charles-Victor Prévôt d'Arlincourt had a great success in 1821 with the spectacular and violent melodrama *The Hermit*.

27. Victor Cousin taught at the Sorbonne from 1815 to 1821. The newspaper *The Globe* was founded by the liberals in 1824.

28. In the *Debates*, 8 July 1818. [Stendhal's note.]

29. Louis-Simon Auger delivered a vehement attack on romanticism at the French Academy, 24 April 1824.

30. Vincent Voiture and Jean-Louis Guez de Balzac were minor writers in the first half of the seventeenth century.

31. By Prosper de Barante (1824).

32. In Rousseau's novel *La Nouvelle Héloise*.

33. By Walter Scott (1823).

34. A tragedy by Pierre Lebrun (1825).

35. This line was the climax of Talma's performance of the title role in Antoine de LaFosse's *Manlius Capitolanus*.

4

CHARLES-AUGUSTIN SAINTE-BEUVE

Charles-Augustin Sainte-Beuve (1801–1870) is one of the most important literary critics of the nineteenth century in France and one of the few men of letters in this period whose reputation is almost wholly founded on his critical writing. He is now remembered as the creator of the literary portrait (his first collection of portraits was published in 1832) and a major contributor to the development of the biographical method in criticism. In addition to the various collections of portraits (1839, 1844, 1846), his publications include the history Port-Royal *(1840–1842), and* Chateaubriand and his Literary Group during the Empire *(1860). In 1849 he began to provide Paris newspapers with a series of articles which have been collected as* Monday Chats *(15 volumes, 1851–1860) and* New Mondays *(13 volumes, 1863–1870). These collections and his early criticism, published posthumously in* First Mondays *(1874), provide a vivid portrait of the literary world in France during the July Monarchy and the Second Empire.*

Like so many Frenchmen, Sainte-Beuve proved to be a classicist at heart. But as a young critic for the Globe, *a liberal newspaper founded in 1824, he was dazzled and inspired by Victor Hugo and joined the romantic faction in 1827. He supported the cause of reform in literature through the battles of 1829 and 1830. His* Historical Portrait of French Poetry and Theatre of the 16th Century *(1828) helped introduce the French romantics to the work of the pre-classical French writers. Under Hugo's influence, Sainte-Beuve began to write poetry and published* The Life, Poetry and Thoughts of Joseph Delorme *(1829) and* Consolations *(1830). He published a novel,* Voluptuousness, *in 1834.*

Although Sainte-Beuve withdrew his support from the romantics early in the 1830s, his work for the Globe *provides a clear analysis of the state*

of the theatre in France during the Restoration and outlines the pressing
need for reform. The article that follows is one of Sainte-Beuve's first
published statements of allegiance to the romantic cause. It appeared in the
Globe, *5 July 1828. Alexandre Duval (1767–1842) was elected to the*
Academy in 1812. His comedy Charles II *opened at the Odéon Theatre,*
11 March 1828.

"Alexandre Duval of the French Academy: *Charles II, or the Labyrinth at Woodstock*" (1828)

A few months ago, Duval's *Charles II*, which had a kind of demi-success at the Odéon, was discussed in the *Globe*. The "Notice" which serves as its Preface, rather than the play, will be the subject of our discussion here. From the outset, the author does not dissimulate how much "courage" is needed, in times such as these, to dare express healthy ideas concerning the art of the drama. But, "taking up the quill, he was resigned to submit to the consequences of his temerity." And, although the neo-classical play which he has promised us "perhaps within a month" might be sacrificed to the fanaticism of the angry cabal, the truth must prevail. He is determined to proclaim it loudly. Listen to this:

Once there was a great lady who welcomed all comers to her salon. It was there that a Teutonic innovator preached, indoctrinating the young. The seed bore fruit. Beardless professors, sent forth from Madame de Staël's salon, have disseminated its doctrines. And, since the *Globe*'s appearance, the evil has been overwhelming. There you have, in a few words, the history of romanticism, according to M. Duval. Here follows its disastrous effects: "Since the young editors of a scholarly literary periodical exercise so much talent and wit in proving that all French writing is devoid of common sense and in proposing as models foreign writers who know only our theatre," the result is: (1) that "at present, everything aims at being original or bizarre"; that "probability and reason have been banished"; and that "by virtue of seeking the truth, one ends up with the trivial, which all too soon borders on the absurd"; (2) that "young people, led astray by the preachers of the new doctrines, no longer know which is the best road, the one their fathers followed or the one pointed out to them, limit themselves to collaborating on vaudevilles or to placing brief articles in the literary press while waiting for the solution to their dilemma"; and, notably, that one of them, through wit or know-how, has succeeded—cry scandal!—"in making his fortune and that of several theatres as well"; (3) finally, added to this miserable anarchy one finds "impudent plagiarism, tickets given to the claque," and "the purchasing of praise in the newspapers." But, from this sort of literary '93, allow yourself to be carried back mentally to the Golden Age before the Revolution! Oh, let us regret not having witnessed those days. And, if we have seen them, let us regret that we are not still living in them! But at this point the portraits become so flattering, the descriptions so gay, that we would fear doing them harm in retelling them. We hasten to pass the pen, or rather, the brush and lyre, to M. Duval:

On his graduation from college, where he had already acquired a taste for the theatre which he had studied, and full of admiration for the classical authors as well as for the masterpieces of Racine, Corneille, and Molière, a young man would be eager to compose a tragedy or a comedy in the traditional mold. After devoting several years to this work, and thanks to his former professors or a few college friends in high society, he would succeed in finding a patron. If the work possessed some merit, the author would give a reading at the home of an acknowledged connoisseur. If this reading was a success, the nobility and successful financiers vied for the honor of presenting the new work to their circles. After earning a reputation at these diverse gatherings, the play, having been heard by one of the leading actors of the Comédie-Française, would be received by the actor's colleagues. Once received by the theatre, the play became the subject of discussion in all the salons. The readings began again. The most eloquent passages, the most notable verses, were memorized. The play dominated conversation at dinner parties. The author was led about and lionized all over Paris. He suffered immortality in advance. He was pampered and praised like a new star. ("To pamper," "to praise like a star," note this in passing, you members of the Academy!) In the salons, the triumph could last for several years. But finally the author's fate would be sealed by the production, confirming or contradicting the amateur judgement.

If the play was not a success, its young author, too well known not to have made a few friends, would find a place in government or business as a recompense for his ill luck. And, if he was wise, he abandoned forever a career in which he could not make his fortune.

On the other hand, if the play was a success, its author took his place in society, from that moment on a fashionable man. Only one sort of occupation was suitable: he became the companion, or rather, the secretary of a nobleman. His life, always filled—rather more by duties of the world than the labors of literature—flowed by rapidly midst pleasures whose expenses were borne by the rich and the powerful. Light verse, a few couplets, some trivial pamphlets, two tragedies and some comedies in one, two, or three acts gently bore him to the Academy, where esteem and pensions awaited him.

There is something paradoxical and almost epigrammatic in this last phrase which could be misleading. But M. Duval has not intended any malice. To fully justify his intention, it would suffice to recall another passage, where, speaking of "that aura known as fame," he finds it "desirable, in effect, when it can lead to the only recompense a man of letters should want: the Academy."

When the Revolution came and disturbed these minor literary lives, instead of readings in the salons, one had "Sunday luncheons." For at least fifteen years, at these luncheons, the literary guests exchanged confidences "between the fruit and the cheese." At these luncheons, "one told one's friends the subject and plan of one's work before a single line of it was written. No sooner had the first acts been scribbled down than a reading was given." Moreover, there was no fear of any abuse of confidence; there was no larceny; plagiarism had not been invented.

M. Duval's "Notice" is followed by "An Account of a Trip Through the Netherlands and Part of Germany." The aim is to show that the German theatre is largely made up of translations from the French and that the few original works seen there are mediocre or absurd. Through this he believes he has greatly compromised his adversaries. But he too easily forgets that we ourselves have never praised the current foreign theatre. And, if we have proposed Shakespeare, Goethe, and Schiller, not for imitation, but for admiration, and reflection to our poets, we were the first to indicate, at the time of the arrival of the English actors,[1] this mania for exotic imports, leaden travesties of vaudevilles, which seem to give the academician subject for triumph. In passing, M. Duval does not spare us souvenirs and eulogies of the inhabitants who gave him an agreeable welcome. We will not fault him for this chatter, however unimportant it may seem to the public; from it one can conclude that this lowly world is still tolerable for a man possessing some talent and a reputation, although, unhappily, the time of the "Sunday luncheons" has passed. The conversation concerning the unities, in which the author engages with a lady distinguished by her wit and advocacy of the new ideas, will further prove that one can argue courteously and rail without offending. We owe M. Duval the justice of acknowledging that his polemic never oversteps the limits of polite opposition. His tone is tinged with sadness rather than anger. If he takes exception to and condemns certain doctrines, he absolves individuals. We would simply wish him to be slightly more aware of the effective and quiet power of the truth in a "fad" he indulgently attributes to certain pretentious talents.

It would be both lengthy and tedious to re-establish here our own ideas, in their proper terms, so often expressed, yet so poorly comprehended. It is both simpler and more useful to take up in turn the question dealt with by M. Duval, and, after having determined the present state of drama in France, to predict its future—to guess at its failure or triumph—in order to indicate possible remedies and resources. Although indirect, the refutation will lose none of its impact.

We will start with an incontrovertible fact, and which, judged many ways, interpreted favorably or unfavorably, at least is self-evident. There is no question that the complete decadence of the Comédie-Française can no longer be denied. Classical tragedy, especially, has fallen into disrepute. The complete boredom on the stage is not only the result of so many empty exaggerations now being written, or even of Voltaire's tragedies, so-called masterpieces, but also of the truly beautiful and polished works of Racine. This can be deplored with more or less bitterness, but it cannot be overlooked. At the moment, I am not seeking to lay the blame with the authors, the actors, or the audience. There may be no fault on any side. One side may be guilty only of having grown old and the other of being young.

However that may be, if you could still overlook, a few years ago, the general symptoms of boredom and hostility—seeing in them a temporary attack of anglo- or germano-philia to which you responded in good faith "to the cabal"—it is no longer possible to harbor any doubts about the pronounced antipathy, or at least the profound indifference, of the public toward our noblest dramatic genre. Box office receipts speak more plainly than arguments. A writer of tragedies, who in 1821 made four or five thousand francs profit from his plays, has seen this source of income successively diminish and dry up. At present, to obtain what looks like a success, he is reduced to distributing complimentary tickets to the first performances, the cost of which will not be repaid to him by the public. For, we should note in passing, the abuse of the "claque," the scandal of complimentary tickets—against which M. Duval employs neither enough eloquence nor tears—is only a miserable expedient of the old school, now at the end of its tether: as its distress increases, it must recruit for pay the general portion of its army. But people are not fooled, and demi-successes are tantamount to failures. For ten years now, how many reputations thus begun, have we not seen pass by, one by one, and die? Moving forward, the public has left behind what it at first supported. The author writes no worse than at his debut, but more is demanded of him. Had the *Sicilian Vespers* premiered this year it might have met with the same sort of success as *Princess Aurelia*.[2] It remains, then, clearly proven that, for better or worse, the case for dramatic traditions is singularly compromised and that the hope for their restoration grows less every day. Also, certain clever classicists, being skillful tightrope walkers, have decided to fortify themselves for battle with this fact: they stress the current decadence in order to deny any eventual renewal, and no longer daring to count on success, they want there to be no winners. According to them, an aged society like ours, and one so completely addicted to political discussion, can and must do without a great and serious theatre. The trivialities of the Gymnase are sufficient each evening to dissipate the headaches of our statesmen. And as for the masses, less refined and more avid for emotional release, do they not have *The Two Convicts* and *The Gambler*?[3] These wittily superficial arguments would be favorably received by a few members of the younger generation whose thoughts are dominated by philosophical and political attitudes and who are all too disposed to sell their literary opinions cheaply: we will answer them with some particulars.

If the renewal of the theatre in terms of ideas called "romantic" is not practical in France, it must be attributed to one or several of four following factors: first, our social climate; second, public taste; third, the lack of authors; fourth, theatre management.

But first, the social climate, that is to say the freedom of the press and the two houses of government, far from being an obstacle, a distraction in opposition to great dramatic compositions, must be seen as an essential condition, a powerful inspiration for them. If we did not have the two chambers, and if we were still living under a monarchy like that of Louis XIV or Louis XV, what more would we require, I ask you, than the admirable emotional analyses of Racine, or the philosophic dramas of Voltaire? Even after the Revolution, during the ten years of the Empire, wasn't the very absence of freedom enough to revive, in the context of Austerlitz and Jena, the classical tragedy of the monarchy which, excepting Corneille, was so foreign and incongruous? Had not several years of freedom prior to the Empire been enough to engender *Pinto*?[4]

The constitution and the theatre stand. It is precisely because plays are no longer written for Madame de Pompadour or for the schoolgirls at St. Cyr, but for statesmen, philosophers, young people, and the masses that we demand reform and that it cannot fail to take place. The constitution calls for it, rather than resisting it.

Up to the present, it is true that politics, whose influence had been felt everywhere, has curbed art. It is true that politics, in the new order, has not made as broad, comfortable, and splendid a place for art as it deserves and will have. But, that is because the new order itself was in question until now. All social forces were joined in the struggle which would determine the future. Now that the victory seems clear and security is imminent, politics and art will be discrete, without being isolated. Free from the vortex, art, still youthful, yet ripe with experience, will pursue her peaceful work in solitude. This work will be animated with all life's colors and all mankind's passions. This product of leisure and meditation will doubtless encompass and intermingle in thousands of charming or sublime effects the true and the ideal, reason and fantasy, the observation of men and the poet's dreams. At its appearance in the real world and exposed to the scrutiny of all, this work will enchant and garner much praise. The most serious, philosophic, learned, and historical minds will find diversion in the contemplation of art, for the beautiful is never fatiguing. Politicians, especially, though seeking only pleasure in art, will find in it more than one luminous insight which, transplanted and transformed without their realizing it, will not remain sterile. It will affect the understanding of history and the development of eloquence. In a word, the tribunal and the stage, rivals rather than enemies, will be able to sound together and sometimes to harmonize.

Second, public taste impels and marvelously prepares the way for this future of drama we have pleasantly imagined. Although there is still much progress to be made in terms of public taste, the public is both timid and bold. It is content with and fearful of, very few things. But, up until now, it expresses itself through its dislikes much more than in its predilections. Nevertheless, you must admit that its judgement is sound and that it encourages the new as constantly as it repulses the exhausted remains of the past. It would suffice to invoke the success of a number of books in which the drama—banished from the stage—has found refuge. In these books the public gratefully welcomes its long-anticipated image. M. Scribe's vogue, far from being the scandal M. Duval sees in it, is a new proof for us of this good sense and good taste on which we must rely. We have dared admit that in the secondary genre of comedy-vaudeville, there is at present more novelty and more pointed truth than in the cold and boring comedies of "character" or in the trivial, sentimental or domestic compositions. We have dared whisper it at first, then have loudly proclaimed it, and in consequence have not believed it to be condescending to leave the Comédie-Française for the boulevard theatre. This is not to say that Scribe, despite his wit and talent, creates a complete illusion or that he seems to be a modern Shakespeare: we know what is of value in his refined and sparkling wit; but while hoping for better, we profit from and amuse ourselves with what there is. The minor work before the masterpiece. There is no doubt that the great play will appear. The question is when and the answer is that we don't know. But the public is patient because it is young. The public seems to say to the Director of Fine Arts: "Sir, I will wait." It has been said that the Abbé de Bernis, while waiting, went to the cabaret; the nineteenth-century audience goes to the Gymnase.

Third, where are they to be found, these pontiffs of the temple, these writers of the future? That is truly a fine objection! To this point, time alone can provide an answer. But, although in such cases critics are not required to awaken genius with a stroke of their pens and exhibit it at a set hour—this is rather the business of genius itself and of the God who has engendered it—we would not be embarrassed to dare to look ahead and name a good number of the mainstays and ornaments of this new art. This is because the work has already ripened in the shade and because so much has been done to prepare the way. Thus, neither in the political constitution of the state, nor in public taste, nor in the talent of writers, is there anything contrary to the renewal of the theatre. On the contrary, everything contributes to this renewal. It will, then, take place, however much longer the administration may offer resistance through support of the monopoly and through censorship. In a future article, we will examine the influence of this latter fact, and consider whether even accepting it as necessary or not, there would be a means of correcting its negative effect.

Notes

1. A company of English actors began a successful season in Paris in September 1827.

2. Plays by Casimir Delavigne. *The Sicilian Vespers* was a great success in 1819; *Princess Aurelia* failed in 1828.

3. Melodramas; the former by Pierre-Frédéric-Adolphe Carmouche, Eugène Cantiran de Boirie, and Alphonse-André-Véran Poujol; the latter, *Thirty Years, or The Life of a Gambler*, by Victor Ducange.

4. A successful political drama by Népomucène Lemercier.

VICTOR HUGO

In 1824 the younger generation of French romantic poets began to group together to discuss and disseminate their literary theories. The periodical the French Muse *was established as a means of communicating their ideas. Once formed, the group began to look to Victor Hugo (1802–1885) as its leader and spokesman. By 1824 Hugo had published two collections of poetry,* Odes and Diverse Poetry *(1822) and* New Odes *(1824). His novel* Han of Iceland *appeared in 1823. The primacy of Hugo's position in the 1820s was confirmed by the publications which followed: two editions of the poems,* Odes and Ballads *(1826, 1828), and a collection of poems,* The Orientals *(1829); the novels,* Bug Jargal *(1826) and* The Last Day of a Condemned Man *(1829); and the unproduced verse drama,* Cromwell *(1827) which, with its Preface, constituted the major and most publicized statement of the romantic theory of drama.*

In 1829 Hugo wrote two verse dramas, Marion Delorme *and* Hernani; *the former was accepted for production at the Comédie-Française, but banned by the government censor. It was not produced until 1831 at the Porte-Saint-Martin Theatre. The production of* Hernani *at the Comédie-Française in February 1830 marks the end of the first phase in the history of the French romantic theatre. Its enormous success signaled the triumph of romanticism over classicism in France.*

Hugo's subsequent work helped him retain his position as the most important of the French romantic poets. His collections of verse appeared regularly until his death. Notable among them were Inner Voices *(1837),* Contemplations *(1856), and* The Legend of the Centuries *(1859). His novels* Notre Dame de Paris *(1831) and* Les Miserables *(1862) were great popular successes. For the theatre he wrote three prose dramas,*

Lucretia Borgia *(1833)*, Mary Tudor *(1833)*, *and* Angelo *(1835)*, *as well as three plays in verse,* The King Amuses Himself *(1832)*, Ruy Blas *(1838)*, *and* The Burgraves *(1834)*. Hernani *and* Ruy Blas *are the only poetic dramas from the French romantic period to remain consistently in the repertory until the present.*

Preface to *Cromwell* (1827)

The publisher Hetzel issued Cromwell *on 4 December 1827.*

The drama you are about to read has nothing to commend it to the attention or the goodwill of the public. It does not have the advantage of the government censor's veto, which would earn it the attention of political factions. Nor does it have the honor of having been officially rejected by an infallible reading committee which, from the start, would win for it the sympathy of men of taste.

It is offered for study, therefore, alone, poor and naked like the cripple of the Gospel: *solus, pauper, nudus.*

Nevertheless, it is not without hesitation that the author of this drama resolved to burden it with notes and a Preface. Ordinarily, such things are of little importance to readers. They are more concerned with a writer's talent than with his point of view; and, whether the work be good or bad, the ideas on which it is based or the mind in which it was conceived are of little import to the reader. One seldom visits the basement of a house after visiting its rooms, and, while one is eating the fruit of a tree one cares little about its roots.

On the other hand, notes and prefaces are sometimes a convenient way of adding to the weight of a book and, at least in appearance, of increasing the importance of a work. This is a tactic similar to that of the general who, to make his battlefront more imposing, puts everything, even his baggage-train, into the line. Then, while critics focus on the preface and scholars on the notes, it may be possible for the work itself to escape them, passing uninjured through the crossfire, like an army extricating itself from a dangerous position between skirmishes of outposts and rear guards.

These motives, however considerable they may be, are not those which influenced this author. This volume did not need to be *inflated*; it is already too thick. Furthermore, and the author does not know why it

occurs, his frank and naïve prefaces have always served rather to com-
promise him with the critics, rather than protect him from them. Far
from being strong and trusty protection, they have played him the nasty
trick, like the unusual uniform which draws attention on the battlefield
to the soldier wearing it, of attracting the fire to him and protecting him
from nothing.

Considerations of a different sort influenced this author. It seemed
to him that, if in fact, one hardly visits the basement of a house for
pleasure, one might still find it necessary to occasionally examine its
foundations. Therefore, he will expose himself once more, with a preface, to the wrath of literary critics. *Che sarà, sarà.* He has never given
much thought to the fortune of his works. He has little fear of the literary
attitude: "what will people say about it." In the discussion now raging,
in which are opposed the theatres and the schools, the public and the
academies, you will hear, perhaps not without some interest, the voice
of a solitary apprentice of nature and truth, who early in his career has
withdrawn from the literary world through love of letters, and who offers
sincerity for want of *good taste*, conviction for want of talent, study for
want of expertise.

He will limit himself, however, to general considerations about art
without in any way attempting to pave the way for his own works, without
pretending to write an indictment or a plea, for or against any individual.
The attack upon or defense of his work is less important to him than to
anybody else. Moreover, personal controversy is not at all to his taste.
It is always a piteous spectacle to see two egos crossing swords. He
protests, then, in advance against all interpretations of his ideas, all
applications of his words, saying with the Spanish fabulist:

> *Quien haga aplicaciones*
> *Con su pan se lo coma.*[1]

In truth, several of the leading champions of "sound literary doctrine"
have done him the honor of casting down the gauntlet to him, even in
his profound obscurity—to him, a simple and uninfluential observer of
this curious battle. He will not have the presumption to take up the
challenge. There will be found in the following pages the observations
with which he might oppose them: his slingshot and his stone. But others,
if they wish, may hurl them at the head of the *classical* Goliaths.

This said, let us proceed.

Let us begin with this fact: the same type of civilization, or, to use a
more precise, albeit more general expression, the same society has not
always existed. The human species as a whole has grown, developed,
and matured like each and every one of us. It has been a child; it has
been a man; we are now witnessing its impressive old age. Before that
epoch called "ancient" by modern society, another epoch existed which

the ancients called "legendary" and which ought more exactly to be called "primitive." We have had, then, three great successive divisions in civilization, from its origins to the present. Now, as poetry is always superimposed on society, we propose to try to demonstrate from the form of its society, what the character of its poetry must have been in those three great ages of the world: the primitive period, the ancient period, and the modern period.

In the primitive period, when man awakens in a world which has just been created, poetry awakens with him. In the face of the marvellous things which astonish and intoxicate him, his first speech is a hymn. He is still so close to God that all his meditations are ecstatic, all his dreams are visions. His heart opens; he sings as he breathes. His lyre has only three strings: God, the soul, creation. But this threefold mystery envelops everything. The earth is still practically unpopulated. There are families, but not nations, patriarchs but not kings. Each race exists comfortably; there is no property, no law, no conflict, no war. Everything belongs to each person and to all people. Society is a community. Man is restricted in nothing. He leads that pastoral and nomadic life by which all civilizations begin, and which is so well suited to solitary contemplations, to fanciful revery. He offers no resistance, he lets himself go. His thought, like his life, resembles a cloud which changes shape as it moves at the mercy of the prevailing wind. Such is the first man, such is the first poet. He is young, he is lyrical. Prayer is his sole religion, the ode his sole form of poetry.

This poem, this ode of the primitive period, is called *Genesis*.

Gradually, however, this adolescence of the world passes away. All spheres broaden; the family becomes a tribe, the tribe a nation. Each of these groups of men settles around a common center, and kingdoms appear. The social instinct replaces the nomadic instinct. The camp gives way to the city, the tent to the palace, the ark to the temple. The leaders of these nascent states are still shepherds, but shepherds of peoples; the pastoral staff has already assumed the shape of a scepter. Everything becomes stationary and fixed. Religion assumes a definite form; prayer is governed by rites; dogma defines the limits of worship. Thus the priest and the king share the paternity of the people; thus patriarchy is replaced with theocracy.

Meanwhile, nations are beginning to be packed too closely on the earth's surface. They irritate and disturb one another, and war, the collision of empires, ensues.[2]* They overflow, one upon the other, and voyages, the migration of nations, result.[3]* Poetry reflects these momentous events; from ideas it passes to things. It sings of ages, of nations, of empires. It becomes epic, it gives birth to Homer.

Homer, in effect, dominates ancient society. In that society, everything is simple, everything is epic. Poetry is religion, religion is law. The virginity of the first age has been succeeded by the chastity of the second. A sort of solemn gravity is visible everywhere, in domestic customs as in public matters. The nations have preserved nothing of their wandering life save respect for the foreigner and the traveller. The family has a homeland; everything is related to it; there is a cult of the hearth; a cult of the tomb.

We repeat, such civilization can find its expression only in the epic. The epic will assume various forms, but it will never lose its character. Pindar is more sacerdotal than patriarchal, more epic than lyric. If the chroniclers, the necessary contemporaries of the world's second age, set about gathering traditions and begin to think in terms of centuries, they are working in vain; chronology cannot drive out poetry; history remains epic. Herodotus is a Homer.

But it is especially in ancient tragedy that the epic is ever-present. It appears on the Greek stage without losing anything of its gigantic, immeasurable proportions. Its characters are still heroes, demigods, gods; its means are dreams, oracles, destiny; its scenes are catalogues, funerals, battles. What the rhapsodists formerly sang, the actors declaim—that is the sole difference.

There is more. When all the actions and all the spectacle of the epic poem have passed on the stage, what remains is taken up by the chorus. The chorus comments on the tragedy, encourages the hero, summons and dismisses daylight, rejoices, laments, on occasion furnishes the scenery, explains the moral sense of the subject, flatters the audience. Now what is the chorus, this strange character placed between the spectacle and the spectator, if not the poet completing his epic poem?

The theatre of the ancients is, like their drama, grandiose, pontifical, epic. It can hold 30,000 spectators; the plays are staged in the open air, in broad daylight; the performances last all day. The actors' voices are amplified, their features are masked, their height increased; they are made gigantic, like their roles. The stage is immense. It can represent simultaneously the interior and exterior of a temple, a palace, a military camp, a city. Vast spectacles are unfolded on it. There is—and we cite from memory—Prometheus on his mountain, there is Antigone, atop a tower, seeking her brother Polyneices in the enemy camp (*The Phoenician Women*); there is Evadne throwing herself from a cliff into the flames where the body of Capaneus burns (*The Suppliant Women* of Euripides); there is a ship one sees entering port from which descend fifty princesses and their retinues (Aeschylus' *The Suppliants*). Architecture, poetry, everything assumes a monumental character. In all antiquity there is nothing more solemn or majestic. Its religion and its history are joined on the stage. Its first actors are priests; its scenic performances are religious ceremonies, national festivals.

A final observation will complete our demonstration of the epic character of this period. In the subjects it treats, no less than in the forms it adopts, tragedy simply repeats the epic. All the ancient tragic writers derive their plots from Homer. The same stories, the same catastrophes, the same heroes—all are drawn from the Homeric stream. The *Iliad* and the *Odyssey* are always in evidence. Greek tragedy circles Troy, like Achilles drawing Hector behind him.

But the age of epic poetry draws to a close. Like the society it represents, this form of poetry feeds on itself, and is exhausted. Rome copies Greece, Virgil imitates Homer, and in order to come to a seemly end, epic poetry expires in this last incarnation.

It was time. Another era is about to begin for the world and for poetry.

A spiritual religion, supplanting the materialism and superficiality of paganism, makes its way into the heart of ancient society, kills it, and plants the germ of modern civilization in the cadaver of a decrepit civilization. This religion is complete because it is true; morality is firmly placed between its dogma and its ritual. And first, as a fundamental truth, it teaches man that he has two lives to live, one transitory, the other immortal; one on earth, the other in heaven. It shows him his duality, like his destiny, that he possesses an animal nature and an intelligence, a body and a soul; in short, that he is the point of an intersection, the common link of the two chains which encompass all creation, of the chain of material beings and the chain of incorporeal beings; the first starting from the rock to arrive at man, the second starting from man to end at God.

It is possible that a certain portion of these truths had been suspected by certain wise men of antiquity, but their full, luminous and grand revelation dates from the Gospels. Pagan philosophy groped in darkness, clinging to falsehoods as to truths in its haphazard journey. Some of its philosophers occasionally cast a feeble light on one facet of a subject only to place the rest of it in a deeper shadow. Hence all the phantoms created by ancient philosophy. Nothing but divine wisdom was able to substitute a vast and consistent light for all the flickering lights of human wisdom. Pythagoras, Epicurus, Socrates, Plato are torches; Christ is the light of day.

Moreover, nothing is more materialistic than ancient theology. Far from proposing, as does Christianity, to separate the spirit from the body, it gives a form and feature to everything, even to essences, even to ideas. In it everything is visible, palpable, in the flesh. Its gods need a cloud to be hidden from view. They eat, drink, and sleep. When wounded, they bleed; when crippled, they limp for eternity. That religion has both gods and demigods. Its thunderbolts are forged on an anvil from three sheets of twisted rain ("*tres imbris torti radios*").[4] Its Jupiter suspends the world from a golden chain; its sun drives a four-horse chariot; its Hell is a precipice, the brink of which is geographically determined on the globe; its Heaven is a mountain.

Thus paganism, which molded all of its creations from the same clay, minimizes divinity and magnifies man. The heroes of Homer are almost indistinguishable from his gods. Ajax defies Jupiter. Achilles is the equal of Mars. Christianity, on the contrary, as we have just seen, clearly distinguishes spirit from matter. It places an abyss between man and God.

In order to omit nothing from the sketch which we have begun, we will note that, at that epoch, with the advent of Christianity and by means of it, a sentiment unknown to the ancients, but singularly developed in the moderns, entered into the social consciousness, a sentiment which is more than seriousness, but less than sadness: melancholy. And, in truth, could not the human heart, hitherto untouched by hierarchal and sacerdotal religions, awaken and feel some unexpected faculty come to life, inspired by a religion that is human because it is divine, a religion that makes of the poor man's prayer, the wealth of the rich, a religion of equality, liberty, and charity? Might it not see everything in a new light, since the Gospel had revealed the soul to it through the senses, eternity behind life?

And, at that very moment, the world was undergoing so great a revolution that it was impossible for there not to be a change in human consciousness. Hitherto the catastrophes of empires had rarely touched the hearts of the people; it was kings who fell; kingdoms which vanished, nothing more. The lightning struck only in high places, and, as we have already indicated, events seemed to unfold with all the solemnity of epic poetry. In ancient society, the individual was of so lowly a position that to be affected, adversity had to descend to the level of his immediate family. The result was that he knew little of misfortune outside of domestic troubles. It was almost unheard of for the wider ills of the state to affect his life. But as soon as Christian society became firmly established, the ancient world was thrown into confusion. Everything was uprooted. Events destined to destroy ancient Europe and construct a new Europe tumbled together in a ceaseless rush, pushing nations about pell-mell, casting some into light, others into darkness. The earth was filled with such an uproar that it was impossible for something of the tumult not to be perceived in the hearts of the people. It was more than an echo, it was a repercussion. Man, withdrawing into himself in the face of these great vicissitudes, began to take pity on mankind, to reflect on the bitter ironies of life. From this feeling, which had been despair to the heartless Cato, Christianity fashioned melancholy.

At the same time, the spirit of inquiry and curiosity was born. The great catastrophes were also great spectacles, striking reversals. The North was invading the South; the Roman world was changing shape; an entire world was in the last convulsions of its death agony. As soon as that world was dead, swarms of rhetoricians, grammarians and sophists, like flies, enveloped its immense cadaver. They could be seen hovering and buzzing in the putrefaction. They competed with one another in examining, commenting, and disputing. Each limb, each muscle, each fibre of the gigantic prostrate body was scrutinized from every viewpoint. Surely it must have been a pleasure for these anatomists of thought to be able, from the start, to make experiments on a grand scale; to have a dead society to dissect as their first *subject*.

Thus, we see the genius of melancholy and of meditation, the demons of analysis and controversy, appear at the same time and, as it were, hand in hand. At one end of this transitional period stands Longinus, at the other Augustine. We must, however, refrain from casting a disdainful eye on this epoch when seeds were sown which have since borne fruit; an epoch whose humblest writers—if we may be allowed a vulgar, but expressive phrase—provided manure for the harvest that was to follow. The Middle Ages were grafted onto the declining empire.

There is, then, a new religion and a new society. From this dual foundation a new poetry inevitably will arise. Previously—we beg your pardon for setting forth a result that the reader himself must have already foreseen in what we stated above—previously, and in a manner similar to that of ancient polytheism and philosophy, the purely epic muse of the ancients had studied nature in only one aspect, mercilessly eliminating everything in the world subject to imitation by art which did not conform to a certain conception of beauty. This conception of beauty was magnificent at first, but, as always happens when something is systematized, in later times became false, trivial, and conventional. Christianity leads poetry to truth. Like it, the modern muse will view things from a higher and broader vantage point. She will see that everything in creation is not humanly *beautiful*, that the ugly exists beside the beautiful, deformity beside gracefulness, the grotesque on the reverse side of the sublime, evil with good, light with shadow. She will ask herself if the narrow and relative reason of the artist should prevail over the infinite, absolute reason of the Creator; if it is for man to correct God; if a mutilated nature will not seem all the more beautiful; if art has the right to duplicate, so to speak, man, life, creation; if things will function better with their muscle and vigor removed; finally, if being incomplete is a function of achieving harmony. That is when, with its gaze fixed on events, both risible and awesome, and under the influence of the spirit of Christian melancholy and philosophical criticism which we described above, poetry will take a giant step, a step which, like the trembling of an earthquake, will alter the whole face of the intellectual world. It will begin to act as nature does, mixing, but not confounding in its creations shadow and light, the grotesque and the sublime, in other words, body and soul, beast and reason. For religion and poetry have always the same starting point. All things are connected.

Thus we see a principle unknown to the ancients, a new subject introduced into poetry. And, as an additional element in a being modifies the entire being, a new form of art evolves. That subject is the grotesque; its form is comedy.

And we ask leave to stress this point; for we have just indicated the characteristic feature, the fundamental difference which, in our opinion, separates modern art from ancient art, present form from past form, or, to use the vaguer, but more acceptable terms, *romantic* literature from *classical* literature.

"Finally!" say those men who for some time now have *seen* where we were *heading*. "We have you now. You are caught in the act. Thus you allow the *ugly* as a type for imitation and the *grotesque* as an element of art![5]* What of the graces...what about good taste....Aren't you aware that art ought to correct nature? That it must be ennobled? That it is necessary to be *selective*? Have the ancients ever exhibited the ugly and the grotesque? Have they ever mixed comedy with tragedy? The example of the ancients, gentlemen! Consider Aristotle...and Boileau...and LaHarpe...my word!"[6]

These arguments are, doubtless, sound and, above all, extremely novel. But it is not our place to answer them. We are not constructing a system here—heaven preserve us from systems! We are stating a fact. We act as an historian not as a critic. Little matter whether this fact pleases or displeases; it is a fact—Let us resume, then, and attempt to illustrate that the fruitful union of the grotesque type with the sublime type produces the modern genius—so complex and varied in its forms, so inexhaustible in its creations, and in that, directly opposed to the uniform simplicity of the genius of the ancients. Let us demonstrate that this must be the point of departure to establish the real and radical difference between the two forms of literature.

This does not mean that comedy and the grotesque were completely unknown to the ancients. In fact, such a thing would be impossible. Nothing grows without roots; the germ of the second epoch is always present in the first. In the *Iliad* Thersites and Vulcan provide comedy, one to mortals, the other to gods. There is too much of nature and originality in Greek tragedy for it not to sometimes include the comic. For example, to cite only what immediately comes to mind, the scene between Menelaus and the palace attendant (*Helen*, Act I), and the scene of the Phrygian (*Orestes*, Act IV). Mermen, satyrs, cyclops are grotesques; sirens, furies, fates, harpies are grotesques. Polyphemus is a terrifying, Silenus a buffoonish, grotesque.

But one senses that this part of the art is still in its infancy. The epic, which in this period imposes its form on everything, the epic bears down upon it and stifles it. The grotesque of the ancients is timid and always seeking to hide itself. One senses that it is not on familiar ground because it is not in its natural surroundings. It is hidden as much as possible. Satyrs, mermen, and sirens are hardly deformed. The fates and the harpies are rather more hideous in their characters than in their features; the furies are beautiful and called "*eumenides*," that is, "kindly." There is a veil of grandeur or divinity over the other grotesques. Polyphemus is a giant; Midas is a king; Silenus is a god.

Thus comedy is almost imperceptible in the great epic ensemble of antiquity. What is Thespis' wagon compared with Olympian chariots? What are Aristophanes and Plautus beside the Homeric colossi, Aeschylus, Sophocles, and Euripides?[7]* Homer bears them along, as Hercules bore the pygmies, hidden in his lion skin.

In modern thought, however, the grotesque plays an important role. It is found everywhere; on the one hand, it produces the deformed and the horrible; on the other, the comic and buffoonish. It clothes religion with a thousand original superstitions, poetry with a thousand picturesque fancies. It is the grotesque which scatters freely in air, water, earth, and fire those myriads of intermediary creatures which we find again living in the popular traditions of the Middle Ages. It is the grotesque which sets in motion in the shadows the horrifying dance of the Witches' Sabbath, which gives Satan horns, goat's hooves, and bat's wings. It is the grotesque, always the grotesque, which places in the Christian Hell those hideous figures that the austere genius of Dante and Milton will evoke, or peoples Hell with those ridiculous figures which inspire the creations of Callot, the burlesque Michaelangelo. If it passes from the unreal world to the real world, it unfolds an inexhaustible supply of parodies of mankind. Its fantasies give birth to Scaramouches, Crispins, Harlequins—grimacing silhouettes of men, types completely unknown to serious-minded antiquity, though they originated in classical Italy. It is the grotesque, finally, which causes Sganarelle to dance about Don Juan, Mephistopheles to slink after Faust, coloring the same play alternately with the imagination of the South and the North.[8]*

And how free and frank is its behavior! How boldly it throws into relief all those strange forms that earlier periods in timidity had wrapped in swaddling. Ancient poetry, obliged to provide the lame Vulcan with companions, attempted to disguise deformity so to speak, by developing it on a colossal scale. The modern genius retains this myth of supernatural blacksmiths, but gives it a completely different character which renders it more striking. Giants are changed into dwarfs, cyclopes are turned into gnomes. With similar originality, it replaces the rather banal Lernaean hydra with all the local dragons of our legends—the gargoyle of Rouen, the *gra-ouilli* of Metz, the *chair sallée* of Troyes, the *drée* of Montlhéry, the *tarasque* of Tarascon—monsters of diverse form, given additional character by their baroque names. All these creations draw from their own nature the energetic and significant coloring which antiquity often studiously avoided. Certainly the Greek Eumenides are much less horrible, and consequently, less true, than the witches of *Macbeth*. Pluto is not the Devil.

In our opinion, a very novel book could be written on the place of the grotesque in art. One could demonstrate what powerful effects the moderns obtain from this fruitful type, although it is still ruthlessly condemned by narrow-minded critics in our day. Our subject may soon cause us to note in passing some of the features of this vast picture. We will simply say here that when placed beside the sublime, as a means of contrast, the grotesque, in our opinion, is the richest source that we can open to art. Rubens doubtless understood this when he placed some hideous figure like a court dwarf amid his displays of royal pomp, coronations, and dazzling ceremonials. The universal beauty which the ancients solemnly imparted to everything was not without monotony. The same effect, constantly repeated, can be fatiguing in the end. It is difficult to develop contrast when sublime effect follows sublime effect. Everything can benefit from repose, even the beautiful. On the other hand, the grotesque seems to be a stopping point, a point for comparison, a point of departure, from which one approaches the beautiful with a fresher and keener perception. The salamander sets off the water-nymph; the gnome heightens the effect of the sylph.

And it would be correct to say that contact with the deformed has endowed modern sublimity with something more pure, more grand, more sublime, in short, than the beauty of the ancients; and that is as it should be. When art is consistent in itself, it more surely draws each element to its goal. If the Homeric Elysium is far from possessing the ethereal charm and angelic sweetness of Milton's paradise, it is because beneath Eden lies a hell far more terrible than the Tartarus of the pagans. Do you believe that Francesca da Rimini and Beatrice would be as enchanting in a poet who would not imprison us in the Tower of Hunger and compel us to share in Ugolino's revolting meal? Dante would have less charm, if he had less vigor. Do the fleshy naiads, the robust mermen, the wanton zephyrs, have the diaphanous sinuousity of our water-nymphs and sylphs? Is it not because the modern imagination can picture vampires, ogres, *aulnes*, snake-charmers, ghouls, *brucolaques*, and *espioles* hideously prowling about cemeteries, that it can give its fairies that incorporeal form, that essential purity, so rarely found in pagan nymphs? The antique Venus is beautiful, admirable, no doubt, but what has imparted that slender, vaporous, other-worldly elegance to the figures of Jean Goujon? What has given them that hitherto unfamiliar lifelike character and grandeur, if not the proximity of the rough and powerful sculptures of the Middle Ages?

If the thread of our argument has not been broken for the reader by these necessary digressions—which could be rendered in much greater detail—he has doubtless understood how powerfully the grotesque—that germ of comedy fostered by the modern muse—must have sprouted and grown since its transplanting in a more propitious soil than that of paganism and epic poetry. In effect, in the new poetry, while the sublime represents the soul as it is, purified by Christian morality, the grotesque will play the role of the animal in man. The former type, free from the admixture of all impurities, will have as its domain all that is charming, graceful, and beautiful; it must one day be able to create Juliet, Desdemona, Ophelia. The latter type assumes all that is ridiculous, infirm, and ugly. In this partition of mankind and creation, to the latter will fall passions, vices, and crimes; it will be lustful, servile, gluttonous, miserly, perfidious, mischievous, and hypocritical. It will be, in turn, Iago, Tartuffe, Basile; Harpagon, Polonius, Bartholo; Falstaff, Scapin, Figaro.[9] The beautiful has only one type; the ugly has thousands. The fact is that the beautiful, in human terms, is merely form considered in its simplest aspect, in its most absolute symmetry, in its most perfect harmony with our constitution. Thus it always presents us with a whole which is complete, but limited, as we are. What we call ugly is, on the contrary, a detail of a larger whole which escapes our perception, and which is in harmony, not with mankind, but with all creation. That is why it constantly presents us with new, but incomplete aspects.

It is interesting to study the advent and progress of the grotesque in modern times. At first, it is an invasion, an overflow, an excess; it is a torrent which has burst its banks. At its inception, it passes over the dying tradition of Latin literature, imparts some coloring to Persius, Petronius, Juvenal, and leaves behind *The Golden Ass* of Apuleius. Thence it is diffused through the imagination of the new peoples who are rebuilding Europe. It flows in waves through the work of the fabulists, the chroniclers, and the writers of romances. We see it spread from the South to the North. It flickers through the dreams of the Teutonic nations and, at the same time, breathes life into those admirable Spanish *romanceros*, the veritable Iliad of the age of chivalry. For example, it is what, in the *Roman de la Rose*, portrays the election of a king, an august ceremonial, in the following terms:

> A great villain did they elect,
> The boniest man of them all.

Above all, it imparts its character to that marvelous architecture which, in the Middle Ages, represented all the arts. It fixes its work on the face of cathedrals, frames its hells and purgatories in the ogives of the great doors, portrays them in a blaze of color in stained glass windows, exhibits its monsters and demons on capitals, in friezes, and along the edges of roofs. Its infinite forms are displayed on the modern fronts of houses, on the stone faces of castles, and on the marble facades of palaces. From the arts it passes into manners and, while causing the people to applaud the *graciosos* of comedy, it gives court jesters to kings. Later, in the age of ceremony, it will show us Scarron perched on the edge of Louis XIV's bed. Meanwhile, it decorates coats of arms and traces on the knight's shields the symbolic hieroglyphics of feudalism. From manners it passes into laws; numerous bizarre practices attest to its presence in the institutions of the Middle Ages. In the same way, it caused Thespis to leap from his cart, his face smeared with wine lees, to dance with the legal fraternity on that famous marble table for royal banquets. Finally, having been assimilated into the arts, manners, and laws of the people, it enters the church. In every Catholic city, we see it organize some one of those curious ceremonies, those strange processions, in which religion is accompanied by all varieties of superstition, the sublime is encircled by all forms of the grotesque. To paint it with a single stroke: such is its verve, its vigor, its creative force, at the dawn of letters, that, from the outset, it casts on the threshold of modern poetry three burlesque Homers: Ariosto in Italy; Cervantes in Spain; Rabelais in France.[10]*

It would be excessive to dwell further on the influence of the grotesque in the third civilization. In the epoch called *romantic*, everything attests to its intimate alliance with the beautiful. Even among the most naïve popular legends, we find explained this mystery of modern art and sometimes with an instinctive perception. Antiquity could not have produced *Beauty and the Beast*.

It is true that in the epoch we have been speaking about the predominance of the grotesque over the sublime, in literature, is quite conspicuous. But this is a feverish reaction, a passion for novelty which passes, a first wave which gradually recedes. The type of the beautiful will soon recapture its place and its rights, not excluding the other principle, but prevailing over it. It is time that the grotesque be content with a corner of the picture in Murillo's royal frescoes, in the sacred works of Veronese; to be part of two notable *Last Judgements*, in Michaelangelo's scene of rapine and horror, embellishing the Vatican, in the awesome catastrophes traced by Rubens across the vault of Antwerp cathedral. The moment has come for an equilibrium to be established between these two principles. A man, a poet-king, "*poeta soverano*," as Dante says of Homer, will settle everything. The two rival geniuses will unite their double flame; and from the flame issues Shakespeare.

We have now reached the poetic summit of modern times. Shakespeare is the *drame*, and the *drame*, which assimilates in the same inspiration the grotesque and the sublime, the fearful and the absurd, tragedy and comedy, the *drame* is characteristic of the third poetic epoch, the literature of the present.

To hastily summarize the facts we have thus far noted, poetry has three ages, each corresponding to an epoch in society: the ode, the epic, the drama. Primitive periods are lyrical, ancient times are epic, modern times are dramatic. The ode sings of eternity, the epic solemnizes history, the *drame* paints life.[11]* The characteristic of the first type of poetry is naïveté; the characteristic of the second is simplicity; the characteristic of the third is faithfulness to life. The rhapsodists mark the transition from lyric to epic poets, as do the romancers from epic to dramatic poets. Historians are born with the second epoch; chroniclers and critics with the third. The characters of the ode are colossi: Adam, Cain, Noah; those of the epic poems are giants: Achilles, Atreus, Orestes; those of the *drame* are men: Hamlet, Macbeth, Othello. The ode takes life from the ideal, the epic from the grandiose, the *drame* from the real. Lastly, this threefold poetry flows from three great sources: the Bible, Homer, Shakespeare.

Such then—and we will limit ourselves to drawing only one conclusion—such are the diverse aspects of thought in the different ages of mankind and society. Such are its three faces, in youth, in manhood, and in old age. Whether you examine one specific literature, or all literature, *en masse*, you will always come to the same conclusion: lyric poets precede epic poets, epic poets precede dramatic poets. In France, Malherbe precedes Chapelain, Chapelain precedes Corneille; in ancient Greece, Orpheus precedes Homer, Homer precedes Aeschylus. In the first of all books, Genesis precedes Kings, Kings precedes Job; or, to return to the great scale of all poetic ages, outlined above, the Bible precedes the *Iliad*, the *Iliad* precedes Shakespeare.

In effect, society begins by singing its dreams, then narrates its deeds, and finally sets about describing what it thinks. We must note in passing that it is for this last reason that the *drame*, unifying the most opposing qualities, can be at once both full of depth and rich in surface, philosophical and picturesque.

It would be logical to add here that everything in nature and in life goes through these three phases, the lyric, the epic, and the dramatic, because everything is born, acts, dies. If it were not ridiculous to confound the fanciful conceits of imagination with the stern deductions of reason, a poet might say, for example, that sunrise is a hymn, noon a brilliant epic, sunset a somber *drame* in which night and day, life and death, do battle. But that would be poetry, madness perhaps; and "what does it prove?"[12]

Let us pursue the facts assembled above: complete them, moreover, with an important observation. In no way have we pretended to assign exclusive limits to the three epochs of poetry. We have only tried to establish their dominant characteristics. The Bible, a sacred lyric monument, as we noted earlier, contains the seeds of an epic and a *drame* in Kings and Job. In all Homeric poems one senses the residue of lyric poetry and the germs of dramatic poetry. The ode and the *drame* intersect in the epic. Everything is found in everything; but in each thing there is found a generative element to which all the other elements are subordinated, and which imposes its character upon the whole.

Drame is complete poetry. The ode and the epic contain it only in germ; it contains them both in a highly developed state; it encompasses both of them and epitomizes them. Certainly, the man who said "the French don't have an epic turn of mind" made a subtle and just observation.[13] Had he said "the moderns," a clever phrase would have been profound. It is, however, incontestable that there is epic genius especially evident in that marvelous *Athalia*, so lofty and so simple in its sublimity that it was not understood by its regal century. Certainly Shakespeare's series of history plays contains many epic qualities. But it is lyric poetry which best suits the *drame*. Lyric poetry never impedes the dramatic, adapts to all its caprices, plays in all its forms, sometimes sublime, like Ariel, sometimes grotesque, like Caliban. Our epoch, above all a dramatic one, is, for that, eminently lyrical. There is more than one affinity between the beginning and the end. The sunset recalls in some of its colors the sunrise. The old man returns to infancy. But this final infancy does not resemble the first; it is as sad as the first was joyful. So it is with lyric poetry. Dazzling, dreamlike at the dawn of civilization, it reappears somber and pensive at the decline. The Bible opens happily with Genesis and closes with the menacing Apocalypse. The modern ode continues to be inspired, but it is no longer born of ignorance. It is more meditative than contemplative; its reverie is the result of melancholia. Her children bear evidence that the muse has been mated to drama.

To make these ideas clear through an image, we would compare primitive lyric poetry to a peaceful lake which reflects the clouds and the starry firmament; the epic is the river which flows from it and rushes on, reflecting its banks, forests, the countryside and cities until it reaches the ocean of the *drame*. Finally, like the lake, the *drame* reflects the heavens; like the river, it reflects its banks; but it alone has great depths and tempests.

The *drame*, then, is the end to which everthing in modern poetry leads. *Paradise Lost* is a *drame* before it is an epic. We know that it was first conceived by the poet in the form of a *drame* and as such it remains ever in the reader's imagination, so strongly evident is this early dramatic framework beneath the epic structure given it by Milton! When Dante Alighieri had finished his terrifying Inferno, when he had closed its door and nothing remained but to name his work, his genius made him instinctively aware that this multi-form poem was derived from the drama, not the epic; and on the title page of that gigantic monument, he wrote with his bronze pen: *Divina Commedia.*

Thus we see that the only two poets of modern times equal in stature to Shakespeare follow him in unity of design. They combine with him in imparting a dramatic coloring to all our poetry; like him, they combine the grotesque with the sublime; and, far from standing alone in this great literary tradition derived from Shakespeare, Dante and Milton are, in a way, the twin buttresses of the edifice whose central pillar is Shakespeare: they are the counterforts of the arch of which he is the keystone.

Permit us to take up again some previously stated ideas which it is important to emphasize. We have arrived, and now we must start out again.

On the day when Christianity said to man: Thou art twofold, thou art made up of two beings, one perishable, the other immortal, one carnal, the other ethereal, one enslaved by appetites, cravings, and passions, the other borne aloft on wings of enthusiasm and revery, the former always stooping to earth, its mother, the latter always darting up toward heaven, its fatherland—on that day, the *drame* was created. It is, in fact, anything other than this constant—on every day, for every man—contrast and struggle between two opposing principles which are ever present in life and which dispute possession of man from the cradle to the grave.

The poetry born of Christianity, the poetry of our times, is, therefore, the *drame*. The characteristic of the *drame* is the real: the real results from the completely natural combination of the two types, the sublime and the grotesque, which intersect in the *drame* as they do in life and creation. For true poetry, complete poetry, resides in the harmony of opposites. It is true, then, to proclaim loudly—and it is especially here that the exceptions prove the rule—everything that exists in nature exists in art.

Assuming this point of view in order to judge our petty conventional rules, in order to escape from these pedantic labyrinths, in order to resolve all these trivial problems laboriously constructed around art by the critics of the past two centuries, we are struck by the promptness with which the question of the modern stage is clarified. The drama has but to take a step to free itself from all the webs which the troops of Lilliput placed around it as it slept.

And so let the mindless pedants (one does not exclude the other) maintain that the deformed, the ugly, the grotesque must never be the subject of imitation in art. Our reply to them is that the grotesque is comedy and that comedy is apparently a part of art. Tartuffe is not handsome; Pourceaugnac is not noble;[14] Pourceaugnac and Tartuffe are shining examples of art.

If, driven back from this entrenchment to the second line of their customs-houses, they renew their prohibition on the joining of the grotesque with the sublime, comedy incorporated into tragedy, we prove to them that in the poetry of Christian nations, the first of these two types represents the human animal, the second the soul. These two strains of art, if their branches are kept from intermingling, if they are systematically separated, will produce as fruit, on the one hand, abstractions of vices and follies, and, on the other, abstractions of crime, of heroism, and virtue. The two types, thus isolated, and left to themselves, will each go their own way, leaving the real between them, one to its right, the other to its left.[15]* From this it follows that after these abstractions there remains something to represent: man; after these tragedies and comedies, something to write: the *drame*.

In the *drame*, at least as it is conceived, if not executed, everything is connected and ordered as in reality. The body plays its part no less than the soul; and men and events, set into motion by this double agent, appear alternately clownish or terrible, and sometimes both at once. Thus, the judge will say: "Off with his head! Let's go to dinner!"[16] Thus, the Roman senate will deliberate over Domitian's turbot.[17] Thus, Socrates, drinking the hemlock and discoursing on the immortal soul and the only God, will interrupt himself to request that a cock be sacrificed to Aesculapius.[18] Thus, Elizabeth will curse and speak Latin. Thus, Richelieu will suffer Joseph the Capuchin, Louis XI his barber, Olivier-le-Diable. Thus, Cromwell will say, "I have Parliament in my purse and the King in my pocket"; or, with the hand that signed the death warrant of Charles I, will smear with ink the face of a regicide who, smiling, hands it to him. Thus, Caesar, riding in his triumphal chariot, will fear his downfall. For men of genius, however great they may be, always have within them the beast which mocks their intelligence. In this, they touch mankind; in this, they are dramatic. "It is but a step from the sublime to the ridiculous," Napoleon said, when he was convinced of being merely a man; and that flame from a fiery soul which illuminates both art and history, that cry of anguish, epitomizes the *drame* and life.

It is a striking thing that all these contrasts are encountered in the poets themselves, considered as men. By dint of meditating on existence, of laying bare its bitter irony, of pouring floods of sarcasm and irony on our weaknesses, these men who make us laugh, become profoundly sad. These Democrituses are Heraclituses as well, Beaumarchais was morose, Molière was gloomy, Shakespeare melancholy.

The grotesque, then, is one of the *drame*'s supreme beauties. Not merely an expedient, it is often a necessity. Sometimes it appears in homogenous masses, in entire characters, as Dandin, Prusias, Trissotin, Brid'oison, Juliet's nurse; sometimes marked by terror as Richard III, Bégears, Tartuffe, Mephistopheles; sometimes even in a veil of grace and elegance as Figaro, Osric, Mercutio, Don Juan.[19] It insinuates itself everywhere;

for just as the most commonplace have their moments of sublimity, so the most exalted often pay their tribute to the trivial and the ridiculous. Thus, often impalpable, often imperceptible, it is always present on stage, even when it says nothing, even when it is hidden. Thanks to it, there is no monotony. Sometimes it injects laughter, sometimes horror, into tragedy. It will arrange the confrontation of Romeo with the apothecary, the three witches with Macbeth, the grave-diggers with Hamlet. Finally, it can occasionally, without discord, mingle its shrill voice with the most sublime, the most lugubrious, the dreamiest harmonies of the soul.

That is what Shakespeare, this god of the stage, above all others has been able to do in a manner which is unique and which it would be as useless as it would be impossible to imitate. In Shakespeare, as in a trinity, the three characteristic geniuses of the stage, Corneille, Molière, and Beaumarchais, seem united.

We see how quickly the arbitrary distinction of the genres crumbles before reason and taste. No less easily might the alleged rule of the two unities be destroyed. We say two, not *three*, unities, for the unity of action or of the whole, is the only true and well-founded one, and has been exempt from controversy for a long time.

Distinguished contemporaries, French and foreign, have already attacked in practice and theory, this fundamental law of the pseudo-Aristotelian code. The battle ought not to be a long one, for the timber of that aged academic hovel was so worm-eaten that it crumbled at the first blow.

The strange thing is that the slaves to convention claim their rule of the two unities is founded on probability, whereas it is precisely the real that destroys it. In effect, what is more improbable and more absurd than that the vestibule, peristyle, or antechamber—the banal settings in which our tragedies are obliged to unfold—where conspirators come, one knows not how, to declaim against the tyrant, and the tyrant to declaim against the conspirators, each in turn, as if they were repeating to each other the bucolic phrase:

Alternis cantemus, amant alterna Camenae.[20]

Where have you seen that type of vestibule or peristyle? What is more contrary, we will not say to truth, as the pedants hold it cheap, but to probability? The result is that everything which is too personalized, too intimate, too localized to take place in the antechamber or at the crossroads, that is to say, all the drama, takes place in the wings. On stage we see only the elbows of the drama, so to speak; its hands are elsewhere. Instead of scenes, we have narrations, instead of pictures, descriptions. Solemn characters, placed, like the ancient chorus, between us and the drama, come to tell us what happens in the temple, in the palace, or in the public square, until we are tempted to cry out: "Really! Lead us there then! It must be entertaining there. It must be a beatiful sight to see!" To which they would reply: "It is quite possible that it might amuse or interest you, but that is not the question at all; we are the guardians of the dignity of the French Melpomene." And there you are!

"But," someone will say, "this rule you repudiate is derived from the Greek theatre." In what do the Greek theatre and drama resemble our drama and our theatre? Besides, we have already demonstrated that the prodigious expanse of the ancient stage enabled it to encompass an entire locality, so that the poet could, according to the demands of the action, transport it at will from one part of the theatre to another, which is very nearly the equivalent of set changes. Odd contradiction! The Greek theatre, restricted as it was to a national and religious end, was freer than ours, whose sole object is the entertainment and, if you wish, the instruction of the spectator. The reason is that the one only obeys laws which are suited to it, while the other struggles to maintain conditions which are perfectly foreign to its essence. One is artistry; the other is artifice.

It is beginning to be understood in our time that exact localization is one of the first elements of reality. The speaking or acting characters are not the only things which impress a faithful representation of the facts on the minds of the spectators. The place where this or that catastrophe occurred becomes a terrible and inseparable witness of it; and the absence of silent characters of this sort would make the greatest scenes of history incomplete in the drama. Would the poet dare assassinate Rizzio anywhere but in Mary Stuart's chamber? stab Henry IV anywhere but in the rue de la Ferronerie, obstructed with drays and carriages? burn Joan of Arc anywhere but in the Old Market? dispatch the Duke of Guise anywhere but in the chateau at Blois where his ambition roused a popular assembly to frenzy? decapitate Charles I and Louis XVI anywhere but in those sinister squares from which Whitehall and the Tuileries can be seen, as if their scaffolds were extensions of the palaces?

Unity of time rests on no firmer foundation than does the unity of place. The action forcibly confined within twenty-four hours is as ridiculous as one confined within a vestibule. Every action has its proper duration as well as its appropriate setting. Administer the same dose of time to all events. Apply the same standard to everything! You would laugh at the cobbler who would put the same shoe on every foot. To cross the unity of time with the unity of place, like the bars of a cage, and to pedantically, on the authority of Aristotle, introduce into it all the deeds, all the actions, all the figures which Providence displays to us in such richness in real life, is to mutilate both men and objects and make history wince. It is better to say that everything dies in the execution; and it is thus that the dogmatic mutilators achieve their usual result: what was alive in the chronicle is dead in the tragedy. That is why so often the cage of the unities contains nothing but a skeleton.

And then, if twenty-four hours can be comprised in two, it would be logical for four hours to contain forty-eight. Thus Shakespeare's unity is not the unity of Corneille. Pity!

But these are the wretched quibbles posed to genius for over two centuries by mediocrity, envy, and routine! Thus has the flight of our greatest poets been limited. Their wings have been clipped with the scissors of the unities. And what has been offered in exchange for these eagle feathers clipped from Corneille and Racine? Campistron.[21]

We imagine that it might be said: "There is something in the too frequent changing of sets which confuses and fatigues the spectator, and which can disturb his concentration. Numerous transitions, from one place to another, or from one time to another time, can necessitate boring expositions. It is also necessary to avoid leaving gaps in the middle of the action which prevent the different parts of the drama from adhering closely to one another, and which, moreover, confuse the spectator because he does not yet possess a clear idea of what there could be in those gaps. . . ." But these are precisely the difficulties art faces. These are the obstacles peculiar to one subject or another, and for which universal laws cannot be found. It is for genius to resolve them, not for *poetics* to evade them.

Finally, to demolish the absurdity of the rule of the two unities, a last argument taken from the very bowels of art would be sufficient in itself. This is the existence of the third unity, the unity of action, the only one that is universally admitted because it results from a fact: neither the human eye nor the human mind can grasp more than one whole at a single time. This unity is as necessary as the other two are useless. It is what characterizes the viewpoint of drama; and for that reason excludes the other two unities. There no more can be three unities in drama than three horizons in a painting. Furthermore, we should beware of confusing unity with simplicity of action. The unity of the whole does not exclude in any way secondary actions on which the principal action may depend. It is only necessary that these parts, wisely subordinated to the whole, always gravitate toward the central action and be grouped around it on different levels or, rather, on the diverse planes of the drama. The unity of action is the law of perspective in the theatre.

"But," the customs officer of thought will cry, "great geniuses have nevertheless submitted to these rules you reject." Unfortunately, yes! But what would these admirable men have done, had they been left alone? At least they did not accept your chains without a struggle. You should recall how Pierre Corneille, harrassed after the debut of his marvelous *Cid*, struggled under Mairet, Claveret, d'Aubignac, and Scudéry! How he denounced for posterity the violence of these men, who, he quipped, had turned their hair "all white with Aristotle." You should see how it was said to him, and we cite texts from the period: "Young man, you must learn before you teach, and unless you are a Scaliger or a Heinsius, that is intolerable!" At that Corneille rebelled and asked if it was their desire to make him descend "much lower than Claveret!" Here, Scudéry became indignant at so much pride and reminded the "thrice great author of the *Cid*...using the modest words Tasso, the greatest man of his century, placed at the beginning of his *apologia* for the most beautiful and the greatest of his works against the harshest and most unjust censure that perhaps will ever be pronounced. M. Corneille," he adds, "shows in his *Replies* that he is far from that excellent author's moderation as he is from his merit." The *young man* so *justly* and so *sweetly censured* dared resist; thereupon Scudéry returns to the charge, calling to his aid the *Eminent Academy*: "Pronounce, O MY JUDGES, a verdict worthy of your eminence, and which will inform all Europe that *The Cid* is not a masterpiece by the greatest man in France, but the least judicious play of M. Corneille himself. You must do it, both for your own particular renown, and for that of our nation in general, whose interests are concerned; given that foreigners who could see this beautiful masterpiece— they who have possessed a Tasso or a Guarini—might believe that our greatest masters are only apprentices."[22] These few instructive lines contain all the perennial tactics of envious routine against newborn talent— tactics which are still used today, and which, for example, have added such a curious page to the youthful work of Lord Byron. Scudéry gives us the quintessence. Thus the earlier works of men of genius are always preferred to the new ones, in order to prove that they are declining, rather than improving: *Mélite* and *The Palace Gallery* are ranked above *The Cid*. And the names of the dead are always thrown in the faces of the living: Corneille is abused in the name of Tasso and Guarini (Guarini!), as later Racine would be abused in the name of Corneille, Voltaire in the name of Racine, as today, everything new is abused in the names of Corneille, Racine, and Voltaire. These tactics, as will be seen, are well-worn, but they must be effective, as they are still in use. However, the poor devil of a great man still breathed. Here we must admire how Scudéry, the bully of this tragicomedy, provoked beyond endurance, treated Corneille roughly and abused him, how he pitilessly unleashed his classical artillery, how he "made" the author of *The Cid* "see what the episodes should be, according to Aristotle, who treats it in the tenth and sixteenth chapters of his *Poetics*"; how he crushes Corneille by the name of this same Aristotle "in the eleventh chapter of his *Art of Poetry* where one can find the condemnation of *The Cid*"; in the name of Plato, "in the tenth book of *The Republic*"; in the name of Marcellinus, "as may be seen in the twenty-seventh book"; in the name of "the *Ajax* of Sophocles";

in the name of "the example of Euripides"; in the name of "Heinsius, chapter six of the *Constitution of Tragedy*"; in the name of the younger Scaliger "in his poems"; finally, in the name of the Canonists and Jurisconsuls, under the title "Nuptials." The first arguments are addressed to the Academy, the last was for the Cardinal. After pin-pricks, the hammer-blow. A judge was needed to decide the question. Chapelain gave judgement. Thus, Corneille found himself condemned; the lion was muzzled; or, as was said at the time, the "crow" [*corneille*] was "plucked." Now comes the sad part of this grotesque drama: after having thus been broken in its first flowering, this entirely modern genius, inspired by the Middle Ages and by Spain, was forced to lie to himself and to steep himself in antiquity. He gave us a Castilian Rome, undoubtedly sublime, but where—except perhaps in *Nicomedes*, a play ridiculed in the eighteenth century for its proud and naïve coloring—we find neither the real Rome nor the real Corneille.

Racine experienced the same persecution without, however, offering the same resistance. Neither in his genius nor in his character was there any of Corneille's haughty severity. He submitted in silence and abandoned to the disdain of his epoch his ravishing elegy *Esther* and his magnificent epic, *Athalia*. So that we must believe that, had he not been paralyzed by the prejudices of his century, had he come into contact less frequently with the classical sting-ray, he would not have failed to introduce Locuste into his drama between Narcissus and Nero. Nor would he have relegated to the wings that admirable scene at the banquet when Seneca's pupil poisons Britannicus with the cup of reconciliation. But can we demand of the bird that it fly in a vacuum? What beauties have the men of taste—from Scudéry to LaHarpe—cost us! We could compose a truly beautiful work of all that their arid breath has withered in its germ. Our great poets, however, have nonetheless found a way to make their genius shine through all these obstacles. The attempt to confine them behind the walls of dogma and convention has often been in vain. Like the Hebrew giant, they carried the doors of their prison with them to the mountain.

But the same refrain is still repeated and doubtless will be continued to be repeated for a while longer: "Follow the rules! Copy the models! It was the rules that shaped the models!" Just a moment! In that case there are two kinds of models, those which are made according to the rules, and, prior to them, those according to which the rules were made. Now, in which of these two categories ought genius to seek a place for itself? Although it is always unpleasant to come in contact with pedants, is it not a thousand times better to give them lessons than to receive lessons from them? And then, to imitate? Is the reflection equal to the light? Is the satellite which ceaselessly travels the same orbit equal to the central creative star? For all his poetry, Virgil is still only a satellite of

Homer. And who, pray tell, should we imitate? The ancients? We have just proven that their theatre has nothing in common with ours, Moreover, Voltaire, who would have nothing to do with Shakespeare, would have nothing to do with the ancients, either. Let him tell us why: "The Greeks ventured to produce spectacles no less revolting to us. Hippolytus, crushed by his fall, counts his wounds and utters doleful cries. Philoctetes falls in a fit of pain; black blood flows from his wounds. Oedipus, while blood flows from his empty eye-sockets, complains of gods and men. You hear the cries of Clytemnestra, her throat slit by her son, and Electra shouts out on stage: 'Strike. Don't spare her. She did not spare our father!' Prometheus, nails driven through his arms and stomach, is pinned to a boulder. The Furies answer the bloody ghost of Clytemnestra with inarticulate howls.... Art was in its infancy in Aeschylus' time as in Shakespeare's London."[23] Imitate the moderns? Imitate imitations? Have mercy!

"But," someone will continue to object, "in the way you conceive art, you seem only to seek great poets and always count on genius." Art does not rely on mediocrity. Nothing is proscribed for art. Art does not know mediocrity. It does not even exist for art. Art gives wings, not crutches. Alas, d'Aubignac followed the rules, Campistron imitated models. What does it matter to art! Art does not construct palaces for ants. It lets them build their anthill without knowing whether they have built their parody of its palace at its base.

The critics of the academic school place their poets in a singular position. On the one hand, they constantly cry: "Imitate models!" On the other hand, they are in the habit of proclaiming that "the models are inimitable." Now, if their craftsmen, by dint of hard work, succeed in forcing through this narrow passage some pallid copy, some colorless tracery from the masters, these ingrates criticize the new *refaccimiento* with the cry "that resembles nothing!" or "that resembles everything!" And by means of logic expressly disguised to meet the occasion, each of these two formulae is a criticism.

Let us speak boldly. The time has come, and it would be strange, if in this epoch, liberty, like light, penetrated everywhere except in that one place most naturally free in the world: the domain of thought. Let us take the hammer to theories, poetics, and systems. Let us tear down that old plasterwork which masks the façade of art! There are neither rules nor models; or, rather, there are no rules other than the general laws of nature, which soar above all art and the special laws which, for each composition, result from the conditions appropriate to its subject. The former are essential, eternal, and do not change; the latter are external, variable, and used only once. The former are the framework which supports the house; the latter are the scaffolding used in its construction and constructed anew for each building. In sum, the former are the skeleton, the latter the clothing, of the *drame*. But these rules are not found in the poetics. Richelet does not suspect their existence.[24] Genius, which divines more than it apprehends, finds for each work the general laws in the general order of things and the special laws in the isolated whole of the subject treated; not in the manner of the chemist who lights his furnace, fans his fire, heats his crucible, analyzes and destroys; but in the manner of a bee, who flies on golden wings, lights on each flower and draws out its honey, without the flower losing any of its splendor or the corolla losing any of its fragrance. The poet—let us insist on this point—should, then, take counsel only from nature, from truth, and from inspiration, which is both truth and nature. "*Quando he*," said Lope de Vega,

> *Quanda he de escrivir una comedia,*
> *Encierro los preceptos con seis llaves.*[25]

In effect, to lock up the rules, six keys are none too many. Let the poet be especially wary of imitating anyone, Shakespeare no more than Molière, Schiller no more than Corneille.[26]* If true talent were able to renounce its own nature to that degree, and thus put aside its own personal originalty, in order to be transformed into something other than itself, it would sacrifice all to this role of Sosia. It is the god who is turned into a valet. We must draw our inspiration from the original sources. It is the same sap, spread throughout the soil, that nurtures all the trees of the forest, so diverse in fruit, shape, and foliage. The true poet is a tree which can be whipped by all the winds and watered by all the dews, who bears his works like fruit, as the fabulist bore his fables. Why attach oneself to a master or graft oneself to a model? Better that one be a bramble or a thistle, nourished by the same soil as the cedar or the palm, than be a fungus or a lichen on these great trees. The bramble lives; the fungus vegetates. Moreover, however great the cedar or the palm, it is not with the nourishment that can be extracted from them that one can become great oneself. A parasite on a giant will appear all the more dwarfish. As mighty as the oak is, it can only produce and nourish the mistletoe.

Let there be no misunderstanding. If some of our poets have achieved greatness, even through imitation, it is because, while modeling their work on ancient forms, they have often heeded the voice of nature and of their own genius: they have been true to themselves in some respect. Their branches may have become entwined with those of a neighboring tree, but their roots were plunged into the soil of art. They were ivy, rather than mistletoe. Then came the second-rank imitators who, possessing neither roots in the soil nor genius, had to limit themselves to imitation. As Charles Nodier noted, "After the Athenian school, the Alexandrian school." Then there was a flood of mediocrity, followed by numerous poetics, so troublesome to talent, but so convenient to mediocrity. It has been said that everything has been done and God has been forbidden to create more Molières and Corneilles. Memory has replaced imagination. Even imagination has been subjected to rules and has been a topic for aphorisms, "Imagination," says LaHarpe, "is in essence only remembering."

Nature then! Nature and truth!—And here, for the purpose of demonstrating that new ideas, far from destroying art, only wish to reconstruct it solidly and soundly, let us try to indicate what is the impassable limit which, in our opinion, separates the reality of art from the reality of nature. It is careless to confuse them as some of the less informed partisans of *romanticism* do. Truth in art could never be considered *absolute* reality, as several writers have claimed. Art cannot produce the thing itself. Let us imagine one of those rash promoters of absolute nature, of nature seen apart from art, at the performance of a romantic play, *The Cid*, for example. "What is that?" he will ask at the first word. "The Cid speaks verse! Speaking verse is not natural." —How do you want him to speak? —"In prose." —So be it. A moment later, he will continue, if he is consistent: "What! The Cid speaks French!" —So what? —"Nature demands that he speak his native language. He must speak Spanish." —We will not understand any of it, but so be it again. Do you believe this to be all? No, for before the tenth Castilian phrase, he ought to be up demanding to know if this Cid who speaks is the true Cid, in flesh and blood? By what right does this actor, named Pierre or Jacques, take the name of the Cid? That is *false*. —There is no reason for him not to demand next that the sun replace the footlights and *real* trees and houses replace those deceitful sets. For, once on this path, logic has you by the throat, and you cannot stop.

You must recognize, or risk seeming absurd, that the domain of art and of nature are entirely distinct. Nature and art are two things; if this were not so, one or the other would not exist. Art, in addition to its ideal aspect, has an earthy and practical aspect. Whatever it may do, it is enclosed between grammar and prosody, between Vaugelas and Richelet.[27] For its most capricious creations, it possesses forms, methods of execution, a complete apparatus to set in motion. For genius, these are delicate instruments, for mediocrities, they are tools.

It seems to us that others have already stated that the *drame* is a mirror in which nature is reflected. But, if this mirror is an ordinary mirror with a smooth, uniform surface, it will only reflect a dull image without depth, faithful, but colorless. It is known that color and light are lost in simple reflections. It is necessary, then, that drama be a concentrating mirror which, far from weakening, gathers and condenses colored rays and transforms a glimmer into a light, a light into a flame. Then only is drama recognized by art.

The theatre is an optical point. All that is found in the world, in history, in life, in man, can and ought to be reflected in it, but under the magic wand of art. Art reads the ages, reads nature, examines the chronicles, schools itself in the representation of actual facts—especially of manners and characters, much less given to doubt and contradiction than facts.[28]*
Art restores what the annalists have cut, harmonizes what they have assembled, divines their omissions and replaces them, fills their gaps with imagined scenes painted with appropriate colors, and groups together what had been dispersed. Art reactivates the strings of Providence which control the human marionettes, clothes the whole with a form both natural and poetic, and gives it that brilliant and lifelike truthfulness which produces illusion. Art possesses that prestige of reality which arouses the enthusiasm of the spectator, and of the poet first of all, for the poet is sincere. Thus, the aim of art is almost divine: to bring to life again if writing history; to create, if writing poetry.

It is a marvelous sight to see that amplitude displayed in the *drame*, in which art powerfully develops nature; a *drame* in which the action moves to its conclusion with a firm and easy air, without diffuseness or constraint, a *drame*, in short, in which the poet clearly fulfills the multiple aim of art: that is, to open a double horizon to the spectator, to illuminate at once the internal and the external in men; the external through discourse and action; the internal through asides and monologues; in a word, to bring together in the same picture the drama of life and the drama of the conscience.

You will perceive that, for this type of work, if the poet must *choose* (and he must), he must choose not the *beautiful*, but the *characteristic*. Not that it is advisable, as they say today, "to paint local color"; that is to say, the addition, after the fact, of some discordant touches here and there to a whole which is otherwise perfectly false and conventional. Local color should not merely be on the *drame*'s surface, but at its center, in the very heart of the work, from which it is diffused to the surface itself, naturally and equally, and, so to speak, into every corner of the *drame*, like the sap which rises from the roots to the topmost leaf of a tree. The *drame* should be thoroughly impregnated with this period color; it must in some way be present in the atmosphere of the theatre, so that it is only on entering and leaving the theatre that one is aware of having changed period and atmosphere. If it requires some study and effort to reach that point, so much the better. It is good that the avenues of art are obstructed by those brambles which repulse all but the strong-willed. Moreover, it is that study, seconded by fiery inspiration, which will protect the *drame* from the ordinary, a vice which destroys it. The ordinary is the failing of short-sighted and short-winded poets. For the optic of the theatre, all figures must be reduced to their most salient, their most precise, their most individual traits. Even the vulgar and the trivial must have an intensity. Nothing must be neglected. Like God, the true poet is present everywhere at the same time in his work. Genius resembles the machine which stamps the royal likeness on copper and gold coins alike.

We do not hesitate—and again, this would prove to honest men how little we seek to distort art—we do not hesitate in considering verse to be one of the most appropriate means of preserving the *drame* from the plague we have just mentioned, one of the most powerful barriers against the irruption of the *ordinary*, which, like democracy, always flows freely in men's minds. And here, may the young literary generation, already so rich in men and works, permit us to indicate an error in which it seems to us to have fallen—an error all too justified, however, by the incredible aberations of the old school. The new century is at that stage of growth when things can easily be set right. A singular school of dramatic poetry has recently appeared, a kind of penultimate offshoot of the aged classical trunk, or better, like one of those excrescences, one of those polyps, which develop in decrepitude and which are more a sign of decomposition than a proof of life. This school seems to us to have as its master and founder the poet who marks the transition from the eighteenth to the nineteenth century, Delille, a man given to description and periphrasis. It has been said that near the end of his life he boasted, after the manner of Homer's enumerations, of having *made* twelve camels, four dogs, three horses, including Job's, six tigers, two cats, one chess set, one backgammon board, one checkerboard, one billiard table, several winters, a great many springs, fifty sunsets, and so many sunrises that he had lost count of them!

Delille also wrote tragedy. He is the father (he, and not Racine, for Heaven's sake!) of a so-called school of elegance and good taste which recently flourished. Tragedy is not for this school what it was for the good-natured Will Shakespeare, i.e., a source of all kinds of emotions, but rather a convenient frame for the solution of a multitude of petty descriptive problems which it sets up for itself as it develops. This muse, far from rejecting the trivialities and vulgarities of life, as does the true French classical school, on the contrary, seeks them out and avidly gathers them up. The grotesque, avoided as undesirable company by the tragedy of Louis XIV's day, can quietly pass before this muse. *It must be described*, that is to say, *ennobled*! A scene in a guardhouse, a peasant revolt, the fish market, a galley, the wine-shop, Henry IV's "chicken in every pot," are a windfall for it. It seizes upon this rubble, cleans it up, sews tinsel and spangles over the ugliness; *"purpureus assuitur [sic] pannus."*[29] Its purpose seems to be to deliver patents of nobility to all that is plebeian in the drama; and under a great seal each of these patents becomes a *tirade*.

This muse, you understand, possesses a rare prudery. Accustomed as

it is to the caress of the periphrasis, plain speaking, which would sometimes treat it harshly, horrifies it. Natural speech is not in accord with
its dignity. It *scores* old Corneille for his manner of coarsely saying:

...A *bunch of men* riddled with debts and crimes.[30]
...Chimène, *who'd have thought it?* Rodrigue, *who'd have said it?*[31]
...When their Flaminius *haggled* with Hannibal.[32]
...Ah! Don't *embroil* me with the Republic![33]
Etc., etc.

It still cherishes its "Very good, Sir!"[34] and many "Sirs" and "Madames"
were necessary to pardon our admirable Racine for his so monosyllabic
"dogs"[35] and for that "Claudius" so brutally "bedded" with Agrippina.[36]

This Melpomene, as she is called, would shudder at the thought of
touching a chronicle. She leaves the knowledge of the epoch she is evoking to the care of the costume designer. To her mind, history is ill bred
and in bad taste. How is it possible, for example, to tolerate kings and
queens who curse? Their royal dignity must be elevated to tragic dignity.
It was in furtherance of this goal that she ennobled Henry IV. That is
how the people's king, purified by Legouvé,[37] saw the "*ventre-saint-gris*"
[goddam drunken belly] ignominiously replaced in his mouth by two
maxims. Thus he was sentenced, like the girl in the fairy tale, to let fall
from his royal lips nothing but pearls, rubies, and sapphires; all of them
false, in truth.

In summary, nothing is so *ordinary* as that conventional elegance and
nobility. There is nothing original in it, no imagination, no invention in
style. There is only what can be found anywhere: rhetoric, bombast,
platitudes, florid academic eloquence, and poetry inspired by Latin verses.
Borrowed ideas are clothed in secondhand images. The poets of this
school are elegant in the manner of stage princes and princesses, always
sure of finding in labelled cartons from a warehouse the robes and gilded
crowns, which have no disadvantage other than that of having served
everyone. If these poets do not look at the Bible, they are not without
their own thick book, *The Dictionary of Rhymes*. That is the source of their
poetry, *fontes aquarum.*[38]

You understand that in all this, nature and truth survive as they can.
It would be a piece of good luck if some remnants of either were to
withstand this cataclysm of false art, false style, false poetry. This is what
led to the errors of several of our distinguished reformers. Shocked by
the stiffness, the ostentation, the *pomposo* of this so-called dramatic poetry, they believed the elements of our poetic language to be incompatible
with nature and truth. The alexandrine had bored them so often that
they condemned it, so to speak, without giving it a hearing, and con-
cluded, perhaps a bit rashly, that the *drame* ought to be written in prose.

They were mistaken. If, in fact, the false predominates in the style and development of certain French tragedies, not the verse, but the versifiers, should be blamed. Not the form employed, but those who had employed that form—the workers, not the tool—ought to be condemned.

In order to be convinced how few obstacles the nature of our poetry poses to the free expression of all that is true, you would do better studying much of Corneille and all of Molière, than Racine. Racine, a superb poet, is elegant, lyrical, and epic; Molière is dramatic. It is time to refute the criticisms heaped upon that admirable style by the bad taste of the last century, and to loudly proclaim that Molière occupies the summit of our drama, not just as a poet, but also as a writer. *"Palmas vere habet iste duas."*[39]

With him, the verse encompasses the idea, closely incorporates it, compresses it, simultaneously expands it, giving it a more severe, more complete shape, and gives it to us, in a way, as an elixir. Verse is the optical form of thought. That is why it is especially adapted to the perspective of the stage. Constructed in a certain way, it sets in relief things that without it would be considered insignificant and vulgar. It makes the tissue of style more solid and artistic. It is the knot which stays the thread. It is the belt which holds up the garment and shapes its folds. What, then, could nature and truth lose by entering into verse? We ask the question of our prose writers themselves—what would they lose in Molière's type of poetry? If we may be allowed another trivial illustration, does wine cease to be wine when it is bottled?

If we had the right to say what, in our opinion, dramatic style should be, we would ask for a free, frank, and sincere verse which dares without prudishness to say everything, to express everything without affectation. It would pass from the natural air of comedy to tragedy, from the sublime to the grotesque, by turns practical and poetic. The whole would be artistic and inspired, profound and unexpected, ample and true. It would know how, at the appropriate moment, to break and displace the caesura in order to disguise the monotony of the alexandrine. It would tend to use *enjambement*, which lengthens the line, rather than inversion, which obscures it. It would be faithful to rhyme, that enslaved queen, that supreme grace of our poetry, which generates our metre. It would be a verse inexhaustible in the variety of its turns and whose secrets of elegance and composition are impenetrable. It would assume a thousand shapes, like Proteus, without changing type and character. It would flee the *tirade*, delight in dialogue, always remaining true to the characters, and, above all, keep its place. When it is called upon to be *beautiful*, it would be beautiful as if by chance and despite itself.[40]* It would be lyric, epic, dramatic as appropriate and would run the whole gamut of poetry from high to low, from the most elevated ideas to the most vulgar, from the most clownish to the most serious, from the most superficial to the most abstract, without ever passing beyond the limits of the spoken scene. In a word, it would be the verse of a man magically endowed with Corneille's soul and Molière's mind. It seems to us that such verse would be "as beautiful as prose."[41]

There would be no relation between such poetry and that whose *post mortem* was sketched above. The nuance which separates them will be easy to indicate, if we may borrow from a talented man—to whom the author of this book owes personal thanks—the following clever distinction: the former poetry was descriptive, ours would be picturesque.

Let us repeat above all, verse in the theatre must lay aside all egoism, all unreasonableness, all coquetry. It is simply a form, a form which ought to admit everything, and in no way imposes on the *drame*, rather, it must receive everything from the *drame*, in order to communicate it to the spectator: French, Latin, law texts, royal oaths, popular phrases, comedy, tragedy, laughter, tears, prose, poetry. Woe to the poet whose verse is fastidious! But this form is made of a bronze which frames thought in its metre, beneath which drama is indestructible, which engraves itself deeper in the actor's mind and warns him of what he omits or adds, preventing him from altering his role or substituting himself for the author. It renders each word inviolable and causes the poet's words to remain vivid for a long time in the auditor's memory. The idea, steeped in verse, suddenly takes on a more incisive and daring quality. It is iron which becomes steel.

One feels that prose is far from possessing these resources. It is of necessity more timid, obliged to deprive the *drame* of all lyric or epic poetry and to reduce it to dialogue and the matter-of-fact. Its wings are not so broad. Furthermore, prose is of easier access; mediocrity is comfortable with it. And for the sake of a few distinguished works which have recently appeared, art would very quickly be encumbered with abortions and embryos. Another faction in the reform movement would incline toward a *drame* which combines verse and prose, like Shakespeare. This manner has its advantages; however, it could lead to incongruities in the transitions from one form to another. When the fabric is of even weave, it is much stronger. Besides, it is a secondary question whether the drama should be written in prose or verse, or in prose and verse combined. A work's status ought to be determined not by its form but by its intrinsic merit. To this sort of question there is only one solution, only one weight that can tip the scales of art: genius.

After all, the first and indispensable merit of a dramatist, be he writer of prose or poetry, is accuracy. Not that merely superficial accuracy, the virtue or vice of the descriptive school, which makes Lhomond and Restaut the wings of its Pegasus,[42] but that intimate, profound, and deliberate accuracy which is permeated with the genius of an idiom and has probed its roots and investigated its etymology. It is always free because it is sure of its actuality and because it is always in agreement with the logic of the language. Our Lady Grammar leads the former with guide ropes; the latter leads grammar by the nose. It can dare, hazard, invent, create its style: it has the right to do so. For, despite what has been said by certain men who do not reflect on what they say, among whom your author must be included, the French language is not *fixed* and will not be fixed. A language does not become fixed. The human spirit is always on the march, or, if you prefer, in movement, and language moves with it. How would it be possible not to change the clothing when the body changes? The Frenchman of the nineteenth century can no more be the Frenchman of the eighteenth century than the latter be the Frenchman of the seventeenth century or this latter be the Frenchman of the sixteenth century. Montaigne's language is no longer that of Rabelais; Pascal's language is no longer that of Montaigne; Montesquieu's language is no longer that of Pascal. Each of these four languages, taken in itself, is admirable because it is original. Each epoch has its own ideas, and it must also possess its own vocabulary to express these ideas. Languages are like oceans, with their ceaseless risings and fallings. At certain times, they leave the shore of one world of thought and sweep over another. All that their wave thus deserts dries up and vanishes. This is the way ideas are extinguished and words disappear. It is the same with human idioms as with everything else. Each century adds something and takes something away. What can be done since it is a matter of fate? In vain would one seek to petrify the mobile countenance of our idiom in a fixed form. In vain would our literary Joshuas cry out to language to stand still. The day when it is *fixed* is the day it dies—that is why the French of a certain contemporary school is a dead language.

Such are, substantially, the *current* ideas of the author of this book concerning the drama. They lack, however, the complete development that would prove the argument for him. He is far, however, from presuming to offer his dramatic essay as being derived from these ideas, which, on the contrary, may themselves, in a simple sense, only be a result of its execution. Doubtless it would be very convenient and more clever for him to rest his book on his Preface and defend the one with the other. He prefers to be less clever and more frank. He wishes, then, to be the first to demonstrate the tenuousness of the tie which links his Preface to the *drame*. His original plan, dictated by laziness, was to present the work alone to the public; "*el demonio sin las cuernas*," as Iriarte said.[43] Only after having duly completed it, at the solicitation of a few, most probably ill-advised, friends, did he decide to reckon with himself in a Preface; to trace, so to speak, the map of the poetic voyage he had taken, to take account of the good or bad acquisitions he had brought back and of the new aspects in which the domain of art had presented itself to his mind. Doubtless this admission will be used to repeat the reproach already addressed him by a German critic of having written "a poetic in defence of his poetry." What does it matter? His original intention had been rather to dispose with, rather that write, a *poetics*. Moreover, would it not always be better to write poetics based on poetry than to write poetry based on poetics? But no, we repeat he has neither the talent to create nor the pretension to establish systems. "Systems," Voltaire noted wittily, "are like rats which pass through twenty holes, only to find two or three among them that will not let them pass through."[44] Therefore, it would have been a useless task and one much beyond his powers. What he has pleaded, on the contrary, is liberty in art against the despotism of systems, codes, and rules. He is in the habit of following, at all risks, whatever he takes for his inspiration, and to change molds as often as compositions. Above all, he flees dogmatism in the arts. God forbid that he aspire to being one of those men, romantic or classicist, who compose *works according to their system*, who condemn themselves to having but one form in mind, to be forever *proving* something, to be following laws other than those of their own temperament and nature. The artificial work of these men, whatever talent they display elsewhere, does not exist for art. It is a theory, not poetry.

After having tried, in all the preceding, to indicate what to us has been the origin of drama, what its character is, and what its style could be, it is now time to descend from these exalted general observations on art to the particular case which elicited them. There remains for us to speak with the reader about our work, about this *Cromwell*; and since it is not a subject in which we take pleasure, we will say very little of it in a very few words.

Oliver Cromwell is one of those characters in history who are at once very famous and very little known. The majority of his biographers, some of whom are historians, have left this great figure incomplete. It seems that they dared not assemble all the features of this strange and colossal prototype of the religious reformation and revolution in England. Almost all of them limit themselves to reproducing on a vaster scale the simple and sinister profile drawn by Bossuet from his monarchist and Catholic viewpoint, from his bishop's throne, supported by the throne of Louis XIV.[45]

Like everyone else, the author of this book went no further. The name Oliver Cromwell only aroused in him the simple conception of a fanatical regicide and a great military leader. In perusing the chronicles—a labor of love—in randomly investigating English seventeenth-century memoirs, he was struck to see a completely new Cromwell unfold gradually before his eyes. This was no longer only the military and political Cromwell of Bossuet; it was a complex, heterogeneous, multi-faceted being, composed of many contradictions. In him was joined much that was bad and much that was good; a greatness and a pettiness of soul. He was a sort of Tiberius-Dandin; a tyrant to Europe and a toy to his family; an old regicide humiliating all royal ambassadors, tormented by his royalist daughter. He was austere and somber in manner, but maintained four court jesters in his circle. He was a writer of bad verse. He was sober, simple, frugal, yet a stickler for etiquette. He was a rough soldier and a shrewd politician. He was experienced in theological disputation and took pleasure in it; a dull, diffuse, muddled orator, but skillful in speaking the language of those he wished to seduce. He was hypocritical and fanatical, a visionary swayed by phantoms from his childhood, believing in astrologers, but banishing them. He was excessively suspicious, always menacing, but rarely sanguinary. He was a strict observer of Puritan morality, while solemnly wasting several hours a day in buffoonery. He was brusque and contemptuous with his intimates, while flattering the sectarians whom he feared. He qualified his remorse with subtleties and deceived his conscience. He was inexhaustible in ingenuity, in deceptions, in resources. He mastered his imagination with his intellect. He was grotesque and sublime. In sum, he was one of those men called "square at their base" by Napoleon, the prototype and leader of all such complete men, whose language was as authentically exact as it was poetic.

This writer, confronted with this rare and striking whole, felt that Bossuet's passionate silhouette was no longer sufficient. He began to range about this lofty figure and was possessed with the burning desire to paint this giant with all his faces, with all his characteristics. The material was rich. Besides the warrior and statesman, one could sketch the theologian, the pedant, the bad poet, the visionary, the buffoon, the father, the husband, the human Proteus, in a word, the twofold Oliver Cromwell, *homo et vir*.

There is one period in his life, especially, when this singular character was manifest in all its forms. It is not, as one might first think, at the trial of Charles I, though that scene is shot through with a somber and terrible fascination. It is the moment when the ambitious man attempted to harvest the fruit of this death. It is that moment when Cromwell, having reached what would have been for others the height of success, master of England, whose innumerable factions lay silent at his feet, master of Scotland, which he governed like a pasha, and of Ireland, which he made a penal colony, master of Europe by means of his navy, his armies, and his diplomacy, it is that moment when he tried finally to accomplish the first dream of his youth, the last goal of his life: to make himself king. History has never concealed a loftier lesson in a nobler drama. First, the Protector arranges to be urged to accept the crown; the august farce begins with the addresses from the municipalities and the shires. An Act of Parliament follows. Cromwell, the anonymous author of the piece, feigns displeasure. He is seen advancing and withdrawing a hand from the scepter. He approaches the throne obliquely, the throne from which he has swept the legitimate dynasty. At last he makes a brusque decision. At his command Westminster is decked with flags, the dais is set up, the crown ordered from the goldsmith, the day for the ceremony is appointed. Strange dénouement! On that very day, before the populace, the troops, the House of Commons, in the great hall of Westminster, on that platform from which he intended to descend a king, suddenly, with a start, he seemed to waken at the sight of the crown, asked if he were dreaming, what meaning had this ceremony, and, in a discourse lasting three hours, declined the royal title.—Was it because his spies warned him that two conspiracies, plotted by Cavaliers and Puritans, would have broken out that day, profiting from his error? Was it a reversal caused in him by the silence or the murmurs of the people, disconcerted to see their regicide assume the throne? Was it simply the wisdom of genius, the instinct of a prudent, albeit unbridled ambition, which knows how much one additional move changes the position and attitude of a man and which dares not expose its plebeian structure to the winds of unpopularity? Was it all these at once? That is what no contemporary document completely illuminates. So much the better! The poet's freedom is all the more complete and the drama benefits from the leeway left it by history. It is clearly an enormous and unique freedom. This is surely the decisive hour, the great peripety of Cromwell's life. It is the moment when his chimera escapes him, when the present kills the future for him, when, to use an expressive vulgarism, his destiny *misfires*. All of Cromwell is at play in this comedy enacted between England and himself.

That, then, is the man, that is the period we have tried to sketch in this book.

The author has let himself be carried away by the child-like pleasure of fingering the keys of this great harpsichord. Certainly, more skillful men would have been able to produce a lofty and profound harmony from it—not one of those harmonies which caress the ear, but one of those intimate harmonies which rouse the whole man, as if each key of the keyboard were attached by a thread to his heart. The author himself ceded to the desire to paint that fanaticism, all those superstitions, diseases of religion which occur at certain periods, and, as Hamlet said, "To make playthings of all men." He ceded to the desire to set up above and around Cromwell—himself the center and pivot of that court, of that nation, of that world, and who rallied all to his cause, coloring everything with his ambition—that double conspiracy plotted by two factions who despised each other but which were in league to overthrow the man who thwarts them, united but not joined. There was the Puritan faction, of diverse minds, fanatical, somber, unselfish, choosing for a leader the most insignificant man for a great role, the egotistical and cowardly Lambert. There was the Cavalier faction, light-headed, joyous, unscrupulous, insouciant, loyal, led by the man who, except for his zeal, was least representative of them, the upright and severe Ormonde. To these are added the ambassadors, humble when confronting the soldier of fortune; and that strange court, a mixture of soldiers of fortune and great lords, vying with each other in servility; and the four jesters whom history's right has allowed me to invent; and the family, each member of which is a thorn in Cromwell's flesh; and Thurloe, the Protector's Achates; and the Jewish rabbi, Israël-Ben-Manasseh, spy, usurer, and astrologer, two parts vile and one part sublime; and Rochester, that bizarre Rochester, ridiculous and clever, elegant and filthy, constantly swearing, always in love and always drunk, as he himself boasted to Bishop Burnet, a bad poet and a good gentleman, vicious and naïve, staking his head and caring little about winning providing the game amused him, capable of anything, of guile and carelessness, of madness and calculation, of villany and generosity; and the savage Carr, of whom history has recorded only one trait, albeit a characteristic and suggestive one; all classes and types of fanatics: Harrison, a fanatical pillager; Barebones, a fanatical merchant; Syndercomb, a murderer; Augustine Garland, the tearful and pious assassin; brave Colonel Overton, literate but somewhat declamatory; the austere and strict Ludlow, who left his ashes and his epitaph at Lausanne. And lastly, there were "Milton and a few other clever men" as noted in a pamphlet dated 1675 (*Cromwell the Politician*) which reminds us of the *Dante quemdam* of the Italian chronicle.

We have not mentioned many of the more secondary figures, each of whom, however, has his own story and marked individuality, and all of whom have contributed to the grip on the author's imagination exercised by this vast historical scene. Out of this scene he has constructed his drama. He writes it in verse because he prefers it thus. Moreover, in reading it, you will discover how little he thought of the play while writing the Preface, for example, with what disinterestedness he combatted the dogma of the unities. His *drame* does not leave London; it begins on the 25th of June 1657 at three in the morning and ends at noon on the 26th. Note that it would fit within the classical formula as it is now laid down by the professors of poetry. They need not, however, thank him for it. It is not with Aristotle's sanction, but with that of history, that the author constructed his *drame* thus; and, because the interest being equal, he prefers a concentrated subject to a diffuse one.

It is evident that, in its present proportions, this *drame* could not be staged in our theatre. It is too long. You will perhaps recognize, however, that it has been composed in all its parts with an eye for the stage. As he approached his subject for closer study, the author recognized, or thought he recognized, the impossibility of its faithful representation being allowed on our stage, given the exceptional status of this theatre, placed as it is between the academic Charybdis and the administrative Scylla, between literary judges and political censors. He had to choose: either the wheedling, cunning, false tragedy and be staged; or the insolently realistic *drame* and be censored. The former was not worth doing; he prefered to attempt the latter. That is why, despairing of ever being staged, he abandoned himself, freely and docilely, to the whims of composition, to the pleasure of unfurling it in large folds, and to the development which the subject required and which, if they result in preventing the *drame* from being staged, at least give it the advantage of being almost complete in historical terms. Besides, reading committees are only a secondary obstacle. If it were to come to pass that dramatic censorship, understanding how far outside our period this innocent, exact and conscientious portrait of Cromwell is drawn, were to permit its staging, only in that case would the author be able to extract a play from this *drame*, a play which would then hazard production and would be hissed.

Until then he will continue to stand apart from the theatre. And it will always be too soon if he quits his modest and well-loved retreat for the agitations of this new world. God grant that he never repent of having exposed the virginal obscurity of his name and person to the shoals, squalls, and tempests of the pit, and especially (for what does failure matter?) to the miserable bickerings of the wings. God grant that he never repent having entered this unsettled, foggy, stormy atmosphere, where ignorance dogmatizes, where envy hisses, where cabals are rampant, where legitimate talent has often gone unrecognized, where the noble candor of genius is sometimes out of place, where mediocrity triumphs by reducing to its level the superiority which eclipses it, where there are so many small men for each great one, so many nonentities for one Talma, so many Myrmidons for one Achilles! Perhaps this sketch will seem surly and far from flattering; but does it not succeed in delineating the differences which separate our theatre, a place of intrigue and battles, from the solemn serentiy of the ancient theatre?

Whatever may happen, he believes that he must give warning in advance to the small number of persons who might be tempted by such a spectacle, that a play drawn from *Cromwell* would occupy no less time than an ordinary production. It is difficult for a *romantic* theatre to be established otherwise. Certainly, if you seek something other than those tragedies, in which one or two characters, abstractions of a metaphysical idea, solemnly strut on a narrow stage, barely filled with a few confidants, pale tracings of heroes entrusted with filling the gaps of an action, simple, uniform and monotonous; if you are bored by all that, a whole evening is not too much time to devote entirely and with some completeness to this elite among men, to this period of crisis. This man possesses character and genius, which is linked to his character, both of which are dominated by his beliefs, his passions which disrupt his beliefs, his character, and his genius, his tastes which color his passions, his habits which regulate his tastes and muzzle his passions. He is surrounded by an endless cortege of types of men stirred up by these various character traits. The period has its customs, its laws, its fashion, its spirit, its achievements, its superstitions, its events, and its people, which all the above first causes mold like soft wax. You imagine that such a portrait will be gigantic. Instead of one personality, like that with which the drama of the old school is content, you will have twenty, forty, fifty, who knows how many, in all shapes and sizes. The *drame* will be crowded. Would it not be petty to allot two hours of the performance time to a comic opera or a farce, to abridge Shakespeare for Bobèche?[46] And, don't imagine that, if the action is well managed, the multitude of characters set in motion will cause fatigue to the spectator or cause confusion in the *drame*. Shakespeare, who abounds in minor details, is, at the same time, and for that very reason, imposing through the greatness of the whole. He is the oak which casts an enormous shadow composed of thousands of tiny, etched leaves.

Let us hope that the French will not delay becoming accustomed to devoting a whole evening in the theatre to a single play. In England and in Germany there are plays lasting six hours. The Greeks, who are so often held up to us as models—and in the manner of Scudéry, we cite at this point the classicist Dacier, Chapter VII of his *Poetics*[47]—the Greeks sometimes went so far as to perform twelve or sixteen plays in a single day. The attention-span of people who are fond of the theatre is more *lively* than is usually believed. *The Marriage of Figaro*, the connecting link of Beaumarchais's great trilogy, fills an entire evening, and who was ever bored or fatigued by it? Beaumarchais had the merit to venture the first step toward that goal of modern art where it is impossible to develop in only two hours that undying interest which results from a vast, true, and multi-leveled action. But, you say, such a performance, consisting of a single play would be monotonous and seem long. That is an error! On the contrary, it would lose its present tedium and monotony. In effect, what is done now? The spectator's pleasure is divided into two distinct parts. He is first given two hours of serious pleasure which is followed by one hour of comic pleasure; with an hour of intermission which we do not count in the entertainment, the total is four hours. What would the romantic drama do? It would artfully mingle these two kinds of pleasure. It would constantly move the audience from the serious to the comic, from buffoonish excitement to heart-rending emotions, *from grave to tender, from pleasant to severe.* For, as we have already established, the *drame* is the grotesque, joined with the sublime, the soul within the body; it is tragedy beneath comedy. Do you not see that offering you respite from one impression by means of another, by sharpening the tragic on the comic and vice versa, even by making use of the charms of the opera when need be, that these performances although made up of only one play, would have the value of many more? The romantic stage would make a piquant, savoury, and diversified dish of what on the classical stage has been a medicine divided into two pills.

Thus has the author quickly exhausted what he said to the reader. He does not know how the critics will receive this *drame* and these ideas, summarily presented, stripped of their corollaries, bereft of their ramifications, assembled on the run and in haste to have done with them. They will no doubt seem most impudent and strange to "the disciples of LaHarpe." But if, by chance, as naked and undeveloped as they are, they were able to contribute to setting the public on the path of truth— this public whose education is already so advanced, which has already been prepared for art by so many remarkable critical and practical writings, books, and newspapers—let the public follow this impulsion without being concerned that it is the product of an unknown man, from a voice without authority, from a work of little merit. It is a copper bell which calls the populace to the true temple and the true God.

Both the old literary regime and the old political regime exist today. At almost every point the last century weighs down on the new one. The oppression is most notable in criticism. For example, you will find living men who repeat to you the definition of taste from Voltaire: "Taste in poetry is no different from what it is in women's clothing."[48] Taste, then, is coquetry. Remarkable words, which marvellously portray the rouged, beauty-marked, powdered poetry of the eighteenth century, that literature of panniers, pom-poms and flounces. They offer an admirable summary of an age which reduced to pettiness, at least in some aspects, even its loftiest geniuses. It was an age when Montesquieu was able and compelled to compose *The Temple of Gnide*, Voltaire, *The Temple of Taste*, and Jean-Jacques, *The Village Soothsayer*.

Taste is the common sense of genius. That is what will soon be established by another school of criticism, a strong, frank, knowledgeable criticism, a criticism of this century, whose vigorous sprouts are beginning to push through the dessicated branches of the old school. This youthful criticism, as serious as the other is frivolous, as erudite as the other is ignorant, has already created journals that are heeded. And one is sometimes suprised to find in the most negligible publications excellent articles by its adherents. Joining hands with all that is superior and courageous in letters, it will deliver us from two plagues: decrepit *classicism* and false *romanticism*, which dares show itself at the feet of the true. For modern genius has its shadow, its pale imitation, its parasite, its *classic*, which copies its makeup, smears itself with its colors, assumes its livery, picks up its crumbs, and, like *the sorcerer's apprentice*, puts into play, using words retained from memory, elements of action whose secret

it does not possess. Thus it produces nonsense which frequently causes
its master much trouble in setting right. But what must be destroyed
above all is the old false taste. It must be scrubbed from the surface of
contemporary literature; it corrodes and tarnishes in vain. It is addressing a young, severe, vigorous, generation which does not understand it.
The train of the eighteenth century is still dragging in the nineteenth;
but we young men who have seen Bonaparte are not the ones who will
carry it.

We are approaching, then, the moment when we will see the new
criticism prevail, posed as it is on a broad, solid, and deep foundation.
It will soon be understood that writers ought to be judged, not according
to rules and genres, things which are contrary to nature and art, but
according to the immutable principles of that art and the special laws
of their individual temperaments. The sound general judgement will be
ashamed of the criticism which buried Pierre Corneille alive, muzzled
Racine, and ridiculously rehabilitated John Milton only by virtue of the
epic code of Father LeBossu. People will agree to place themselves in
the author's position to get a clear view of the work, to see it through
the author's eyes. One will put aside, as Chateaubriand noted, "the petty
criticism of defects for the great and fruitful criticism of the beauties."[49]
It is time for all intelligent people to grasp the thread which frequently
links what we, according to our fancy, call a "defect" to what we call a
"beauty." Defects, at least what we give that name, are often the inborn,
necessary, inevitable conditions of good qualities.

Scit genius, natale comes qui temperat astrum.[50]

Who ever saw a medal without a reverse side; or a talent whose light
does not have its shadow, the smoke with the flame? Such a blemish can
only be the inseparable consequence of beauty. A crude brushstroke,
which offends at close range, completes the effect and gives relief to the
whole. Eliminate one, and the other is eliminated. Originality consists
in such things. Genius by definition is uneven. There are no high mountains without deep valleys. Fill the valley with the mountain and you will
have nothing but a steppe, a wasteland, the Sablon plain rather than the
Alps, larks, not eagles.

It is also necessary to make allowances for the weather, the climate,
local influences. The Bible and Homer sometimes pain us precisely because of their sublimities. Who would want to cut a word of them? Our
weakness is often fearful of the boldness genius inspires because of our
inability to seize objects with a similarly vast intelligence. And then, once
again, there is the matter of those *defects* which only take root in masterpieces; it is a given of certain geniuses to have certain defects. Shake-

speare is reproached for his abuse of metaphysics, and of wit, for borrowed scenes, for obscenity, for the use of mythological nonsense in vogue in his time, for extravagance, obscurity, bad taste, bombast, and stylistic unevenness. The oak, that giant tree we compared earlier to Shakespeare and which bears more than one resemblance to him, the oak has an odd shape, gnarled branches, dark leaves, hard and rough bark; but it is an oak.

And it is because of these qualities that it is an oak. If you want a smooth trunk, straight branches, satiny leaves, look to the pale birch, the hollow elder, the weeping willow; but leave the mighty oak in peace. Don't abuse what offers you protection.

The author of this book knows as well as anyone the numerous and sizable defects of his works. If he rarely happens to correct them, it is because he loathes returning after the fact to something he has finished.[51]* He has not mastered the art of concealing a blemish with a beauty, and he has never been able to revive inspiration when it has cooled. Moreover, what has he written which would merit such effort? The labor he would expend in eliminating these imperfections in his books, he prefers to employ in cleansing his intellect of its defects. His method is to correct one work by another work.

Nonetheless, no matter how his book is received, he vows here not to defend it in whole or in part. If his *drame* is bad, what is the use of defending it? If it is good, why defend it? Time will do the book justice or will wreak justice upon it. Success of the moment is the business of the publisher alone. If, then, the wrath of critics is aroused by the publication of this essay, he will leave them alone. How would he answer them? He is not one of those who speak, as the Castilian poet says, "Through the mouths of their wounds."

Per la boca de su herida.[52]

One last word. You may have noticed that in this somewhat long journey through so many diverse questions the author has generally refrained from backing up his personal opinion with texts, citations, or authorities. It is not because they were not available—"If the poet establishes things that are impossible according to the rules of art, he unquestionably is in error; but it ceases to be an error when by this means he achieves the end he had in view; for he has found what he sought."—"They take for nonsense all that the weakness of their intellect does not allow them to comprehend. They especially treat as ridiculous those marvelous places where the poet, in order to better approach reason, sets aside, if one must speak thus, reason itself. In fact that precept, which sometimes makes not observing the rules a rule in itself, is one of art's mysteries that it is difficult to communicate to men of absolutely no taste. . .and whom a sort of abnormality of mind renders insensible to what ordinarily impresses men."—Who said the former? Aristotle. Who said the latter? Boileau. You see from this single example that the author of this drama, like others, could have armed himself with proper names and taken refuge behind others' reputations. But he preferred to leave that style of argument to those who think it invincible, universal, and all-powerful. As for him, he prefers reasons to authorities; he has always cared more for arms than for coats-of-arms.

October 1827

Preface to *Hernani* (1830)

Hernani *premiered at the Comédie-Française on 25 February 1830. It was published by Mame and Delaunay-Vallée in March 1830.*

The author of this play wrote the following statement a few weeks ago about a poet who had died prematurely:[53]

. . .During this period of conflict and turmoil in the literary world, who are to be pitied, those who succumb or those who fight? No doubt it is sad to witness the departure of a twenty-year-old poet. A lyre has been broken. A future ended. But doesn't repose have something to be said for it? Yet what of those men who remain and are constantly exposed to slanders, insults, hatred, jealousies, cabals, and treachery? They are honest men against whom a dishonest war is waged. They are dedicated men, who, after all, only want to gain an additional freedom for the nation—intellectual and artistic freedom. They are hardworking men who peacefully pursue their conscientious work, at prey, on one side, to the vile machinations of police censorship and too often exposed, on the other side, to the ingratitude of the very audience for whom they work. Is it not permitted to them to sometimes look back with envy on those who have fallen behind them and rest in the tomb? "*Invideo*," Luther said in the cemetary at Worms, "*invideo quia quiescunt.*"[54]

Yet what does it matter? Young men, be brave! However harsh the present is made for us, the future will be fine. Romanticism, so frequently poorly defined, is, in the main, no more than *liberalism* in literature—and that is its real definition, if you only consider it in its militant aspect. This truth is already understood by nearly all clever men, and their number is great. And soon, for the work is already well under way, liberalism in literature will be no less popular than political liberalism. Liberty in art; liberty in society; these are the double goals toward which all rational and logical minds must strive together. That is the double banner under which rally all the strong and steadfast youth of our time, excepting a very few intellects (who will be enlightened in time). There, with the youth and at their head, are the elite of the preceding generation, all those wise old men who, after the first moment of suspicion and scrutiny, recognized that what their sons were doing is a consequence of what they themselves did, and that liberty in literature is the daughter of political liberty. This is the principle of the century and will prevail. The various factions of *ultras*, classicists or monarchists, will lend help in vain to the reconstruction, in all its aspects, of the old regime, in society as in literature. Each improvement in the nation, each intellectual development, each step taken by liberty will cause the collapse of the entire scaffolding they have erected. And, definitely, their reactionary efforts will have proven to have been of no use. In a revolution, all movement leads forward. Truth and liberty possess the excellent quality of having all that is done for them and all that is done against them serve them equally. Well, after so many great deeds done by our fathers—deeds we have witnessed—we find ourselves freed from the old forms of society. How could we not help but free ourselves from political forms? For a new people, a new art. While admiring the literature of the age of Louis XIV, so well adapted to the monarchy, France today will be able to have her own, personal and national, literature, this France of the nineteenth century, given liberty by Mirabeau and strength by Napoleon.

The author of this play begs your pardon for citing himself. His words are so unmemorable that he often needs to repeat them. Moreover, it is perhaps not inappropriate today to offer the reader the two pages just transcribed. Not that this *drame* might in any way merit the fine appellation, *new art, new poetry*. Far from it. But the principle of liberty in literature has just advanced a step; progress has been made, not for art, this *drame* is too small a thing, but for the public. In this respect at least, a part of the predictions put forward above have just been realized.

There was, in fact, danger in such an abrupt change of audience, in risking experiments in the theatre which had heretofore only been entrusted to the page, *which suffers all*. The reading public is very different from the theatre-going public, and it was to be feared that the latter might reject what the former had accepted. This did not happen. The principle of liberty, in literature, already understood by the reflective, reading public, has been no less thoroughly embraced by that enormous crowd which floods Parisian theatres every evening, avid for the pure emotions of art. The loud, powerful voice of the people, which resembles that of God, henceforth wants poetry to have the same motto as politics: TOLERANCE AND LIBERTY.

Now let the poet appear! He has a public.

And the public will have this liberty as it ought to be, in harmony with the concept of order in the state and with art in literature. Liberty has a wisdom peculiar to it and without which it is incomplete. Let the old rules of d'Aubignac die with the old customs of Cujas;[55] it is well. Let a literature of the people succeed a court literature, that is even better. But, above all, let there be an internal logic at the heart of all these novelties. Let the principle of liberty do its work, and let it be well done.

In letters, as in society, let there be no ceremony and no anarchy; let this be law. Neither red heels nor red caps.

That is what the public wants and this desire is good. As for us, in deference to this public which has welcomed with so much indulgence an endeavor which merited so little, we offer it today this *drame* as it was acted. Perhaps the day will come when it can be published as it was conceived by the author with indications and discussion of the modifications it was subject to for performance. These critical details might not be without interest nor without educational value, but they would seem trivial today. Liberty in art is admitted. The principal question is resolved: what need have we to stop for secondary questions? We will return to the rest someday. And we will also speak in great detail, ruining it with reason and with fact, of the censorship of drama which is the only obstacle left to liberty in the theatre, now that the public is no longer an obstacle. We will attempt, at our own risk and peril, and through our devotion to artistic matters, to characterize the thousand abuses of this petty inquisition, which has, like the other Holy Office, its secret judges, its masked executioners, its tortures and mutilations, and its death penalty. If it is possible, we will tear off these swaddling clothes wrapped around the theatre by the police. It is a shame that in the nineteenth century we still find the theatre encumbered by them.

Today must be the occasion for gratitude and thanks. The author of this *drame* addresses his to the public from the depths of his heart. Not because of its literary worth, but because of its sincerity and freedom, this work has been generously protected from great hostility by the public, itself sincere and free. My thanks then be given to it, as to this powerful group of youths who brought aid and protection to the work of a young man who, like them, is sincere and independent! He works especially for them. It would be a very great honor to receive the applause of this youthful elite. They are intelligent, logical, rational, truly liberal in literature as in politics, a noble generation which does not refuse to open its eyes to the truth and receive illumination from all sides.

As for his work itself, he will not speak about it. He accepts the criticisms it has received, the most severe with the kindest, as one can profit from anything. He does not flatter himself that everyone understood this *drame* from the start. Its true key is in the *Romancero general*. He would sincerely urge those people who have been shocked by this work to re-read *The Cid*, *Don Sanche*, *Nicomedes*, or, rather, all of Corneille and Molière, both great poets. Such a reading, if, however, they will first wish to make allowance for the enormous inferiority of *Hernani*'s author, will perhaps render them less severe in regard to certain things which may have offended them in either the form or the background of this drama. In sum, the moment has perhaps not come to judge it. *Hernani* is, at present, only the first stone of an edifice which exists already completed in the mind of the author, but whose entirety alone can give value to this *drame*! Perhaps one day it will not seem unfortunate that his fantasy, like that of the architect of Bourges, placed an almost moorish door on his gothic cathedral.

In the meantime, he knows that what he has done counts for very little. May he not lack the time and the fortitude to complete his work! It will be all the more highly regarded when it is finished. It is not the work of one of those privileged poets who can die or be interrupted before finishing their work without harm to their memory. It is not the work of one of those men who remain great without having completed their work, happy men, of whom it can be said as Virgil said of the construction of Carthage:

> *Pendent opera interrupta minæque*
> *Murorum ingentes!*[56]

9 March 1830

Notes

1. "You break bread with the industrious man." Tomás de Iriarte (1750–1791), "*Fabula Primera: El elefante y otros animales*."
2. *The Iliad*. [Hugo's note.]
3. *The Odyssey*. [Hugo's note.]
4. Virgil *Aeneid* 8. 429.
5. Without doubt yes, yes again, always yes! Acknowledgement is due here to an illustrious foreign author who had the kindness to notice this writer. We wish to prove our gratitude and esteem by noting an error into which he seems to have fallen. The honored critic "noted down," such are his exact words, this author's declaration in the Preface of another work, that: "There is neither *classical* nor *romantic*, in literature, as in all things, but two divisions, the good and the bad, the beautiful and the deformed, the true and the false." So much solemnity in declaring this profession of faith was not necessary. The author has never and will never deviate from it. It is wonderfully in tune with "what allows the *ugly* as a type for imitation and the *grotesque* as an element of art." One does not contradict the other. The division between the beautiful and the ugly in art is not symmetrical with that division in nature. Execution in art determines whether something is beautiful or ugly. A deformed, horrible, hideous thing transported with truth and poetry into the domain of art, will become beautiful, admirable, and sublime, without losing any of its monstrousness. And, conversely, the most beautiful things in the world, falsely and systematically arranged in an artificial composition, will be ridiculous, burlesque, hybrid, *ugly*. The Callot orgies, Salvator Rosa's "Temptation" with its terrifying demon, the same painter's "Battlepiece" with its repulsive images of death and carnage,

Bonifacio's "Triboulet," Murillo's vermin-ridden beggar, and Benvenuto Cellini's sculptures, where laughter is aroused by the hideous figures in the arabesques and acanthuses, these are the ugly in nature, but beautiful in art. While nothing is more ugly than all the Greek and Roman profiles, than the patchwork idea of beauty, displayed in the purplish and mealy colors of the followers of David's second period. Job and Philoctetes, with their suppurating, foetid wounds are beautiful; the kings and queens of Campistron in their purple robes and tinsel crowns are very ugly. Something well done, something poorly done: these are the beautiful and the ugly in art. This author has already explained his idea by assimilating this distinction in that between the *true* and the *false*, the *good* and the *bad*. Furthermore, in art as in nature, the grotesque is an element, but not an end. That which is only grotesque is incomplete. [Hugo's note.]

6. Boileau's *Art of Poetry* (1674) was an important statement of French neo-classical attitudes. Jean-François de LaHarpe (1739–1803) was a playwright and critic in the late eighteenth century. His *Lycée, or Lectures on Ancient and Modern Literature* was published from 1799 to 1804.

7. These two names are united here, but should not be confused. Aristophanes is incomparably superior to Plautus. Aristophanes holds a distinct position in ancient poetry, like Diogenes in philosophy. You will sense why Terence is not named in this passage with the two popular comic writers of antiquity. Terence is the poet of the Scipios, an elegant and stylish sculptor, in whose hands the unpolished comedy of the early Romans is eliminated. [Hugo's note.]

8. This great drama of the man who is damned dominates the imagination of the Middle Ages. Pulcinella, carried off by the Devil to the great pleasure of the crowds in our public squares, is a trivial and popular version of this drama. What is singularly striking when you compare the twin comedies, *Don Juan* and *Faust*, is that Juan is the materialist and Faust the spiritualist. The former has tasted all the pleasures, the latter all the sciences. Both have attacked the tree of good and evil; one has made off with its fruits, the other has dug up its roots. The first is damned for enjoying, the second for knowing. One is a great lord, the other is a philosopher. Don Juan is the body; Faust is the soul. These two plays complement one another. [Hugo's note.]

9. Harpagon is the title character in Molière's *Miser*. Scapin is the comic servant in several Molière comedies. Basile, Bartholo, and Figaro are characters in Beaumarchais's *Marriage of Figaro*.

10. This striking expression, "burlesque Homer," is from Charles Nodier, who employed it in speaking of Rabelais and who will pardon our extending it to Cervantes and Ariosto. [Hugo's note.]

11. But, you will say, drama also portrays the history of men. Yes, but as *life*, not as *history*. It leaves the historian the exact series of general facts, the order of the dates, the arousal of large crowds, battles, conquests, the breaking-up of empires, all the surface of history. Drama takes history up from within. What history overlooks or disdains—details of dress, customs, appearances, the underside of events, in a word, life—belongs to drama. And drama can be enormous in its scope when these trivial things are taken up by a great hand, *prensa manu magna*. But one must be wary of seeking pure history in drama, even if it is "historical." Drama is written from legends, not records. It is a chronicle, not chronological. [Hugo's note.]

12. LaHarpe, *Lycée*, book XII, chapter 15.

13. Voltaire, "Essay on Epic Poetry."

14. Title characters in Molière comedies.

15. Why is it that Molière is much truer than our tragic authors? Let us go further and ask why it is that he is almost always true? The reason is, that although entirely restricted by the prejudices of his time with respect to pity and fear, he nonetheless adds to his grotesques grandly sublime scenes which round out the humanity of his drama. Comedy is also much closer to nature than tragedy. In effect, one can conceive of actions in which the characters can constantly laugh or excite our laughter, without ceasing to be natural. And furthermore, Molière's characters sometimes weep. But how can one conceive an event, no matter how fearful or limited, where not only the principal characters never smile, even from irony or sarcasm, but where there is no human being—from *prince* to *confidant*—who is subject either to fits of laughter or even of human nature?

Finally, Molière is truer than our tragic authors because he exploits the new principle, the modern principle, the dramatic principle: grotesque, comedy; while the latter use up their energy and their genius returning to the ancient epic circle which is closed, an aged and exhausted mold, from which the truth our epoch needs will not escape, because it is not in the form of modern society. [Hugo's note.]

16. This is an allusion to Voltaire's *Socrates*.

17. Juvenal *Satire* 4.

18. Plato *Phaedo* 66.

19. Dandin is the ridiculous judge in Racine's *Litigants*; Prusias the king in Corneille's *Nicomedes*; Trissotin the poet in Molière's *Learned Ladies*; Brid'oison the judge in Beaumarchais's *Marriage of Figaro*; and Bégears a character in Beaumarchais's *Guilty Mother*.

20. "Sing in alternating couplets; the Muses like alternation." Virgil *Bucolics* 3. 59.

21. Jean Galbert de Campistron was a writer of neo-classical tragedies in the late seventeenth and early eighteenth centuries.

22. This is a reference to the debate in the form of pamphlets that followed the première of Corneille's *The Cid* in 1637. Jean Mairet, Jean de Claveret, Georges de Scudéry, and the Abbé d'Aubignac were the writers involved in the attack on Corneille's play.

23. From the "Discourse to Lord Bolingbroke on the Subject of Tragedy" (1731).

24. Richelet is the author of *Treatise of French Versification* (1692).

25. "When I have to write a play, I lock the rules up with six keys." From "The New Art of Writing Plays" (1609).

26. It is not by adapting novels, even those of Walter Scott, to the stage that the art will make progress. It is alright for a first or second effort, especially when the adaptors have other and more solid qualifications; but it is fundamentally little more than the substitution of one imitation for another. When we say that you should neither copy Shakespeare nor Schiller, we are addressing those clumsy imitators who, seeking rules where those poets have only used genius, reproduce the form without the essence, the bark without the sap. We are not referring to those skillful translations which can be undertaken by true

poets. Madame Tastu has made excellent translations of several scenes from Shakepeare. Emile Deschamps is currently working on a *Romeo and Juliet* for our stage. And such is the powerful suppleness of his talent, he can encompass Shakespeare in his verses, as he has already done with Horace. Certainly, this is artistic and poetic work, a labor which excludes neither originality, life or creativity. That is the manner used by the Psalmists to translate Job. [Hugo's note.]

27. Vaugelas was a seventeenth-century grammarian and one of the first members of the French Academy.

28. We were astonished by the following lines from Goethe: "Properly speaking, there are no historical characters in poetry. Rather, when the poet wishes to represent the world he has conceived, he honors certain individuals he has found in history by borrowing their names for his creations." (*On Art and Antiquity*.) You see where this doctrine might lead were it taken seriously: straight to the false and the fantastic. Happily, the famous poet, for whom this doubtless once seemed true from a certain perspective, since he did say it, certainly did not practice it. He would certainly not write a Mahomet like a Werther, a Napoleon like a Faust. [Hugo's note.]

29. The complete citation reads: "Inceptis gravibus plerumque et magna professis / purpureus, late qui splendeat, unus et alter / adsuitor pannus,... ("Works with noble beginnings and grand promises often have one or two purple patches so stitched as to glitter far and wide....") Horace *The Art of Poetry* 14–16.

30. Corneille, *Cinna* V 1. 1493.

31. Corneille, *The Cid* III 4. 987.

32. Corneille, *Nicomedes* I 1. 22.

33. *Nicomedes* I 3. 564.

34. Corneille, *Horace* III 6. 1009.

35. Racine, *Athalia* II 5. 506.

36. Racine, *Britannicus* IV 2. 1137.

37. Gabriel Legouvé, *The Death of Henry IV* (1806).

38. Psalms 42:2.

39. "He truly merits both honors."

40. The author of this *drame* was speaking about it with Talma one day, and, in a conversation he will publish later, when he can no longer be accused of falling back on authorities to support his work or his words, he outlined some of his ideas about dramatic style to the great actor. "Oh yes!" Talma cried, interrupting him, "That is what I myself was telling them: no beautiful verses!" *No beautiful verses*! The instinct of a genius uncovered this profound precept. In effect, it is *"beautiful verses"* which kill beautiful plays. [Hugo's note.]

41. LaHarpe, *Lycée*, book XII, chapter 5.

42. Charles-François Lhomond and Pierre Restaut were grammarians. Restaut's book *General and Reasoned Principles of French Language* (1730) was widely used in the universities at the beginning of the nineteenth century.

43. "The Devil without his horns."

44. Inexact quotation from "Beard," *The Philosophical Dictionary*.

45. Bossuet's portrait of Cromwell appears in his "Funeral Oration for Henrietta of France" (1670).

46. Bobèche (1791–1841) was a performer of *parades* on the Boulevard du Temple and creator of the comic character Jocrisse.

47. André Dacier was a seventeenth-century critic who published annotated translations of Horace and Aristotle.

48. From the Notice to Voltaire's *Selected Letters*.

49. Hugo misquotes slightly from a review of Dussault's *Literary Annals* which Chateaubriand published in June 1819. This review was reprinted in Volume 8 of Chateaubriand's *Oeuvres Complètes* (Paris: Pourrat, 1836). The correct citation reads as follows: "...the petty and easy criticism of *defects* for the great and difficult criticism of *beauties*."

50. "Why so, the Genius alone knows—who rules our star of birth." Horace *Epistles* 2. 2. 187.

51. This is another infraction of Boileau's rules. It is not his fault if this author does not submit to the following articles: "Twenty times to craft," etc., "Polish ceaselessly," etc. No one is responsible for his infirmities or inadequacies. Moreover, we will be the first to honor this Nicolas Boileau, this rare and excellent mind, this Jansenist of our poetry. It is not his fault if the rhetoricians adorned him with the ridiculous sobriquet of "Legislator of Parnassus." He can't do anything about it.

Certainly, if one examines the remarkable poem of Boileau as a code, one will find strange things in it. What can we say, for example, of the reproach he addresses to one who

Had his shepherd speak *as one speaks in a village*?

Should we make them speak as one speaks at court? There you have operatic shepherds turned into types. Let us also say that Boileau did not understand either of the two original poets of his time, Molière and La Fontaine. Of the former he said:

It is thus that Molière, in sketching out his works,
Might have won the prize for his art. . . .

He did not deign to mention the latter. It is true that Molière and La Fontaine did not know how to *correct* or *polish* their work. [Hugo's note.]

52. Guillén de Castro, *Mocedades del Cid*, "First Day," scene 1.

53. Charles Dovalle, who died in November 1829. Hugo wrote the Preface to an edition of Dovalle's poems published in January 1830.

54. "I envy them, I envy those who know peace."

55. François Hédelin, Abbé d'Aubignac, is the author of *The Whole Art of the Stage* (1657), a comprehensive statement of French neo-classical theory. Jacques Cujas was a famous sixteenth-century jurist.

56. "The work stands, unfinished; the walls, colossal, menace." Virgil *Aeneid* 4. 89.

6

EMILE DESCHAMPS

Emile Deschamps (1791–1871) is the only minor figure in this collection. Henri Girard, his only biographer, has aptly labelled him a "bourgeois dilettante." If he is at all remembered it is as the author of the text for Berlioz's Romeo and Juliet *symphony. But during the 1820s Deschamps was a reasonably important figure and an active champion of the romantic cause.*

He was a member of the group of young poets and writers that formed around Victor Hugo and in 1823–1824 was one of the principal editors of the French Muse, *a periodical which provided a much-needed forum for the younger generation of poets.*

Deschamps's original poetry does not compare with the work of his contemporaries Hugo and Vigny. But in his translations of Goethe and Schiller and the Spanish Romancero, *he helped to continue the expansion of French knowledge of foreign literatures. At the beginning of 1828 he collaborated with Vigny on a translation of* Romeo and Juliet *which was accepted by the Comédie-Française but never produced. The manuscript of this first translation of Shakespeare by two French romantic poets has been lost, but in 1844 Deschamps published his versions of both* Romeo and Juliet *and* Macbeth.

In November of 1828 Deschamps published his first collection of poetry and translations, Studies, French and Foreign *(Paris: U. Canel). Its four editions of 1828–1829 attest to the fact of its success. The Preface, which is here translated in part, takes its place as a major statement from the romantic faction during the crucial period between the publication of* Cromwell *in 1827 and the première of* Hernani *in 1830.*

From the Preface to *Studies, French and Foreign* **(1828)**

II

It is time to turn our attention to the French theatre and consider what our great writers have done, what is being done today, and what remains to be done.

After having shown that, for the past two centuries, France was infinitely superior in prose writing to all other nations, we had to admit France's obvious inferiority in the higher poetic genres, which were not really cultivated until the present generation. We are happy to be able to acknowledge France's superiority in dramatic literature.

In Europe, France is preeminent in dramatic writing. No one in any period can dispute France's claim to the palm for comedy. It would be slander to simply call Molière the first comic poet of the world. You must call him the only one, so much is he above the others. No doubt Shakespeare is the greatest tragic genius of modern times. The masters of our stage are far from being his equal in the creation of characters, in the invention of plots, in the language of passion, and in poetic style. But, you must consider that after Shakespeare, England has no other truly great writers, while our tragic theatre has been illustrious continuously for two centuries, with an unbroken succession of first-rate poets. This fact renders the French Melpomene much more imposing and rich. It is also necessary to note that the beautiful proportions and regularity given our tragedy by the authors of *Cinna* and *Andromache* distinguish it from its contemporary literature. We will consider later whether or not this advantage has proven to have been purchased at too dear a price by depriving us of a great many dramatic resources. It remains true that although the fathers of French tragedy did not create a multitude of characters or plots, they cannot be denied an enormous contribution in the development of an entire system whose majestic forms have stood unaltered for two hundred years. Let me cite a few lines written by Sainte-Beuve which express our thoughts much more eloquently than we could:

At that time—and it was unheard of until that time—a modern literature could be seen imposing the most exquisite taste on its noblest masterpieces. Reason informed and aided genius, and, like a vigilant mother, taught it loftiness and chasteness in feelings and grace and melody of language. The imitation of the ancients gave evidence of becoming original and creative and to reflect, while further embellishing, that most splendid civilization of our monarchy. From this harmonious fusion of the depiction of antiquity and the present age, there developed a ravishing and pure ideal, an object of delight and enchantment for all cultivated and discriminating people. Finally, although France has not had poets like Dante, Ariosto, and Tasso, and especially Shakespeare, she has had Racine. And, for the first time, the perfection of Virgil was equalled.[1]

The admirable *Cid* excepted—and to which we will return shortly—the first and finest masterpieces of our stage are Roman, Greek, or Hebrew. Racine and Corneille magnificently exploited these three ancient cultures, arranging, without distorting, them according to the taste of their time. Dramatic poets (and this is what greatly hinders the life of their works) cannot always go very far in developing fidelity of customs and realistic language. To be heard and enjoyed, they are obliged to choose for their style and characters a mean between the period they are depicting and the period in which they live. That was what Corneille and Racine did with prodigious art, although each used different means. These two immortal poets have nothing in common; that is why they can be treated as equals.

Voltaire, after them, located his touching and spirited dramas in all the nations and periods not touched by his predecessors. He brought to the stage a great number of modern cultures. That, specifically, earned him his place on the throne of tragedy. Innovation is always the primary road to fame. But Voltaire, although inventive in his conceptions, inventive in his plots, and original in his thinking, remained inferior to Corneille and Racine as a poet and a writer. It is uncertain whether Nature endowed him with the same degree of poetic talent as these two great men, or that, writing in an excessively witty, but artistically shallow period, he had intentionally neglected poetic form and color, which would have only been indifferently understood, in order to devote himself entirely to the theatrical ingenuity and philosophic declamation then in favor with the public. It is certain that he further exaggerated the error of localization and individualization which is the original sin of tragedy. His Turks, Chinese, Arabs, and Americans are much more French than the Greeks and Romans of Racine and Corneille, and, since they are Frenchmen of the age of Louis XV, rather than of Louis XIV, their language is less grand, less pure, and less idealized. They are addressing Madame de Pompadour rather than Madame de Vallière. Nevertheless, one is justified in making an exception of Voltaire's *chevaliers*, characters which are drawn with great charm and a faithfulness of coloring more than sufficient for the period. On the whole, Voltaire must have earned the successful impression that he made, despite numerous flaws of execution and the weakness of a style which too often contrasts with the boldness of his conceptions. And it is impossible not to acknowledge that, if he did not make it greater, he did enlarge the scope of our tragic theatre and made both the dialogue and the situations more compelling. Finally, he opened up a new and abundant source of emotion; to him we owe the experience of strong and noble feelings which had not been expressed to the same degree hitherto.

We must stop to remark that the genius of our great tragic writers was expressed in the proportions and forms suited to the period in which they were writing. There is no analogy between the nature of their beauties, nor, for that matter, of their defects. How, then, do we obtain a place beside them if not by doing what they have not done and what they would do now?

For too long now, we have been offered the same tragedies under different names. For too long now, those who carry on the tragic tradition have presented ancient characters dressed as moderns, or modern characters speaking an outmoded language, exaggerating what was defective in our masterpieces without reproducing their virtues. Progressing from imitation to imitation, French tragedy has become, with few exceptions, no more than a banal pattern into which motivated entrances and exits fit extremely well, but in which there is little concern for making the characters act and speak in a new and compelling manner. This is the reason for the public's indifference to the Comédie-Française, which for so long had been our glory and our noblest entertainment.

In all nations, the arts, during certain periods, change in their forms and in their methods, while their goals and effects remain the same. The same is true of laws. From time to time new forms of entertainment, new conditions for success become necessary. In the arts, we are at such a point today. the revolution in music led by Rossini and the one presently taking place in painting are irrefutable proofs of this truth. The enormous revolution in French literatre produced by the historians, the philosophers, and the poets of the new school cannot be denied. Why should dramatic art not have its turn?. . . . But this revolution has already been attempted, more or less happily, in our theatres. Alone, the Comédie-Française still remains immobile amidst the general movement. It is the last stronghold of the *academics*. It will not be able to hold out much longer; it will have to capitulate as a result of famine.

Things have already progressed rather far. We are now well aware of what is no longer wanted, if we do not yet know what is wanted. The ground has been cleared. Nothing remains but to lay out the paths. It is the responsibility of the artist to illuminate and guide the public. Theories are not very effective, however, when they are not accompanied by examples. A few good models of the new sort of tragic beauty are needed for the enrichment of our theatre; without them it will die. They will speak more loudly than all rational arguments. That is why the dramatic revolution could not be inaugurated in a better way than with the presentation of Shakespeare's masterpieces, faithfully and audaciously translated into French verse.

"What," you will cry, "more imitations, never any originality!" We will reply, first, that nothing would be more original and novel for the public than the unaffected presentation in our theatre of a major Shakespearean tragedy with all the spectacle of a detailed staging. For both the English performances, where three-quarters of the spectators do not understand a word, and prose translations, deprived of the magic of style and acting, always give an imperfect and sometimes very false impression of the great poet. Moreover, where are the original French tragedies among those which have been designated "new" during the past thirty years? How many have outlived their initial success? The list would be very difficult to draw up. Let us admit that under different titles, we are constantly seeing the same thing on our stage, the work of imitators. . . . In reality, the translations should be given preference until a creative genius appears. As for immortal masterpieces, those who follow tradition in France give us, with a minimum of quality, exactly what we have had for a long time. At least translators will give us what we have not yet had. It is not because an author selects a new subject that he creates a new tragedy. If the characters, situation and style are not at all innovative; if he has borrowed from twenty earlier French works to produce his own work; if *Mithridates* and *Alzire*,[2] with names and customs changed, are continually brought to mind; if almost every verse presumes, as if it could be predicted, the following verse, certainly such a work cannot reasonably be considered a work of the imagination. Tragic plots are extremely rare and men of genius are also very rare. Dramatic poets might be grouped into three classes: first, those who invent, or rather, find plots and treat them in an inventive way—there have only been three or four of these; next are those who openly treat great and beautiful subjects which had been weakly treated before them; and who are, at least, creators in execution, for they embellish and rejuvenate their subjects with the vigor of their thoughts and the new forms of their talent—two or three authors of this sort are found in each period; finally, there are those who treat supposedly original subjects and write in an ordinary and conventional manner, supplying only an original title; an originality which disappears with the poster—this class of writers has always been numerous.

Finding subjects for tragedy in everything is peculiar to mediocre authors; true dramatic poets know, on the contrary, how few tragic plots—destined to inspire terror in every circumstance, like *Oedipus* and

Macbeth—there are. That is why they search for these rare and beautiful subjects; that is why, when they do not find equally noble new subjects, they prefer to re-write those which had not been well executed in the past—at least on our stage—with the conviction that, in the arts, it is an original manner of treating subjects, much more than the novelty of the subjects as such, which should be sought. Great musicians often re-write the opera scores left by their predecessors. Raphaël re-painted the same subject thirty times, yet what a prodigious variety there is in this apparent monotony! Finally, the classic poets of Greece ceaselessly reproduced the same plots in their theatre. Thus it is true, in poetry as in painting, the execution is almost all. Doubtless, if everything is original and beautiful—subject as well as execution—merit and renown reach a superior level: that is where Sophocles and Shakespeare are found. But when you can create *Iphigenia* or *Phaedra*, *Oedipus* or *Mérope*,[3] which have already had numerous productions over the past two thousand years, you are, nonetheless, Racine and Voltaire. If these magnificent subjects had not become magnificent tragedies in the hands of our two great masters, it would be up to our living poets to work upon them until they succeeded in naturalizing the subjects to our stage: there would be no greater contemporary triumphs. Here again, the facts come to the aid of the theories.

Which of the contemporary tragedies produced at the Comédie-Française will long remain in the repertory? The answer is self-evident: Lemercier's *Agamemnon*, Soumet's *Clytemnestra*, and Lebrun's *Mary Stuart*.[4] That is to say, two imitations from the Greek, two ancient and universal subjects which had often been found wanting and which were waiting for two extremely talented men to take them up and place them on the French stage beside our older masterpieces; and a skillful translation from the German which arouses interest and emotion through the natural and colorful poetry later employed by the same author in his *Travels in Greece*.

If we turn to the Odéon, what will we find in the first rank of viable tragedies? Two secondhand subjects: *The Maccabees*, a very remarkable work by Guiraud, and that grand and powerful composition, *Saul*, in which Soumet has proven himself equally adept as a dramatic, epic, and lyric poet—a marvelous union of qualities found to perfection in *Athalia*.[5] A single entirely original tragedy, among the hundreds produced in the same period, will outlast the criticism and praise it has received: this is Casimir Delavigne's *Pariah*.[6] No doubt the conception of its plot is far from being irreproachable, precisely because it is invented. No doubt the drama does not proceed as smoothly as might be desired. And the entire play errs in vulgar interest and in *vis tragica*. But what should above all be noted in this tragedy are well-drawn characters, a great freshness in imagery and feelings, truly original situations, a pure and picturesque poetry, interlaced with passionate dialogue and an exquisitely delicate vocabulary, and, finally, something youthful and unusual in our theatre. That is why *The Pariah* has been the least successful of Casimir Delavigne's works but that which will earn him the most fame.

Thus, only a few of the three or four hundred tragedies which have been praised in the past thirty years have survived! What a source of philosophic reflection for our young dramatists! Can this terrifying disproportion be explained? It can be assigned three principal causes: the disheartening superiority of our great masters; the exhaustion of the truly tragic subjects, at least of those in the so-called classical mode; finally, the absence of a poetic turn of mind in almost all the authors. In France, it has been thought that with some stylistic talent and pedestrian versification, and with a bit of wit and what is termed stage sense, one could turn to the writing of tragedies and even of high comedies!...Many have been written and have, initially, succeeded. For thousands of reasons, it is rare for a first performance not to succeed. Then each work has been religiously entombed in its success. The first requisite for the composition of a great dramatic work is that the author be a poet; the rest is acquired through study and experience. If you are not a poet and absolutely wish to work in the theatre, limit yourself to the secondary genres. The Greek and French classical writers, from Aeschylus to Racine, from Aristophanes to Molière, were, above all else, great poets and great writers.

In truth, what is there in common between these geniuses and their unimaginative successors, who have the pretention to imitate them and the presumption to "defend" them?

Certainly, given the current state of affairs and attitudes, it is a great honor to have written one or two tragedies which should remain in the repertory. And this honor belongs only to poets in the most noble sense of the word. For example, who is not aware that, before turning to dramatic literature, Soumet had gloriously received more than one poetic honor and had contributed, in several works glittering with talent, to the general movement occurring now in the realms of ideas and in the forms of language and verse?

To return to the theatrical question, since good subjects for classical tragedy have become very scarce, and, on the other hand, since sustaining the success of mediocre plays has become more and more difficult, henceforth few tragedies will be written. So much the better. It is the best way of restoring to our masterpieces full possession of our theatre until tragedies of a new type appear to share the stage with them, but without harm to them.

This leads naturally to a discussion of another Schiller translation which will no doubt repeat the success of *Mary Stuart*: it is the *William Tell* left by Pichat.[7] We can affirm that the tone, the color, and all the poetry of the German author have been carried over into the French poet's work. It is a powerful tragedy, perfectly executed. Pichat received acclaim at his debut with *Léonidas*. The progress from *Léonidas* to *William Tell* is immense. The Comédie-Française's neglect or ommision of such a work can be explained only through imprudence or error. If Pichat's name and the interests of art mean little to the reading committee of that theatre, they at least ought to understand their own interests. But this was not the case. *William Tell* triumphed everywhere; the Opera, which is so ably directed now, is preparing a version which will eclipse all the others. Yet the Comédie-Française does not wake from its apathy! The Minister of the Interior's first thoughts had been for the dying Pichat; he was at pains to deliver it from the chains placed upon it by the previous censor—a *Tell* oppressed by another Gessler. For the first time in a great while power was seen to align itself with talent: the Muses are Memory's daughters; they will not forget it. We will hope that the Comédie-Française will finally remember that its files contain a fine tragedy, which the public awaits, by a prematurely mourned poet.

III

We now proclaim that Shakespeare must receive the same attention given to Schiller. If a few timorous spirits still need justification for this, let them read Villemain's fine and eloquent lectures on this creator of modern tragedy.[8] They will see how the purest of tastes bows down before genius. The greatest authors have always been the greatest critics, when they so desired. Again, the masters of our stage have, by themselves, created nothing perfect using modern subjects. Voltaire deprived himself of the great resource of contrasts in manners and characters by maintaining a pompous style. Our only continually natural and true play is *The Cid*, but it, too, was adapted from the foreign stage, and Corneille called it a tragi-comedy, so much did this great man sense the necessity of varying theatricality in a subject that was not classical. It is known how he was driven from this new path by the classicists of his time, but we cannot conceive how, for the past two centuries, no author has sought to return to this path. We persist in claiming that the only way to follow it unquestionably is to debut by imitating Shakespeare, in the same way that Racine, in order to develop classical subjects, took his inspiration from Euripides and came as close to him as the age permitted. But, it is not a question of wanting to unseat our great poets at the expense of a usurper, as some men of letters claim to fear. In the empire of the arts, there is a throne for each genius: Voltaire did no damage to Corneille or Racine; he only killed off their imitators; similarly, Shakespeare will not damage the followers of Voltaire. We can be reasonably calm, then. As for the age-old national hostilities, and the medieval loathing of the foreigner, whom would one impress today with this literary patriotism? France is too strong and too rich to be jealous and unjust. It is wonderful to see the speed with which the public's education has been achieved. Six years ago the English actors were received with catcalls and insults!. . .Why shouldn't the public want to see Shakespeare at the Comédie-Française, as it has always seen, and sees every day, Sophocles, Euripides, Guillem de Castro, Maffei, Alfieri, Schiller, etc., etc.; as it admires a painting by Rubens or Raphaël in our museum; as it listens to the music of Mozart or Rossini at our Grand Opera? What possible distinction would the foolish and the insincere seek to establish between such evident analogies?

But, it will be said, *Phaedra, Iphigenia, Oedipus*, etc., were only imitations of the ancients artfully adapted to our system and to our dramatic practices, while you wish the public to accept faithful translations of Shakespeare—doubtless; and here are the reasons: the disposition of the ancient arenas, the intervention of the chorus, the imposing robes and masks of the actors, female roles played by men, and finally, the extreme simplicity of the action and the completely pagan nature of the ideas and emotions would have formed too shocking incongruities to our society and Christian civilization for Greek tragedy to be transferred unchanged to our stage, as though it were but a statue changing its pedestal. Shakespeare, on the contrary, is a genius who reflects all the modern passions and speaks to us in our own language. And furthermore, the means employed in his works are very nearly the same as in our tragedies. A few set changes more or less, that is the whole difference. We must admit, while lamenting it, that our great writers of tragedy often sacrificed the severe portraits of the antiquity they imitated to the taste of their age: hence, the viragos of Corneille, the gallant young male leads of Racine, and the love affairs of the aging Jocasta, so begrudged by Voltaire. We have reached a time when the need for truth in everything is universally desired, and, because of that, today's poets are more fortunate than their predecessors. Thus, it is their fault, and the actor's fault, but not the audience's fault, if the false and the conventional are still too prominent on our stage. And to return to Shakespeare, who does not now recognize that Ducis' imitations, however daring and useful they might have been, are really only the mutilated fragments of a giant? They contain admirable scenes, but one seeks a play in them in vain. As has been judiciously observed in one of the excellent articles often found in the *Globe*: "The time for imitation is over. It is necessary either to create or translate." In effect, nothing is worse than a portrait which bears no likeness to the original. The time has come to offer the French public Shakespeare, as great as he is, with his magnificent developments, with the variety of his characters, with the independence of his conceptions, with the so artfully managed mingling of comic and tragic styles, and finally, with his fresh and original beauties, and even with some of the defects that are inseparable from his virtues, and which, at least, do not resemble the defects of our poets. The time has come for his masterpieces to be faithfully reproduced on our stage, as ours are on foreign stages. All Europe, learned and poetic, is under Shakespeare's domination. Shakespeare is translated into every language. He is found everywhere but on twenty square metres of Paris, at the corner of the *rues* Saint-Honoré and Richelieu.[9] They cannot hold out much longer.

What! you will say again. Is it necessary to offer the French public all the obscene clowning or cold horrors which charmed the Elizabethans!...Certainly not. This was also the debt the great man paid to the poor taste of his time. But such is the art he applied, even to those monstrosities, that they can be stripped away without in any way upsetting the structure of his plays or the movement of their plots. This purification, begun by the author himself and continued later in England, often with little taste or discernment, is necessarily part of the work of a French translator who must not reject or retain all that the English adaptors have rejected or retained. But the translation will be no less than literal, in the sense that if it does not offer all Shakespeare, at least it will contain nothing that is not by Shakespeare.

We foresee the following banal objection being put to us: you advocate production of verse translations of Shakespeare because you have made such translations of several of his tragedies. We will reply in an equally banal manner: we have translated several Shakespearean tragedies into French verse, precisely because we believe their production necessary, for the public, for art, and for the Comédie-Française itself. For the Comédie-Française because, no longer in possession of great tragic actors, it can only hope to remain in vogue by the attention given to genre and a system of playwriting entirely new to our theatre. For the public, because weary of so many pallid, feeble imitations of our masterpieces and weary of the shabby productions of these masterpieces themselves, it prefers to re-read them twenty times with pleasure and not to return to the theatre until something responds to the vague need for novelty which torments it. Finally, for art, because lacking a point of comparison, it is to be feared that this need would be blindly satisfied by so-called romantic works, written without inspiration or study, which would only reproduce the external forms of Shakespeare's dramas, and whose entire novelty would consist in destroying the unities of time and place—no longer a subject for serious consideration—and in mingling the *lazzi* of the boulevard with the ceremonial language of our classical tragedy. It is urgent that a Shakespearean tragedy forestall this danger and prevent opinion being led astray either for the good or bad on this great dramatic debate. Everything will be decided in an evening, and an intelligent, impartial audience will immediately recognize that the question does not reside in the material arrangement of sets and scenes—in the sudden shifts from forest to palace, and from one province to another, all things which are well enough dispensed with when possible—but that it is really found in the individualized depiction of character, in the consistent replacement of narrative with action, in the simplicity of language and its poetic coloring, and finally, in a completely modern style.

The translation of *Romeo and Juliet* that we have made in collaboration with Alfred de Vigny and the other translations which we are individually completing, are works undertaken conscientiously. Like Montaigne, we could write on the title page: this is a sincere work. We have been directed neither by vanity nor anything other than a concern for art. We have no ambition other than making the great English poet known to the French public. If our works are applauded, it is Shakespeare who will be applauded. If Shakespeare is not understood, it will be the fault of his interpreters; others, luckier or more skilled, will appear, and we will be the first to aid and proclaim their victory. But again, time presses; the moment is decisive. Everything can be compromised and delayed by the appearance of a false romanticism. We must hope that the Comédie-Française will finally open its eyes. With the masterpieces of its magnificent repertory aided by the masterpieces of Shakespeare, with the satisfying unity it can still give to its productions, and with the enlightened concern of Taylor (if it can recognize him as its savior), the Comédie-Française would soon recapture that sparkle and popularity which disappear and are lost with each new day through insipid imitation and habit.

Otherwise, and if the Comédie-Française persists in its inaction or in its poorly conceived activity, it is impossible that the current authority, which has so wisely destroyed so many monopolies, will spare much longer the most intolerable of monopolies, and remain deaf to the protests it hears from all sides. The liberal arts, as their name implies, require liberty. Competition is the best protection. Certainly, if a new theatre were to open, under the direction of an intelligent manager; without a reading committee or an administration; without the encumbrance of works received over the past thirty years (and which were old before they were born); with young actors trained in playing a variety of roles, familiar with the expressive pantomime and natural declamation of the great English actors (the only ones since Talma to arouse tragic emotions in us); with the firm resolution to offer only plays consistently new in form and style as "new" plays; certainly such a theatre would need no other support than its own work and its good organization. And there would exist in all the above something strong and vital which would hardly resemble the dying vegetation, the rank fecundity, which sprouts and flourishes under our stage lighting.

When the great test of Shakespeare has been made, when our public comprehends the most beautiful dramatic poetry of modern times—as it has learned the poetry of the ancients from our stage masterpieces—then, all questions having been posed, all treasures exposed, all systems compared and appreciated, a genius will perhaps appear who will combine all these elements and give them a new form. He will be more fortunate than the great masters of our distinguished past. He will effect the growth of true French tragedy, a national drama, based on our history and our customs. He will copy no one, Shakespeare no more than Racine, Schiller no more than Corneille. This is what Victor Hugo says in his admirable Preface to *Cromwell*. And *Cromwell* is a work of poetry, wholly vigorous and well conceived, even in its most criticized parts, which will remain an object of envy and anger for some, and an object of study and admiration for others, an object of animated discussion for all, when oblivion will have consumed the majority of today's successes.

Notes

1. Charles-Augustin Sainte-Beuve, *Historical Portrait of French Poetry and Theatre of the Sixteenth Century* (Paris: Sautelet, 1828), I, pp. 214–15.

2. Tragedies by Racine and Voltaire, respectively.

3. Tragedies, the first two by Racine, the latter two by Voltaire.

4. Népomucène Lemercier's *Agamemnon* was first produced in 1797. Alexandre Soumet's *Clytemnestra* was produced at the Comédie-Française in 1822. Pierre Lebrun's *Mary Stuart* was produced at the Comédie-Française in 1820.

5. Alexandre Soumet's *Saul* was produced at the Odéon Theatre in 1822. Alexandre Guiraud's *Maccabees* was produced at the Odéon Theatre in 1822. *Athalia* is by Racine.

6. Casimir Delavigne's *Pariah* was produced at the Odéon Theatre in 1821.

7. Michel Pichat's *Léonidas* was produced with great success at the Comédie-Française in 1825. *William Tell* had been accepted by the Comédie-Française before the poet's death in January 1828. Its production was delayed, first by the censor, then by difficulties arising in casting the title role. It was produced at the Odéon Theatre in 1830.

8. Abel François Villemain was a conservative historian and critic who published regularly in the *Debates*.

9. The location of the Comédie-Française.

7

ALFRED DE VIGNY

In 1830 Sainte-Beuve coined the phrase "ivory tower poet" in writing about Vigny (1797–1863). It proved to be a prophetic description, for by the mid-1830s Vigny had virtually ceased publishing. It was only with the post-humous publication of Destinies *(1864) that his position as an important French nineteenth-century poet was established.*

In the 1820s, however, Vigny was, with Hugo and Lamartine, at the forefront of the poetic revolution. He had served in the army between 1816 and 1824 but was able to retire and devote himself fully to literature after his marriage to an English heiress in 1825. By the mid-1820s he had contributed articles and poems to the major romantic periodicals and had become a friend of Hugo. His Poems *(1822) and* Poems, Ancient and Modern *(1826), collected in a definitive edition in 1829, established his reputation as a poet of the first order. His novel* Cinq-Mars *(1826) is one of the finest historical novels published in the 1820s. With his translations from Shakespeare, Vigny made a major contribution to the theatrical debate of the late 1820s. He collaborated with Emile Deschamps on a translation of* Romeo and Juliet *which was accepted by the Comédie-Française in 1828 but never produced. His* Merchant of Venice *was planned for production at the Ambigu-Comique Theatre in 1830 but was denied a production authorization by the censor. His translation of* Othello *was produced at the Comédie-Française in October 1829 and was, thus, the first romantic verse drama to receive an important Paris production. After* Othello, *Vigny wrote three prose plays,* The Maréchale d'Ancre *(1831);* A Narrow Escape *(1833), a* proverbe; *and* Chatterton *(1835). During the first half of the 1830s Vigny also published two collections of novellas,* Stello *(1832), and* Military Servitude and Grandeur *(1835).*

The Othello translation of 1829 and its production were a necessary and important step in the development of French drama in the 1820s. The Preface to this translation (Paris: Levavasseur, U. Canel, 1830) clearly establishes this fact and summarizes the attitudes of the French romantics toward Shakespeare.

Preface to *The Moor of Venice, Othello* (1830): "A Letter to Lord ××× concerning the evening of 24 October 1829 and a theory of drama"

You are greatly mistaken in fancying that France is troubling herself about me. Why, she hardly remembers today Czar Nicholas' conquest, yesterday, of the rotting Turkish empire. I have had *my evening*, my dear sir, and that is that. One evening determines the fate of a tragedy. That very evening is, I assure you, its whole life: for, when you examine the question carefully, you will see that an hour earlier it did not exist; an hour later it is no more. Let me explain:

A tragic play is an idea which suddenly metamorphoses into a *machine*: a mechanism as complicated as Marly's defunct *machine* with its royal past,[1] now but the few decayed joists you see floating in the mud. This machine is mounted with a great expenditure of time, ideas, words, gestures, painted cardboard, drops, and embroidered fabrics. A crowd comes to see it. Once the *evening* has arrived, you release a spring and the *machine* is set in motion for about four hours. Words fly, gestures are made, the cardboard flats move on and off, drops are raised and lowered, fabrics are displayed; the ideas express what they can amidst all this. And, if by chance, nothing goes awry, at the end of four hours, the same person pulls the same spring and the *machine* stops. Everyone leaves, everything has been said. The next day, the *crowd* diminishes exactly by half, and the *machine* starts to become sluggish. You adjust a small wheel or a lever and it runs again a limited number of times, after which friction wears out the machinery, which loosens a bit, and begins to squeak at the hinges. After another series of evenings, the *machine*, having continued to decrease in *quality* and the *crowd* in *quantity*, movement suddenly grinds to a halt.

There you have the general fate of all ideas which are reduced to spring-loaded dramatic mechanisms, usually called *tragedy, comedy, drame, opera*, etc., etc. There is not a student in Paris who could not tell you, within two days, how many times one or another of these machines will

Costume Design by Tony Johannot for Othello in Vigny's *The Moor of Venice, Othello*, 1829. (Jean Sangnier collection.)

be able to continue in operation. One will last one hundred nights, which is said to be the maximum, another six, another more, another fewer.

It cannot, then, be denied: staging a tragedy is nothing more than preparing *one evening*: its true title should be the date of the first performance. According to this principle, in place of Shakespeare's title *As You Like It*, had I been at a loss for a choice I would have placed 6 January 1600 on the title page of his comedy. And for me, *The Moor of Venice* should only be known as 24 October 1829.

Today, all is still; the fireworks are burnt out. I will not conceal that, when I was first struck by this notion, I found the preparation for this sort of evening "a bit time-consuming," as our famed Molière often noted. For example, in order to make plans for a *24 October*, I had to regretfully abandon a story or a history (whichever you prefer) in the manner of *Cinq-Mars*, which I was writing for my own amusement if possible, or for the amusement of children. The interruption was costly, but necessary. I had something urgent to say to the public, and the *machine* we have been discussing was the quickest way. It is truly an excellent method to address an assembly of 3,000 persons as there is no way for them to avoid hearing what you have to tell them. A reader has many defenses against you—such as throwing the book in the fire or out the window: I know of no means to forestall such indignant reactions. But, faced with the spectator, you are in a much stronger position. Once inside, he is caught, as though in a mousetrap. It is very difficult for him to leave if he has unsympathetic neighbors whom he might disturb. There are some places where he cannot even use his handkerchief! In this state of restraint, stifled and suffocating, he must listen. The *evening* over, 3,000 heads have been filled with your ideas. Isn't that a wonderful invention?

Now, this is the essence of what I had to say to the enlightened spectator on 24 October 1829:

The following simple question must be resolved:

Will the French stage be receptive or not to a modern tragedy which offers the following: —in its conception, a large-scale portrait of life, rather than a narrow picture focused on a catastrophe and a plot; —in its composition, characters rather than roles, quiet scenes without drama intermingled with tragic and comic scenes; —in its execution, style which is familiar, comic, tragic, and sometimes epic?

In order to answer this triple question an original tragedy would not be sufficient. At openings, the public always focuses its attention on the plot, trying to follow the action and, unfamiliar with the whole work, fails to understand what motivates variations in style.

A new plot would not have the authority to support an equally new style and would necessarily fall under a double criticism: honorable attempts have proven this.

An original work would only prove whether I had written a good or bad tragedy. But debate would infallibly arise to determine if it is a satisfactory example of the dramatic system being established. And these debates would be interminable for us, posterity being the best arbiter.

Now, posterity has established Shakespeare's greatness. Therefore, one of his works, written according to the system I advocate, is example enough.

Concerning myself principally with the question of style in this first experiment, I wanted to choose a generally recognized model, accepted by all mankind and sanctioned by several centuries.

I offer it, not as an ideal for our time, but as the presentation of a foreign masterpiece, constructed of old by the finest hand ever to write for the stage, and in the style I think appropriate to our own period—modified by the changes necessitated by our own philosophic and scientific progress, by some developments in stage practice, and in the refinement of expression.

Listen tonight to the language I think should be that of modern tragedy, in which each character will speak in character and, in art as in life, will shift from everyday simplicity to passionate exaltation—from *recitative* to *song*.

There you have the sense of this undertaking, which, successful or not, is, for my part, an impartial one. For it is possible that, after having touched, examined and tested, with a Shakespearean prelude, this one hundred-voiced organ which is the theatre, I may decide never to take it up to promulgate my own ideas. The art of the stage is too dependent on action not to trouble the poet's meditation. Furthermore, it is the most restrictive of the arts: by definition too circumscribed for philosophic developments because of the audience's impatience and the limits of time, it is further hampered by other fetters. The heaviest are those of theatrical censorship which invariably prevents the analysis of the two characters which form the basis of modern civilization, the *Priest* and the *King*. You can do no more than broadly sketch them, something unworthy of any serious writer, who feels the need to examine everything in depth. I won't even mention the innumerable and minor frustrations which must be overcome to achieve even a transitory success. This modest *translation*, announced as such and as inoffensive as my work, experienced such a tremendous and unexpected opposition that I still ask myself by what miracle it succeeded. Nevertheless, the *evening* of 24 October consecrated it. Little matter that a dozen other evenings followed or that there are others still to come: after what I have said, they are, as you can see, superfluous. Since a tragedy's success takes the shape of a mermaid—*"desinit in piscem mulier formosa superne"*[2]—whether its fishtail begins to diminish above, or below, the waist is hardly important. The question is: will it continue to swim, and if, after having taken the plunge as usual, will it reappear often? Since the answer to this lies in the future and concerns only me, not general matters, I shall say no more about it.

Let us consider the public.

May it finally receive its due. The public has boldly demonstrated the need to see and hear the *truth* which all uncompromising men in the arts are fighting for today. I know not what the public is if it is not the *majority*, and this majority wanted what we want. Something told me that the long-awaited hour had arrived.[3]* Routine retreated this time. Routine is an evil which often afflicts our country. Routine is contrary to art; the latter thrives on movement, the former on immobility. There is no people today more restricted and immobilized by the customs of literature and the arts than we French, whom you consider so fickle. Yes, noble France is sometimes negligent and, in everything, often sleeps. This is best for the peace of the world, for when she wakes, she rouses the world with invasions or intellectual enlightenment. But for the rest of the time, she is too often governed by the most politically unscrupulous and intellectually least distinguished of men. From time to time, the healthy and active portion of the public feels the need to move forward and wants leaders. But almost always, a group of feeble and lazy-minded people, who support one another, form a chain which encircles and halts progress. Their soporific galvanism expands, ennervating the public, which returns to its bed and falls into a deep sleep. These invalids—formerly sound men—like to hear today what was heard yesterday, the same ideas, the same expressions, the same sounds. Everything new seems ridiculous to them; everything untried, barbarous. "Everything is Aquilon to them."[4] Feeble and sickly, accustomed only to mild, warm, herbal teas, they cannot stomach hearty wine. They are the ones I sought to cure. It hurts me to see them so pallid and unsteady. Sometimes I caused them such pain they cried out. But, by means of some concession to their taste, at present they find themselves in a much better state of health. I will send you news of their progress from time to time.

Let us put aside the pointless question of performances which I have treated lightly as being by nature frivolous. Sometimes we can smile while speaking of men, never when dealing with ideas. I would like to discuss systems in general and, in particular, the present system of dramatic reform.

It is incredible that through distorting words people have sometimes misunderstood the word "system." *System* (Σύδτημα, from δυν ἵδτημι) from its root means *order*, if I remember my Greek correctly, a linking of principles and consequences to form a doctrine, a dogma. Any man who has ideas and doesn't organize them into a unified system is an incomplete man: he will produce nothing that is not vague; if he does anything tolerable, it will be by chance, by fits and starts; he will always be groping in a fog. On the other hand, watch a new thought germinate in a well-organized mind: it develops in an admirable manner, in an instant, so great is the heat and uninterrupted attention of a vigorous mind bringing it quickly to fruition. The idea, well fertilized, gives birth in turn to subsequent generations of ideas which resemble it and are uniquely dependent on it. However involuntary the poet's inspiration, it is, nevertheless, often unconsciously and unaccountably transmitted through a succession of ideas which form a complete system. This perfect order lacking, the system would be nothing, it would not exist. Thus I think that such a person, who seems completely *instinctual* to you— incapable of writing a theory about his own work once the intoxication of his enthusiasm has dissipated—this person, even though he swore that he had no system, is more dependent on his system than anyone else, precisely because he is unconscious of it. He hasn't analyzed the system which sweeps him along and is not free to demolish it to construct a second system better than the first.

The history of the world is nothing more than a series of multiple systems in action. By reducing each one of these systems to its basic idea, one could reduce history itself to twenty-odd ideas, at most. No great man, whether a thinker or man of action, has appeared who has not created and activated a system. A difference to be noted is that the *thinker* is vastly superior to the man of action since he lives in the realm of ideas and presents them in their pristine state, untouched by life or chance. He owes nothing. The man of action, soldier or statesman, however, is tossed about in a sea of circumstances, raised up by one wave, thrown down by another. Swept away by a current from which he hopes to profit, he changes his route twenty times. He changes his plans and projects, forgetting the principle which he wished to illumine and often ceding his conviction to his fate.

The word "system" thus vindicated, we can return to our subject and apply it to the two systems of drama now causing discord; one in its death throes, the other about to be born.

I want to follow the same order I established earlier with you and speak first of literary composition.

Thank heavens, the old tripod of the unities on which Melpomene was placed, often rather awkwardly, is reduced at present to the one solid basis which can't be denied: the unity of interest in the action. One smiles with pity when one reads in one of our great writers: "The spectator is only at a play for three hours: thus its action must not exceed three hours."[5] You might as well say: "It takes the reader only four hours to complete such and such a poem or novel, therefore its action must not exceed four hours." The latter statement embodies all the errors that follow from the first statement. But it is not enough to be freed from such heavy chains. The limited attitude that created them must be eradicated.

Come and may a pure blood spilled by my own hands
Wash the very marble that his feet have touched.[6]

First, consider that every tragedy in the recently defunct system was the catastrophe resulting from and the dénouement of an action already developed at the curtain's rise. This action hung by a thread and all that remained was to sever it. That is the source of the flaw which strikes you, and all foreigners, in French tragedies; the paucity of scenes and developments, the false delays, and then, suddenly, the haste to finish, mixed with the fear you sense everywhere of there being insufficient material to fill the framework of five acts. Far from diminishing my esteem for those who followed the former system, such considerations increase it. A kind of prodigious legerdemain and a multitude of skillful devices were necessary for the writer of each tragedy to mask the poverty to which he had condemned himself, rather like eking out a garment from a rag of faded purple fabric.

In the future, the dramatic poet will not follow that path. First, he will take in his broad hand a lengthy period of time and move whole lifetimes through it. He will create men, not as *types*, but as *individuals* (the only way to interest mankind). He will allow his creations to live their own lives and will place in their hearts only those germs of passion from which great events spring. Then, and only then, when the time is ripe, and without our being able to sense his presence accelerating the action, he will show us fate trapping its victims in coils as powerful and inescapable as those in which Laocoön and his sons writhe. Then, far from finding the characters too small for the space they occupy, he will complain that they lack breathing space. For art will resemble life, and in life a major action is surrounded by a whirlwind of innumerable and necessary events. Thus, the creator will find among his characters enough mouthpieces to promulgate all his ideas, enough hearts to give life to all his feelings. His enlivening presence will be sensed throughout. *"Mens agitat molem."*[7]

I am right. Everything was harmonious in the old system of tragedy; but everything was equally harmonious in the feudal and theocratic system, and nevertheless it is defunct. In order to realize an extended catastrophe which had substance only because it was swollen, it was necessary to substitute roles for characters, personified abstract passions for men. But nature has never produced a family—a whole house in the ancient sense (*domus*)—where father and children, master and servants, are found to be equally sensitive; excited to the same degree by the same event. Such people jump right into the middle of things, and react seriously and sincerely to the most obvious surprises and delusions. From such experiences they derive a solemn satisfaction, a solemn sadness, or a solemn rage. These characters retain only the sentiment that has activated them from the beginning to the end, without permitting their imaginations to deviate by a single step. They have but one function;

to at once activate the dénouement and delay it—while continually speaking about it.

Thus, in anterooms that lead nowhere, there must be characters who go no place and speak about nothing. Their ideas are ill defined, their words vague. They may be slightly motivated by bloodless sentiments or calm passions, and thus achieve a graceful death or a false sigh. O vain phantasmagoria! Shadows of men in a shadow of nature! Empty kingdoms!...."*Inania regna!*"[8]

Thus, it is only by dint of genius or talent that the leaders of each epoch succeeded in piercing these shadows with a glimmer of light, outlining beautiful forms in this chaos. Their works were magnificent exceptions which were taken for rules; lesser writers have fallen into the common rut of this false route.

Nevertheless, it is still possible to find men who can speak this dead language well. In the fifteenth century, highly esteemed discourses were written in Latin!

I, myself, believe that it would not be difficult to prove that the force which held us back for so long in this world of convention was Politeness—the muse of second-class tragedy. Yes, certainly, for it alone was capable of altogether banishing true characters as being gross; simple language as trivial; idealism, in philosophy and passion, as extravagant; poetry as caprice.

Politeness, although a child of the court, has and always will have, a *levelling effect*. It smoothes and evens out everything; neither too high nor too low is its motto. It does not hear Nature, like Macbeth, crying out to genius from all sides: "Come high or low!"[9]

Man is exalted or simple; otherwise he is false. Thus, in the future, the poet will know that a representation of man as he is, is, by definition, emotionally affecting. There is no necessity for me to be aware, from the outset, of the secret motivation of a well-drawn character; I am already intrigued by a recognizable person. I love him because he *exists*, and because I recognize him in his walk, in his language, in his whole air—a living being, like myself, thrown into the world as fodder for destiny. Let him *exist* or I will have nothing to do with him. Let him not seek to appear what the Muse of Politeness has labelled, in her falsely noble language, a "hero." Let him be nothing but a man, otherwise he would be much less. Let him act according to his mortal heart and not according to the unreal representation of a poorly invented character. For this latter, the poet truly deserves the name "imitator of phantoms" given him by Plato when banishing him from the Republic.

The manner of the polite school which is so perfectly boring at present is especially evident in the details of style. I don't believe that a foreigner can completely comprehend the degree of falseness achieved by some *versifiers for the stage* (I refuse to call them poets). As one example among thousands of possible examples, when one wanted to say "spies," one said:

Those mortals on whom the state stakes its vigilance.[10]

You may feel that only an extreme courtesy directed toward the class of spies would give birth to such an elegant periphrasis: such *mortals* who, by chance, found themselves in the theatre were assuredly grateful for it. Besides, it is a natural style, for can't you easily conceive of a ruler, Bonaparte, for example, instead of simply saying: "Fouché, tomorrow you will send one hundred spies to the Carrousel for review," say, "My Lord, you will send tomorrow one hundred mortals on whom the state stakes its vigilance." Here we have the *noble*, the *polite*, and the *harmonious*.

Writers, men of talent for the most part—and the one whose example I have used was a man of talent—have also been led astray by the desire to achieve what is called harmony, seduced by the example of a great writer who dealt only with ancient subjects wherein the Greek and Latin phrase was not misplaced. Wanting to preserve this, they have falsified it. Forced by progress, which drags them along despite themselves to take up modern subjects, they continue to use the language imitated from the ancients (and not in itself ancient). From this develops the style in which each word is an anachronism, wherein Chinese, Turks, and American Indians speak in verse of "Hymen and his torches."

This much-desired harmony is, I feel, better suited to the poem than to drama. The lyric poet can, in fact must, chant his verses, recapturing his initial inspiration. To him the following verses apply:

Verses are children of the lyre;
They must be sung, rather than spoken.

But drama will never offer the public more than characters assembled to speak of their affairs: they must, above all, speak. Let us write for them that frank and simple *recitative*, of which Molière provides the most beautiful example in our language. When passion and misfortune fill the characters' hearts and elevate their thoughts, the verse can transport us for a moment to those sublime movements of passion which seem to be *song*, so much do they carry our souls beyond ourselves!

Does not the ordinary conversation of any man contain his favorite formulas and habitual choice of words, a result of his education, his profession, the tastes he has developed in his home? Is it not inspired by his likes and his natural aversions, by his bilious, sanguine, or excitable temperament and dictated by a passionate or cold attitude, by calculation or candor? Does he not have favorite comparisons and an entire everyday

vocabulary by which a friend would recognize him in the unique turn
of phrase repeated, second hand, without needing to hear the sound of
his voice? Is it thus necessary that a character use the same vocabulary,
the same images, as does every other character? No, the character should
be concise or diffuse, negligent or calculating, prodigal or miserly, depending on his age and inclinations. Molière never failed to offer the
solid and recognizable touches learned from attentive observation of
men, and Shakespeare does not produce a proverb or a curse at random.
—But neither of these great men would be able to encompass natural
language in the *epic verse* of our tragedy; for had they, by mistake,
adopted such a verse, it would have been necessary to disguise the *simple
word* beneath the cloak of periphrasis or the mask of the archaic word.
—It is a vicious circle from which no amount of fortitude would have
freed them. —We have an unexceptional example of it. The author of
Esther, the purest source of the dramatico-epic style, was obliged to write
in 1672, a tragedy whose action dated from 1638. He believed that the
modern Oriental names would not harmoniously fit his alexandrine line,
phrased in imitation of the ancients. What did he do? With admirable
good sense he made his decision, and not considering the possibility of
altering the verse in what he termed a dramatic "poem," he changed
the entire vocabulary of his Turks and removed the setting to some
vague antiquity: Bagdad became Babylon, Stamboul dared not be even
Constantinople, but was Byzantium, and the name of "Shah Abbas," who
had laid siege to Bagdad, was absorbed in the names "Osmin" and "Os-
man."[11] That was as it had to be.

There is more. After having given you earlier an example of the
ridiculous errors his imitators fell into, I am going to defend the perpetrator. I think that it was impossible for him to pronounce a rough
and natural word in the style he had chosen to use: it would have had
the effect of a curse in the mouth of a young girl singing a song of
romantic melancholy. He could only have used *simple expressions* by
sounding them from the first verse. But when, for five acts, you have
used "queen" instead of "Your Majesty," "hymen" for "marriage," "im-
molate" for "kill," and thousands of other similar niceties, how can you
offer a word like "spy"? It is absolutely necessary to say "mortal" and
who knows what, equally refined, to modify it.

The author of *Athalia* sensed this so well that in *The Litigants* he broke
the verse at every turn in favor of the *correct modern word*, almost always
too large for its frame, but impossible to abbreviate. Ancient names,
unlike modern names, were not preceded by another name or by a
qualifier affixed to it like the feathers of a bird. Never will a page announce in a single alexandrine verse, "Milady the Duchess of Mont-
morency"; he would most certainly be run off the boards. The poet of
Esther stated in a similar situation:

                        . . .Milady the *Countess*
    of Pimbesche. . .

Even with familiar locutions, that interruption or rearrangement would
distort, he says:

    Next, then, let us not be permitted to *catch*
    Our breath, and let us be forbidden to stretch out.[12]

Do not doubt that if such a talented writer had been forced to put an
entirely modern subject on the tragic stage, he would have used the
common vocabulary and would have broken the regular and monotonous
balance of the alexandrine by the *enjambement* of one verse into another.
He might have disdained the hemistich and perhaps even have (something we haven't dared) reinstated the hiatus like Molière, when he says:
"First we have the deer GIVEN to the dogs"; or when he abbreviates a
syllable, as the following: "I find myself in an isolated part of the wood,
at the HEELS of our dogs, me, alone with Drécar."[13]
    I deeply regret that such an idea did not strike his fancy around 1670.
It would have spared me a great many obscure accusations, signed or
unsigned (anonymous in either case). It would have prevented incredible
labor on the part of the poor poets who followed him.
    For example, would you believe, you English, who are familiar with
the vocabulary of Shakespeare's tragedies, that it took the French Tragic
Muse, Melpomene, ninety-eight years to decide to say "handkerchief"
out loud—she who could baldly say "dog" and "sponge"? Let us examine
the degrees through which she passed with rather amusing difficulty
and prudishness.
    In the year of the Hegira 1147, which corresponds to 1732 A.D., Mel-
pomene required her handkerchief on the occasion of the "hymen" of
a virtuous Turkish lady, who was not called Zahra and who bore a family
resemblance to Desdemona, but, never daring to take it from the pocket
of her skirts, took instead a letter.[14] In 1792 Melpomene again needed
this same handkerchief for the "hymen" of a citizen who claimed to be
a Venetian and a relative of Desdemona—possessing, moreover, a syllable of her name, the syllable "mo," for she was named Hédelmone, a
name which rhymes conveniently with (I will not suggest "*aumône*," "*ané-
mone*,"—that would be both labored and pedantic) "*soupçonne*," "*donne*,"
"*ordonne*," etc. It is now thirty-seven years later. Melpomene was twice
recently on the verge of taking out that handkerchief. But either it was
too audacious to appear with a handkerchief during the Directory or,
on the contrary, since more luxury was in order, she took instead a string
of diamonds (which she wore in bed rather than appearing under-
dressed).[15] In 1820, French tragedy, having openly renounced the so-

briquet Melpomene, and translating from a German source, again had to deal with a handkerchief for the last will and testament of a Scots queen. Good heavens, she grew bold, took the handkerchief herself, in her hand, in full company, wrinkled her brow and loudly and bravely called it "gauze" and "gift."[16] This was a great advance.

Finally, in 1829, the great word has been spoken, arousing the shock and swoons of the delicate, who, on that day, wept long and mournfully, but to the satisfaction of the public who, for the most part, are in the habit of calling a handkerchief a "handkerchief." The word made its debut: ridiculous triumph! Will it always take a century for each common word to be introduced on the stage?

Finally, we can laugh at this prudishness.—The Lord be praised! The poet will be able to follow his imagination as freely as the prose writer. He can run, unobstructed, the gamut of his ideas without feeling the earth give way beneath him. We are not so fortunate as to be able to mix in the same scene, prose with blank verse and rhymed verse. In England you have available these three octaves and among them have a harmony which cannot be achieved in French. In order to translate this it was necessary to loosen the alexandrine to the point of the most familiar carelessness (recitative) then raise it again to the most extreme lyricism (song). That is what I have attempted to do. Prose, when it translates epic passages, has a sizeable defect, especially visible on the stage, of suddenly appearing bombastic, forced, and melodramatic. Verse, on the other hand, is more elastic and lends itself to all forms: when it soars, one is not surprised, for when it *walks, one feels that it has wings*.

You are a little younger and much more timid than I. —Don't be more careful of what you call my reputation than am I. I am not ashamed to have made, by the by, one translation, although I suffered a bit from self-imposed constraint. In the end, the work will remain; it is another diamond for the French treasure-house, a diamond in the rough if you like, but not without value: even had it given us nothing but a portrait of Iago, who in earlier versions had been removed from his position between Othello and Desdemona—something tantamount to suppressing the serpent in Genesis.

Our epoch is one of renaissance and rehabilitation at the same time. I would, however, never insist that the new law must be imperishable: it will die with us, perhaps before us, and will be replaced by a better one. It should be sufficient for one man's name to mark a degree of progress. The more civilization advances, the more one must be resigned to see the ideas that one sows grow like a fecund grain, ripen, yellow, and promplty fall before the eyes of the first cultivator in order to leave room for a new, stronger, and more abundant crop. Unfortunately, this philosophic disinterestedness is lacking in many of the men who survived the preceding two generations. As if to fulfill the infamous statement of one of their century's writers, they wanted to see "in their sons, their enemies, and in their grandsons, their sons' enemies." By rights we might have received their tenderness, but no, not even that. These aged children were irritated in seeing on young brows the gravity proper to their own age. They sought to restrain the virile shoots that were replacing them: one group wanted to smother the young beneath the plaster of centuries past, the others cast them down with the sword of the Empire. Vain effort. The nursery has grown, the forest, on all sides, sends up trees of all sorts whose branches, vigorous shoots and broad leaves shroud in shade various rickety and dying trunks which would still be living had they sought support, rather than isolation.

What has happened? The younger generation has reared up against its unjust predecessors. Taking into account the old men's grey hairs, the young have, in their impatience, laid out the funeral tables, consoling themselves with impious hopes. I have suffered from their cruelty, but why persecute the aged? Were they responsible for the law which pushes them forward with the rest of mankind?

Far from disparaging great reputations, I claim that one ought to acknowledge each writer's work *in the context of its period*. The best proof I can give of the thankless labor I have undertaken, a contemporary homage to past greatness, not European but universal, for, at the same time *The Moor of Venice* was played in Paris, it was also playing in London, Vienna, and the United States. When you have taken the wrong path, you must retrace your steps in order to set out again on the right one. No other verse was available to the tragic stage but that *polite* and often anachronistic verse which I have described to you. Therefore, in order to worthily arm ancient Shakespeare, it was necessary for me to recover the rusty arms of ancient French poets for our arsenal. Corneille, the immortal Corneille, had given to the Cid Othello's truly modern sword "whose Spanish blade was tempered in the Ebro." "*Ebro's temper!*":[17] why did he use it on only one occasion!

This present work is no more than a formal experiment. It was necessary to re-make the instrument (the style) and publically test it before playing an original tune. Had I known a story more often repeated, more read, more acted, more sung, more danced, more cut, more embellished, more distorted than *The Moor of Venice*, I would have chosen it precisely so that undivided attention might be focused on a single point, the *manner of execution*.

You, Milord, should be wary of reading my translation. You would find it as imperfect as I myself do. For there remains this truth to admit, that there is not one good translation in the world for one who knows the original language if translation is meant as a reproduction of the model, a literal translation of each word, each verse, each sentence into words, verses, and sentences of another language. All translation is made for those who do not understand the original language and is made only for them. This is what critics too often lose sight of. If the translator were not an interpreter, he would be useless. A translation is only to the original what a portrait is to living nature. What youth, given the chance to see his mistress, would deign to regard her image? But, in the event of absence or death, the image satisfies. The same is true of translation. You repeat in vain the same song in your own language: it is another instrument; it has another sound and method of playing, other modulations, other harmonies, which must be utilized both to reproduce the foreign music and to *naturalize* it. One thing, however, is always lost: the intimate union of a man's thought with his mother tongue.

I have sought then, to render the spirit, not the letter. This has not, as I foresaw, been understood by everyone. For one group, those who don't know English, I was too literal; for the other, who do know it, I was not literal enough. Thus, this bronze made in imitation of the great statue of Othello has been pressed, beaten, and twisted between the English anvil and the French hammer by the critics. In book form, *The Moor* will doubtless be attacked again. But: *"Parve, sine me, liber, ibis in urbem."*[18] I shall hardly be more aware of it than you. Every once in a while I hear that a pamphleteer has scribbled, that a buffoon has sung, or that an inveterate censor has held forth against me. I know neither what they do, nor what they are, and don't bother about them at all.

I have only tried to present you with an overview of this literary experiment. The whole system will be better explained by works than by theories. In poetry, philosophy, or action, what is a system but manner, genre, tone, and style? These questions are only resolved by a word and that word is always a man's name. Each person's head is a mold in which a mass of ideas is modeled. The head once broken by death, one must no longer seek to re-compose a similar ensemble. It is destroyed forever.

An imitator of Shakespeare would be as wrong for our time as are the imitators of the author of *Athalia*.

Again, we move forward, and, although Shakespeare may have perhaps attained the highest point that can be reached by *modern* tragedy, he attained it according to the tastes of his period. The poetry and moral observation in him is as beautiful as it ever was because inspiration is not affected by "progress" and the nature of individuals doesn't change. But divine or secular philosophy must correspond to the needs of the society in which the poet lived, and societies do advance.

Today the movement is so rapid that a thirty-year-old man has witnessed two opposing centuries, ten years each in length. One was all exterior action, warlike, conquering, rough, strong, and proud, but lifeless, as though frozen inside, almost without progress in poetry and the philosophy of art, or, at best, seeming to be a period of transition. The other was immobile and languishing on the outside, mean and indecisive in action, without energy, without pomp in its deeds, but agitated and devoured internally with a prodigious intellectual activity, a ferment almost without precedent in history. It contained thought in all its forms, in all its shapes and in all its various orders, as in a fiery furnace in which all is recast, elaborated, shaped together and properly combined. The former is similar to a body, the latter to a soul.

How could a whole new generation of ideas not be produced by this dual spectacle? Who can be surprised by all that is being done, unless possessing, like Jerusalem, "eyes for not seeing"? Limiting myself to dramatic art, I think, then, that in the future this art will be more difficult than ever for France, precisely because it is released from the most restricting rules. In the past there was a sort of distinction in producing something in spite of the rules. Having followed them, one could make a reputation. But, at the present, another point of view will be used for considering the composition of a tragedy. It will be all the more necessary for tragedy to possess natural beauties as it will have fewer conventional charms. In the same way that a rather weak and decrepit horse can take on rather elegant grace in a riding school, caparisoned in a velvet saddle, with rosettes, bows, gilt bridle and reins. It can execute practiced curvettes; it jumps with an aura of strength; it gallops at a measured pace which apes speed. But thrust it naked into the open air of a plain in Alsace or Poland, and judge it in comparison with a wild stallion, and you will see what it knows how to do.

Freedom, allowing everything at once, infinitely multiplies the difficulty of choosing and removes all elements of structured support. Perhaps this is the reason why England, after Shakespeare, counts a very small number of *tragedies* and not a *theatre* worthy of the system of this great man,[19]* while we boast a number of second-class writers who have given us their *theatre*, a tolerable collection in the Racinian mode.

I stress this remark as I have foreseen that, when examples appear, critics will arm themselves with these *drames* and their fate in performance in order to combat the rule and the whole system, without taking into account the new problems and the much greater scale by which future works will be measured. In fact, to all that Shakespeare possesses of poetry and observation, it will be no less than is necessary to add the summary of the peaks of what our era possesses of philosophy and what our society has gained through science. These experiments will be numerous and daring; and they will have all the same merit; even failure will not be shameful, because, in this new order of things, the author and his public are learning together and from each other.

I hope that after all I have just told you, you will not continue to repeat the reproach to me and my friends made in your last letter, of having too ardent a zeal for innovation.

Do you remember that tall old clock I often pointed out to you? Well, let that memory help me explain myself to you. For me it is the faithful image of the constant state of society.

Its large face, on which the Roman numerals resemble columns, is eternally traversed by three hands. One, which is very fast, very large, very heavy, and whose tip resembles a lance-head and its body a bundle of arms, advances so slowly that you might deny that it does move. The surest, most fixed, most persevering eye cannot seize in it the least symptom of mobility. It would appear to be sealed, screwed, encrusted in place for eternity, and, nevertheless, at the end of an hour, it will have progressed along a twelfth of the clock's face. Does not this hand represent the mass of people, for whom advancement is accomplished without shocks and by a continual, but imperceptible drive?

The other, freer hand, moves quickly enough so that even with moderate attention one can perceive its movement. This hand travels in five minutes the route that took the first hand an hour. It gives the exact proportion of steps which enlightened men take in advance of the crowd which follows them.

But in addition to these two hands, there is another which is agile in a different way and whose leaps the eye follows with difficulty. It travels sixty times the distance before the second hand moves and drags the third along.

Never, no, never, have I considered this second hand, this so-lively arrow, so restless, so bold, and so responsive at the same time, which thrusts itself forward and quivers as though at the thought of its own audacity or from the pleasure of its conquest of time; never have I considered it without thinking that the poet has always had, and must have, this ready step ahead of the centuries and the common spirit of his nation, ahead even of his most enlightened fellow countrymen.

And could we not see in this heavy pendulum which governs them with a steady movement—if we pursue our idea—a perfect symbol of that inflexible *law of progress* whose movement ceaselessly carries forward with it the three degrees of the human spirit which are indifferent to it, and, after all, only seem to mark successively its progress towards an—alas!—unknown goal?

1 November 1829

Notes

1. An hydraulic engine was erected at Marly in 1684 to raise water from the Seine to an aqueduct which carried it to the palace at Versailles.

2. "So that a woman, lovely above, foully ended in an ugly fish below." Horace *The Art of Poetry* 1. 4.

3. In 1824, in *The French Muse*, I published a piece concerning these same

doctrines now being put into practice. It concerned an honest attempt by M. de Sorsum, a poet and scholar whose life was too brief, who translated several Shakespearean tragedies into prose, blank verse, and rhymed verse: a system different from my own and one I continue to believe unworkable in French. Considering the esteem in which I hold anyone who takes a step forward and tries a new path, I don't hesitate to mention his endeavor to you. [Vigny's note.]

4. La Fontaine, "The Oak and the Reed," 1. 10.

5. Corneille takes a position like this in his "Discourse on the Three Unities." Cf. Abbé d'Aubignac, *The Whole Art of the Stage*, book 2, chapter 8.

6. Racine, *Athalia*: II 8.

7. "Intellect sways the whole mass." Virgil *Aeneid* 6. 727.

8. Virgil *Aeneid* 6. 269.

9. *Macbeth*: IV 2. 67.

10. From Ducis's *Othello* V 5.

11. In Racine's *Bajazet*.

12. These two examples of *enjambement* and familiar vocabulary are from Racine's only comedy, *The Litigants* I 6. 187–88; and II 3. 791–92, respectively.

13. *The Bores* II 6. 513–14; and 541–42.

14. The reference is to Voltaire's *Zaïre*.

15. The reference is to Ducis's *Othello*.

16. The reference is to Pierre Lebrun's *Mary Stuart*.

17. This is Vigny's translation of Shakespeare's line, "It was a sword of Spaine, the Ice brooke's temper" (Othello: V 2. 315). Vigny chose Alexander Pope's emendation of "Ice brooke's" to "Ebro's."

18. "Little book, you will go without me to the city." Ovid *Tristia* 1. 1.

19. The only thing in which I take some pride in this enterprise is to have made the name of the great Shakespeare heard on the French stage, and thus given the French public the chance openly to show that it knows well that languages are only instruments, that ideas are universal, that genius belongs to all mankind and that his renown demands all the world for a stage. [Vigny's note.]

8

ALEXANDRE DUMAS, THE ELDER

Alexandre Dumas (1802–1870) can rightfully claim the first major the-atrical success for the romantics with the production of Henry III and His Court *at the Comédie-Française in February 1829. With this pro-duction he left the relative obscurity of his position as a clerk in the employ of the Duke of Orléans and joined Hugo and Vigny in the battle for theatrical reform.*

Dumas met with enormous success in the theatre during the 1830s. His plays from this period include Christine *(1830),* Napoleon Bonaparte *(1831),* Richard Darlington *(1831),* Antony *(1831),* The Tower of Nesle *(1832),* Catherine Howard *(1834),* Kean *(1836), and* Made-moiselle de Belle-Isle *(1839). Unlike Hugo and Vigny, Dumas was comfortable working in the boulevard theatre and his plays easily absorbed the techniques and the formulas of the melodrama. In this sense, Dumas's plays are representative of the worst tendencies in the romantic theatre and their enormous popular success proved to be short-lived. Dumas is now best remembered as the author of* The Three Musketeers *(1844) and* The Count of Monte Cristo *(1844–1845) and the numerous historical novels that he wrote in the 1850s and 1860s.*

Dumas did not produce a major critical statement during the 1820s, but the scene from Antony, *translated here, gives a sample of his ideas and fervor.* Antony *is one of the rare romantic plays to use a contemporary setting, and this allows Dumas to bring onto the stage a spokesman for his literary generation.*

Antony *was written in 1830 and offered to the Comédie-Française. It was produced in May 1831 at the Porte-Saint-Martin Theatre and pub-lished by Auffray in 1831.*

Antony (1831)

ACT IV

Scene 6

Adele [She turns abruptly to Eugene in order to conceal her anxiety.]
    No doubt you have something almost finished, don't you?

Eugene
    Yes, madame.

Madame de Camps
    Set in the Middle Ages?

Eugene
    Always.

Adele
    Why don't you ever choose a subject from contemporary society?

Countess
    I am constantly asking him that. Write about the present. Wouldn't we pay
    much more attention to characters drawn from our own time, dressed like
    us, and speaking our language?

Baron de Marsanne
    Oh, it's so much easier for him to find subjects in history than to draw them
    from his imagination....Plays are found almost ready-made in history.

Frederick
    Yes, almost.

Baron de Marsanne
    Indeed! For example, take what the *Constitutionalist* had to say about...[1]

Eugene
    Reasons that are much too complicated to explain prevent me from doing
    it.

Countess
    Present your arguments and we will be your judges.

Eugene

Oh, miladies! I hope you will permit my saying that it would be much too serious a lesson for an audience that is dressed for a ball.

Madame de Camps

Not at all. You can see that the dancing has not begun as yet.... And, furthermore, we are all interested in literature, aren't we, countess?

Baron de Marsanne

Patience, miladies. This gentleman will place all his ideas in the preface to his first work.

Countess

Are you writing a preface?

Baron de Marsanne

All the Romantics write prefaces.... The *Constitutionalist* indulged in a joke about it only the other day...

Adele

You see, sir. You have used time in defending yourself that would have been sufficient for you to outline a whole system.

Eugene

You, too, should be careful, madame. You asked for it. I will no longer take responsibility for the boredom.... Here are my assumptions: Comedy paints manners; drama paints passions. The Revolution, passing over France, made men equal, levelled class distinctions. Dress was democratized. Nothing indicates ones profession; no milieus are distinguished by peculiar customs or habits; everything is mixed together. Nuances have replaced bright colors, but colors, not nuances, are what a painter needs to paint a picture.

Adele

You are right.

Baron de Marsanne

Nevertheless, sir, the *Constitutionalist*...

Eugene [*ignoring him*]

I was saying that comedy of manners, if not impossible, has, at least, become very difficult to write because of this. This leaves the drama of passion, but another difficulty accompanies it. History bequeathes us facts. They are ours by right of inheritance. They are incontestable. They belong to the poet: he exhumes men of other epochs, re-clothes them in appropriate garb, and brings them to life with their passions which he increases or diminishes according to where he has chosen to locate the drama. But, if we in modern society, if we were to try to lay bare the human heart beneath our short and ugly frockcoats, it would not be recognized....The resemblance between the hero and the audience in the pit would be too great; the analogy would be too personal. The spectator who follows the development of passion in the actor would want it to stop where it stops in himself. Were it to go beyond his own ability to feel or express it, he would no longer understand it and would say: "It's not true; that is not the way I experience it. When the woman I love deceives me, doubtless I suffer...yes...for a while...but I neither stab her to death nor die myself. The proof is that I am here." This is followed by the cries of "exaggeration" and "melodrama" which drown out the applause of those few men who, more happily, or unhappily, constituted than the rest, feel that passions are the same in the fifteenth and nineteenth centuries and that hearts beat as warmly under a frockcoat as beneath a suit of armour...

Adele

Well, then, the approbation of these few men would amply compensate for the coldness of the others.

Madame de Camps

Then, if there were any doubt, you could prove to them that these passions truly exist in our society. There are still profound passions which cannot be extinguished by an absence of three years. There are still mysterious knights who save the life of the lady who fills their dreams. There are still virtuous women who flee their lovers. And, since a mixture of the natural and the sublime is fashionable, there are still scenes that are all the more dramatic for being set in a hotel room....I would portray one of these women...

Antony [Who has said nothing during the whole literary discussion, but whose face has become progressively animated, comes forward slowly, and leans on the back of Madame de Camps' chair.]
Is there any chance that you would have a brother or a husband here, madame?

Madame de Camps [startled]
What does it matter to you, sir?

Antony
I want to know!

Madame de Camps
No!

Antony
Very well, then, dishonor rather than blood! [*To Eugene*] Sir, madame is correct! And since she has taken it upon herself to outline the general

subject, I will take it upon myself to fill in the details.... Yes, I would take this woman—innocent and pure among women—and I would reveal her loving and honest heart which is misunderstood by this false society with its corrupt, withered heart. In opposition to her I would draw one of those women toward whom all morality is directed; one of those women who would not flee danger because she has become familiar with it over the years; one of those women who would take advantage of her feminine weakness to basely destroy another woman's reputation, like the bravo who takes advantage of his strength to kill a man. I would prove that the first of these two women, the one who would be compromised, would be the honest woman, not because of her virtue, but because of her ignorance.... Then, in the face of society, I would demand judgement between them here and now, while awaiting God's pronouncement from above. [*A moment of silence.*] Come along, miladies, we have talked enough of literature; the music calls; take your places for the quadrille.

Eugene [*vigorously offering his hand to Adele*]
Will you do me the honor, madame?

Adele

Thank you, I will not be dancing. [*Antony takes Eugene's hand and shakes it.*]

Madame de Camps

Farewell, my dear.

Countess

What, are you leaving?

Madame de Camps [*withdrawing*]
I will not stay after this horrible scene ...

Countess [*withdrawing with her*]
You must admit that you helped provoke it.

Note

1. The *Constitutionalist* was a conservative daily newspaper of the period.

SELECTED BIBLIOGRAPHY

General Works

Bertier de Sauvigny, Guillaume de. *La Restauration*. Paris: Flammarion, 1963.
Brockett, Oscar. *History of the Theatre*. 4th ed. Boston: Allyn and Bacon, 1980.
Clark, Barrett. *European Theories of Drama*. Rev. ed. New York: Crown, 1965.
Dukore, Bernard F. *Dramatic Theory and Criticism: Greeks to Grotowski*. New York: Holt, Rinehart and Winston, 1974.
Hauser, Arnold. *The Social History of Art*. 2 vols. New York: Knopf, 1951.
Lucas-Dubreton, Jean. *La Restauration et la Monarchie de Juillet*. Paris: Hachette, 1926.
Vidalenc, Jean. *La Restauration*. Paris: P.U.F., 1966.
Wellek, René. *Concepts of Criticism*. New Haven, Conn.: Yale University Press, 1963.
————. *A History of Modern Criticism: 1750–1950*. 4 vols. New Haven, Conn.: Yale University Press, 1955–1965.

Romanticism

Abrams, Meyer H. *The Mirror and the Lamp: Romantic Theory and Critical Tradition*. New York: Norton, 1958.
Allen, James Smith. *Popular French Romanticism*. Syracuse, N.Y.: Syracuse University Press, 1981.
Barzun, Jacques. *Classic, Romantic, and Modern*. Garden City, N.Y.: Anchor, 1961.
Bray, René. *Chronologie du Romantisme: 1804–1830*. Paris: Nizet, 1963.
Donohue, Joseph W. *Dramatic Character in the English Romantic Age*. Princeton, N.J.: Princeton University Press, 1970.
Eggli, Edmond. *Schiller et le Romantisme français*. 2 vols. Paris: Gamber, 1928.

————, and Martino, Pierre. *Le Débat romantique en France: 1813–1830*. Vol. 1. Paris: Les Belles Lettres, 1933.

Furst, Lilian. *The Contours of European Romanticism*. London: Macmillan, 1979.

————. *Romanticism in Perspective*. New York: Humanities Press, 1970.

Gautier, Théophile. *Histoire du Romantisme*. Paris: Charpentier, 1874.

Gilman, Margaret. *The Idea of Poetry in France from Houdar de la Motte to Baudelaire*. Cambridge, Mass.: Harvard University Press, 1958.

Kroeber, Karl, and Walling, William. *Ideas of Romanticism*. New Haven, Conn.: Yale University Press, 1978.

Moreau, Pierre. *Le Romantisme*. Paris: Duca, 1957.

Peckham, Morse, ed. *Romanticism: The Culture of the Nineteenth Century*. New York: Braziller, 1965.

————. *The Triumph of Romanticism*. Columbia, S.C.: University of South Carolina Press, 1970.

Remak, Henry H. H. "Western European Romanticism: Definitions and Scope." In *Comparative Literature: Method and Practice*, edited by Horst Frenz and Newton P. Stallknecht, pp. 223–59. Carbondale, Ill.: Southern Illinois University Press, 1961.

Schenk, Hans Georg. *The Mind of the European Romantics*. Garden City, N.Y.: Anchor, 1969.

Schlegel, August Wilhelm von. *A Course of Lectures on Dramatic Art and Literature*. London: Bohn, 1846.

Souriau, Maurice. *Histoire du Romantisme en France*. Paris: Spes, 1927.

Tieghem, Paul van. *Le Romantisme dans la littérature européenne*. Paris: Albin Michel, 1971.

Trahard, Pierre. *Le Romantisme défini par "Le Globe."* Paris: Presses Françaises, 1924.

French Theatre

Allévy, Marie-Antoinette. *La Mise en scène en France dans la première moitié du dix-neuvième siècle*. Paris: Droz, 1938.

Arvin, Neil. *Eugène Scribe and the French Theatre: 1815–1860*. Cambridge, Mass.: Harvard University Press, 1924.

Borgerhoff, Joseph-Léopold. *Le Théâtre anglais à Paris*. Paris: Hachette, 1913.

Bowman, Frank P. "Notes Towards a Definition of Romantic Theatre." *Esprit Créateur*, 5 (1965), 121–30.

Carlson, Marvin. "French Stage Composition from Hugo to Zola." *Educational Theatre Journal*, 23 (1971), 363–78.

Descotes, Maurice. *Le Drama romantique et ses grands créateurs*. Paris: P.U.F., 1955.

————. *Le Public de théâtre et son histoire*. Paris: P.U.F., 1964.

Gilman, Margaret. *Othello in French*. Paris: Champion, 1925.

Ginistry, Paul. *Le Mélodrame*. Paris: Louis-Michaud, 1910.

Horn-Monval, Madeleine. *Répertoire bibliographique des traductions et adaptations françaises du théâtre étranger*. 8 vols. Paris: C.N.R.S., 1961–1964.

Joannidès, Alexandre. *La Comédie-Française de 1680 à 1900*. Paris: Plon, 1901.

Jourdain, Eleanor. *Dramatic Theory and Practice in France: 1690–1808*. 1921. Reprint. New York: Blom, 1968.
Jusserand, J. J. *Shakespeare en France*. Paris: A. Colin, 1898.
Leathers, Victor. *British Entertainers in France*. Toronto: University of Toronto Press, 1959.
Lioure, Michel. *Le Drame*. Paris: A. Colin, 1963.
Melcher, Edith. *Stage Realism in France between Diderot and Antoine*. Ph.D. Dissertation, Bryn Mawr College, 1928. Lancaster, Pa.: Lancaster Press, 1928.
Scherer, Jacques. *Le Dramaturgie classique en France*. Paris: Nizet, 1957.
Yarrow, Philip John. "Three Plays of 1829, or Doubts about 1830." *Symposium*, 23 (1969), 373–83.

Benjamin Constant

Constant, Benjamin. *Oeuvres*. Ed. Alfred Boulin. Paris: Gallimard, 1957.
———. *Wallstein*. Ed. Jean-René Debré. Paris: Les Belles Lettres, 1965.

Holdheim, William H. *Benjamin Constant*. London: Bowes and Bowes, 1961.
Nicholson, Harold. *Benjamin Constant*. Garden City, N.Y.: Doubleday, 1949.

Emile Deschamps

Deschamps, Emile. *Etudes françaises et étrangères*. Paris: Canel, 1828.

Girard, Henri. *Un Bourgeois dilettante à l'époque romantique: Emile Deschamps, 1791–1871*. Paris: Champion, 1921.
———. *Un Manifeste du romantisme: La Préface des "Etudes françaises et étrangères" d'Emile Deschamps*. Paris: Presses françaises, 1923.

Alexandre Dumas, the Elder

Dumas, Alexandre. *Antony*. Nouveaux classiques Larousse. Paris: Larousse, 1970.
———. *Mes Mémoires*. 5 vols. Paris: Gallimard, 1954–1967.
———. *Théâtre complet*. Ed. Fernande Bassan. Vol. 1. Paris: Lettres Modernes, 1974.

Bassan, Fernande, and Chevalley, Sylvie. *Alexandre Dumas père et la Comédie-Française*. Paris: Lettres Modernes, 1972.
Bell, A. Craig. *Alexandre Dumas: A Biography and Study*. London: Cassell, 1950.
Maurois, André. *The Titans: A Three-Generation Biography of the Dumas*. Trans. G. Hopkins. New York: Harper, 1957.

Victor Hugo

Hugo, Victor. *Preface to "Cromwell."* Trans. I. G. Burnham. Vol. IX of *Hugo's Works*. Philadelphia: Barrie, 1895.
———. *Preface to "Hernani."* Trans. I. G. Burnham. Vol. I of *Hugo's Works*. Philadelphia: Barrie, 1895.
———. *Oeuvres complètes, édition chronologique*. Vol. III. Paris: Club Français du Livre, 1967.
———. *Préface de "Cromwell," suivie d'extraits d'autres préfaces dramatiques*. Classiques Larousse. Paris: Larousse, 1949.
———. *Théâtre complet*. 2 vols. Paris: Gallimard, 1963.

Affron, Charles. *A Stage for Poets: Studies in the Theatre of Hugo and Musset*. Princeton, N.J.: Princeton University Press, 1971.
Carlson, Marvin. *"Hernani*'s Revolt from the Tradition of French Stage Composition." *Theatre Survey*, 13 (1972), 1–27.
Chahine, Samia. *La Dramaturgie de Victor Hugo*. Paris: Nizet, 1971.
Daniels, Barry V. "Victor Hugo on the Boulevard: *Lucrèce Borgia* at the Porte-Saint-Martin Theatre in 1833." *Theatre Journal*, 32 (1980), 17–42.
Maurois, André. *Olympio, ou La Vie de Victor Hugo*. 2 vols. Paris: Hachette, 1954.
Ubersfeld, Anne. *Le Roi et le Buffon*. Paris: Corti, 1974.

Charles-Augustin Sainte-Beuve

Sainte-Beuve, C.-A. *Ouevres*. 2 vols. Paris: Gallimard, 1956.
———. *Selected Essays*. Trans. F. Steegmuller. Garden City, N.Y.: Doubleday, 1963.

Chadbourne, Richard M. *Charles-Augustin Sainte-Beuve*. Boston: Twayne, 1977.
Lehmann, Andrew George. *Sainte-Beuve: A Portrait of the Critic, 1804–1842*. Oxford: Clarendon Press, 1962.

Madame de Staël

Staël, Anne-Louise-Germaine de. *De l'Allemagne*. Paris: Garnier, 1968.
———. *De l'Allemagne*. Ed. Comtesse Jean de Pange. 3 vols. Paris: Hachette, 1958.
———. *Germany*. Trans. O. W. Wright. New York: Derby, Jackson, 1859.
———. *The Influence of Literature Upon Society*. 2 vols. London: Colburn, 1812.
———. *De la Littérature considérée dans ses rapports avec les institutions sociales*. Ed. Paul van Tieghem. 2 vols. Paris: Minard, 1959.
———. *On Politics, Literature, and National Character*. Ed. Monroe Berger. Garden City, N.Y.: Doubleday, 1964.

Herold, J. Christopher. *Mistress to an Age: A Life of Madame de Staël*. New York: Bobbs-Merrill, 1958.

Postgate, Helen B. *Madame de Staël*. New York: Twayne, 1968.

Stendhal

Stendhal. *Racine and Shakespeare*. Trans. Guy Daniels. New York: Crowell-Collier, 1972.
———. *Racine et Shakespeare*. Ed. Pierre Martino. 2 vols. Paris: Champion, 1925.

Adams, Robert M. *Stendhal: Notes on a Novelist*. New York: Minerva Press, 1968.
Richardson, Joanna. *Stendhal*. New York: Coward, McCann and Geoghegan, 1974.

Alfred de Vigny

Vigny, Alfred de. *Oeuvres complètes*. Ed. F. Baldensperger. 8 vols. Paris: Conard, 1914–1935.
———. *Oeuvres complètes*. Paris: Gallimard, 1948.

Daniels, Barry V. "An Exemplary French Romantic Production: Alfred de Vigny's *Chatterton*." *Theatre Survey*, 16 (1975), 65–88.
———. "Shakespeare à la romantique: *Le More de Venise* d'Alfred de Vigny." *Revue d'Histoire du Théâtre*, 27 (1975), 125–55.
Germain, François. *L'Imagination d'Alfred de Vigny*. Paris: Corti, 1961.
Hays, Michael L. "An Appraisal of Alfred de Vigny's *Le More de Venise* and its Place in the History of the French Theatre." *Rackham Literary Studies*, no. 3 (1972), pp. 51–63.
Jarry, André. "De Shakespeare à Vigny: Le miroir et son voile." In *Vigny, Les Pyrénées, et l'Angleterre*, pp. 7–23. Paris: Touzot, 1978.
———. "*Roméo et Juliette*: De Shakespeare à Vigny et Deschamps, en passant par les traductions Letourneur." *Bulletin de l'Association des Amis d'Alfred de Vigny*, no. 6 (1974–75), pp. 40–54.
La Salle, Bertrand de. *Alfred de Vigny*. Paris: Fayard, 1963.
Lauvrière, Emile. *Alfred de Vigny, sa vie et son oeuvre*. 2 vols. Paris: Grasset, 1945.

INDEX

Contributions in Drama and Theatre Studies
Series Editor: Joseph Donohue

American Popular Entertainment: Papers and Proceedings of the Conference on the History of American Popular Entertainment
Myron Matlaw, editor

George Frederick Cooke: Machiavel of the Stage
Don B. Wilmeth

Greek Theatre Practice
J. Michael Walton

Gordon Craig's Moscow *Hamlet*: A Reconstruction
Laurence Senelick

Theatrical Touring and Founding in North America
L. W. Conolly, editor

Bernhardt and the Theatre of Her Time
Eric Salmon, editor

About the Author

BARRY V. DANIELS is Associate Professor of Theatre at Kent State University. His articles on theatre history have been published in *Theatre Survey, Theatre Journal, Revue d'Histoire du Theatre, Theatre Research International,* and *Educational Theatre Journal.*